Lacanian Psychoanalysis and Eastern Orthodox Christian Anthropology in Dialogue

This book vigorously engages Lacan with a spiritual tradition that has yet to be thoroughly addressed within psychoanalytic literature—the Eastern Orthodox Christian tradition.

The book offers a unique engagement with a faith system that highlights and extends analytic thinking. For those in formation within the Orthodox tradition, this book brings psychoanalytic insights to bear on matters of faith that may at times seem opaque or difficult to understand. Ultimately, the authors seek to elicit in the reader the reflective and contemplative posture of Orthodoxy, as well as the listening ear of analysis, while considering the human subject.

This work is relevant and important for those training in psychoanalysis and Orthodox theology or ministry, as well as for those interested in the intersection between psychoanalysis and religion.

Carl Waitz, PsyD is an Attending Psychologist at Boston Children's Hospital, Clinical Instructor at Harvard Medical School, and maintains a small private practice in Brookline, MA. His research and clinical interests include depression, suicidal thoughts and behaviors, Lacanian psychoanalysis, and treatment of adolescents and young adults.

Theresa Clement Tisdale, PhD, PsyD is a licensed clinical psychologist and clinical psychoanalyst in private practice in Glendora, CA. She is also Professor of Clinical Psychology at Azusa Pacific University in Azusa, CA. Her clinical, teaching, and research interests are psychoanalysis and religion/spirituality, psychoanalytic psychotherapy, spiritual formation, and addressing religion/spirituality in clinical practice.

Lacanian Psychoanalysis and Eastern Orthodox Christian Anthropology in Dialogue

Carl Waitz and
Theresa Clement Tisdale

LONDON AND NEW YORK

First published 2022
by Routledge
2 Park Square, Milton Park, Abingdon, Oxon OX14 4RN

and by Routledge
605 Third Avenue, New York, NY 10158

Routledge is an imprint of the Taylor & Francis Group, an informa business

© 2022 Carl Waitz and Theresa Clement Tisdale

The right of Carl Waitz and Theresa Clement Tisdale to be
identified as authors of this work has been asserted by them in
accordance with sections 77 and 78 of the Copyright, Designs and
Patents Act 1988.

All rights reserved. No part of this book may be reprinted
or reproduced or utilised in any form or by any electronic,
mechanical, or other means, now known or hereafter invented,
including photocopying and recording, or in any information
storage or retrieval system, without permission in writing from
the publishers.

Trademark notice: Product or corporate names may be trademarks
or registered trademarks, and are used only for identification and
explanation without intent to infringe.

British Library Cataloguing-in-Publication Data
A catalogue record for this book is available from the British Library

Library of Congress Cataloging-in-Publication Data
Names: Waitz, Carl, author. | Tisdale, Theresa Clement, author.
Title: Lacanian psychoanalysis and Eastern Orthodox Christian
    anthropology in dialogue / Carl Waitz and Theresa Clement
    Tisdale.
Description: First Edition. | New York, NY : Routledge, 2022. |
    Includes bibliographical references and index.
Identifiers: LCCN 2021020525 (print) | LCCN 2021020526 (ebook) |
    ISBN 9781032102429 (hardback) | ISBN 9781032102412 (paperback) |
    ISBN 9781003214359 (ebook)
Subjects: LCSH: Psychoanalysis. | Theological anthropology—
    Christianity. | Orthodox Eastern Church—Doctrines. |
    Thought and thinking. | Lacan, Jacques, 1901–1981.
Classification: LCC BF175 .W258 2022 (print) | LCC BF175 (ebook) |
    DDC 150.19/5—dc23
LC record available at https://lccn.loc.gov/2021020525
LC ebook record available at https://lccn.loc.gov/2021020526

ISBN: 978-1-032-10242-9 (hbk)
ISBN: 978-1-032-10241-2 (pbk)
ISBN: 978-1-003-21435-9 (ebk)

DOI: 10.4324/9781003214359

Typeset in Times New Roman
by Apex CoVantage, LLC

To an Unknown God
The Victory he gave me
And my family

—Carl Waitz

I would like to dedicate this monograph to those who are
  raising their voices and pens to further the dialogue
  between psychoanalysis and religion/spirituality in
  theoretical, clinical, academic, and empirical arenas.
  Because of your creativity and courage, both fields will
  be enriched.

—Theresa Clement Tisdale

Contents

List of figure and tables	viii
Acknowledgments	ix
Another to Echo	x

PART I	1
1 Introduction	3
2 Lacanian psychoanalysis: an overview	9
3 Eastern Orthodox Christian theology: an overview	38
4 Lacanian psychoanalysis and Christianity	54

PART II	89
5 Oedipus at Eden	91
6 God in analysis	108
7 Jouissance and the body of the Church	121
8 The ethics of Orthodoxy	141
9 Ego and ego fate	148
10 Concluding reflections	163

Index	166

Figure and tables

Figure

7.1   Diagram of sexuation   122

Tables

2.1   Three types of lack of object   25
5.1   Three types of lack of object   97
5.2   First stage   99
5.3   Second stage   100
5.4   Full table   101

Acknowledgments

We have many people to acknowledge for assisting us through this process. We would like to recognize Christopher Meyer and Joy Bustrum who were members of the committee overseeing this project when it was first developed as Carl Waitz's dissertation and who provided guidance and feedback in its earliest stages.

Carl Waitz would like to acknowledge Christopher Meyer, whose psychoanalytic seminar he (Carl) attended during the development of this project and that oriented him to the work of Lacan. Similarly, Carl is grateful to the California Circle of the *École freudienne du Québec*, whose reading group he attended over the same period.

Theresa Clement Tisdale would like to acknowledge with gratitude those who have inspired, informed, and shaped her interest in psychoanalysis and religion/spirituality, particularly Beth Fletcher Brokaw, Ana-Maria Rizzuto, Randy Sorenson, James Jones, Moshe Halevi Spero, Marie and Lowell Hoffman, Brad Strawn, and Lew Aron.

Special acknowledgments also belong to those who have made it possible for our work to incorporate figures and tables from Lacan's work. We would like to thank Polity Press for permitting our use of the table of "Three Types of Object Lack" and its adaptations, appearing originally in Jacques Lacan, (2021), *The object relation: The seminar of Jacques Lacan, book IV*. (A. Price, Trans.). Malden, MA: Polity Press.

Similarly, we are grateful to Taylor & Francis Group for permitting the use of the version of the diagram of sexuation appearing originally in Evolving Lacanian Perspectives for Clinical Psychoanalysis, Raul Moncayo, Copyright (2008) and Imprint. Reproduced by permission of Taylor & Francis Group.

Finally, we also express thanks to Copper Canyon Press, The Permissions Company, The Wylie Agency, and the W. S. Merwin Estate for the generous permission for us to reproduce, in full, the poem "Another to Echo" from *The Moon Before Morning*. Copyright © 2014 by W. S. Merwin. It is reprinted with the permission of The Permissions Company, LLC on behalf of Copper Canyon Press and used with permission of The Wylie Agency LLC. This poem, which we first came across while writing this book, offers a beautiful entry into what we hope will be a study befitting its reflective tone.

Another to Echo[1]

How beautiful you must be
to have been able to lead me
this far with only
the sound of your going away
heard once at a time and then
remembered in silence
when the time was gone
you whom I have never seen
o forever invisible one
whom I have never mistaken
for another voice
nor hesitated to follow
beyond precept and prudence
over seas and deserts
you incomparable one
for whom the waters fall
and the winds search
and the words were made
listening

Note

1 W. S. Merwin, "Another to Echo" from *The Moon Before Morning*. Copyright © 2014 by W. S. Merwin. Reprinted with the permission of The Permissions Company, LLC on behalf of Copper Canyon Press, coppercanyonpress.org. Used by permission of The Wylie Agency LLC.

"Another to Echo" by W. S. Merwin, currently collected in THE MOON BEFORE MORNING. Copyright © 2014 by W. S. Merwin, used by permission of The Wylie Agency LLC.

Part I

Chapter 1

Introduction

Jacques Lacan (2005/2013) once remarked that Christianity is "the true religion" (p. 66). What might appear at first glance as an endorsement is rather a sharp critique—"it's the worst that can be said about it" (Lacan, 1975/1998, p. 107). As Lacan explained, Christianity—and particularly the Roman Catholic Church he grew up with (Roudinesco, 1993/1997)—is adept at providing *meaning*, in the sense that "meaning serves the purpose of *rationalization*, which keeps the unconscious at bay" (Fink, 2014, p. 7). The ability of Christianity to explain and provide understanding satisfies the ego because it covers up the ruptures of the inexplicable into one's sense of reality—ruptures that cause a wealth of anxiety. For Lacan, "the true religion," by its ability to explain, often amounts to anxiety avoidance and the prevention of hearing the speech of the unconscious. It is because of its function of reassuring the ego that Lacan averred "the triumph of religion" (Lacan, 2005/2013, p. 63).

In contrast, psychoanalysis does not seek to rationalize or explain the inexplicable ruptures, but to attend closely to them, to speak them but not to explain them (Fink, 2014); as such, the question for psychoanalysis is not one of triumph—Lacan conceded that it will not triumph—but one of survival: "either it will survive or it won't" (Lacan, 2005/2013, p. 64). The survival of psychoanalysis depends to a large degree on the totality with which the inexplicable, which Lacan called the real,[1] is paved over when it irrupts—a function served by the "Roman" religion, as Lacan puts it (Lacan, 2005/2013, p. 64). In contrast to this form of religion, the relationship of the real to psychoanalysis is one of symptomatology; that is, "psychoanalysis is a symptom" (Lacan, 2005/2013, p. 65). It is a consequence of the real's irruption into our sense of reality—an irruption following the rapid change in the human context due to the exponential revolution in science and technology. The advancements in these areas "introduce all kinds of distressing things into each person's life" (Lacan, 2005/2013, p. 64), widening the opening that reveals the real. In response to this emergence or irruption of the real, Christianity in its Western garb has sought to cover over the looming gaps with meaning—for example, explaining the yawning questions about the origins of life and the universe—which lessens the anxiety people feel in the face of the real. Psychoanalysis seeks another perspective: "We must be able to get used to

DOI: 10.4324/9781003214359-2

4 Introduction

the real" (Lacan, 2005/2013, p. 77). Thus, as the Church and other explanatory models rush to catch up to the universe opened by the ruptures in meaning generated by science, psychoanalysis, as an expression of the real, may find its end.

Indeed, psychoanalysis faces a field increasingly determined by reductionisms to manualized interventions, evidenced-based practices, and brief courses of treatment. All these reductions essentially serve to provide meaning: that chemical imbalances are the agent of malaise, that symptoms do not carry significance, that complex psychic structures can be rendered manageable through emotion regulation, and so forth. Although some of these explanations may bear on historical facts of the human organism, their status as *meaning* in the Lacanian sense comes from their function as stoppers of the unconscious. The explanations they offer satisfy prematurely, preventing further exploration. As such, Lacan's expression of concern regarding the survival of psychoanalysis was prescient. However, is Christianity by necessity a method of hiding the real? Is it impossible to write the relationship between Christianity and psychoanalysis, in the Lacanian sense, in terms different from contradiction? Or is there a Christianity that might be consonant with Lacanian psychoanalysis' insistence as a symptom?

In addressing the question of Lacanian analysis' relationship to something of the realm of religion, some authors have been so broad as to approach religion as a whole concept, that is, from the perspective of some synthetic collection of religions that lacks acknowledgment of differentiation, which also covers over the real in its own way. Lacan himself argued that "to try to put all religions in the same basket and do what is called 'the history of religions' is truly awful" (2005/2013, p. 66). The attempt to view all religions as a single phenomenon or whole entity that is capable of "integration" with another field, such as psychoanalysis, is inherently problematic. Because of this, a *particular* view of religion is more suitable for developing a dialogue.

Various bodies of work have sought this particular interaction between Lacanian analysis and specific religious traditions. Raul Moncayo (1998a, 1998b, 2003, 2012) has contributed significantly to the discussion of Buddhism and Lacanian psychoanalysis; Moshe Spero has written on Orthodox Judaism and Lacanian psychoanalysis (Spero, 1996; see Cohen, 2008); and various authors have written of Western Christianity and Lacanian psychoanalysis. This latter category includes a notable segment that appears to be based on secular theology, such as contained in Wyschogrod et al.'s (1989) volume; in Parker (1999); in Rashkow (2007); and in Davis et al.'s (2014b) volume. Although these authors make genuine attempts to form connections between these fields, the subject of religion about which they write is often at odds with what many who describe themselves as Christians believe in day-to-day practice. Zizek's (2003) work is perhaps the quintessence of this approach.

Seeking to connect Lacanian analysis to Christianity by utilizing a theology predicated on academic interest will only ever be an academic exercise. These are works implicitly by and for theologians. Such excursions are largely confined to a limited audience, despite the adroitness of their observations.

Furthermore, the use of such theology divests Christianity of its religious content—that is, the belief in its core beliefs—effectively precluding authentic connection with the tradition by removing its heart. This is problematic, as any search for consonance between psychoanalysis and Christianity will succeed only if the violence occurring is not the violence of divestment but the violence of the real as exposed between the fields and in their overlapping claims. Something as thoroughgoing as secular theology's logical working through of systems of thought, even if expressed in Lacanian terms, leaves little room for the violence of the real as it seeks to account for everything; ironically, this approach then contributes to the paving over of the real.

Other authors have taken an approach to dialogue between Lacanian analysis and Christianity that seems to be grounded in traditional rather than secular theology. These include Dunlap (2014) and DeLay (2015), whose work is further explored in Chapter 4. However, all of the authors writing from both secular and more traditional theological perspectives rely on Western conceptions of Christianity as descended from the Western Church after the East–West Schism of 1054. Although Lacan described Catholicism as religion *par excellence*, the systematic approach to theology broadly taken in both Protestant and Catholic Western Christianity lends itself to the same process of explaining and, therefore, hiding the real. There has been remarkably little engagement between Lacanian analysis and Christianity descended from the Eastern tradition (Dunlap, 2014). Given the starkly contrasting theological foundations of Eastern and Western Christianity, Eastern Christianity is uniquely suited for dialogical engagement with Lacanian psychoanalysis. Might Eastern Orthodox Christianity prove more open to the reality of Lacanian psychoanalysis?

We believe so! The Eastern Orthodox Church is historically, theologically, and experientially different from the Western forms of Christianity as manifested in Roman Catholicism and Protestantism, which, "to an Orthodox . . . appear as two sides of the same coin" (Ware, 1993, p. 2). Eastern Orthodoxy offers an inversion of the more typically antinomical relationship between Christianity and Lacanian analysis. Indeed, we hope to demonstrate that these traditions can be enlightening to one another in speaking about human experiences. In Orthodoxy, Lacanian psychoanalysis can discover a form of Christianity not devoted by necessity to paving over the real. Similarly, beyond the acceptance of psychoanalysis as a treatment suitable for Orthodox Christians, Orthodoxy can find in Lacanian psychoanalysis a pathway to further the development of Orthodox thought on human nature. To explore the ways these traditions may supplement one another, this study provides an investigation of a common point of interest to both: anthropology. Religious anthropology has enjoyed some previous exposure in the literature through Lacanian interpretations of the creation story in Genesis (Parker, 1999; Rashkow, 2007; Spero, 1996), but almost none from an Orthodox perspective. Orthodox theologians and authors are not, for their part, uniformly skeptical of psychoanalysis; Fr. Vasileios Thermos (2002) engaged in dialogue with the Winnicottian tradition, and Pia Sophia Chaudhari (2019) examined analytical psychology

6 Introduction

for resonance with the Orthodox faith. Some Orthodox authors have examined Lacanian psychoanalysis, such as Yannaras (1996), Kalinich (1988, 1990), and Schneider (2009); while these chapters and articles are excellent theological works, they are quite brief and illustrative, calling for a greater investment in examining the potential creative space between Lacanian analysis and Eastern Orthodox Christianity.

To assist in structuring the dialogue between Lacanian psychoanalysis and Orthodoxy, we will use the creation story as a beginning point in the second half of the book. Several other Lacanians have engaged with the creation narrative. Points of resonance between the fields are examined by viewing anthropology from both a position within Lacanian psychoanalysis and from within an Orthodox perspective. Ultimately, Eastern Orthodoxy is shown to share with Lacanian analysis a remarkable emphasis on the real.

Because Lacanian psychoanalysis and Eastern Orthodox theology are two particular traditions resting in more general fields, this book is designed to gradually introduce themes and ideas pertinent to dialogue between them. In this spirit, Chapters 2 and 3 are paired overviews; Chapter 2 provides an introduction to critical concepts in Lacanian psychoanalysis, and Chapter 3 explores important components of Eastern Orthodox theology, including points of divergence from the Western Christian tradition. Rather than attempting to provide exhaustive reviews, these two chapters provide a basic framework to enable those unfamiliar with one or the other field to effectively engage with the remainder of the book.

Chapter 4 contains a review of the literature regarding Lacanian analysis and religion, with particular emphasis on the limited literature that already exists at the nexus of Eastern Orthodoxy and Lacanian analysis. It also addresses previous Lacanian interpretations of the creation and fall narratives in Genesis to examine the state of anthropology as intersected by both Lacanian analysis and Orthodox theology. This chapter will provide contextual understanding for the direct dialogue between Lacanian psychoanalysis and Eastern Orthodoxy.

The remaining chapters of this book contain the bulk of our theoretical development. Chapter 5 provides a new reading of the story of the creation and fall of humanity, utilizing the Orthodox Church's unique perspective of the narratives to highlight new interpretations of the texts. Chapter 6 provides an extended reflection on the position of God in psychoanalysis. Specifically, the Orthodox doctrine of the essence/energies distinction is put in conversation with Lacan's conceptions of the Thing and the unconscious. Chapter 7 addresses how Lacanian psychoanalysis' knowledge of sex, sexuation, and sexuality may supplement and enlarge the Church's mind with respect to sexual praxis. Chapter 8 explores the role of ethics between Eastern Orthodox theology and Lacanian psychoanalysis using Lacan's teaching and the Orthodox hagiographies of two saints. Chapter 9 discusses the ego and its fate; the ego is viewed as symptomatic in Lacanian analysis and the individual person is vital in the Orthodox Christian faith.

The book concludes with a reflection on the implications of the theoretical development presented, its limitations, and further directions that might be explored. As is the case throughout the book, the focus will be on ways in which Lacanian psychoanalysis and Eastern Orthodoxy might continue to be mutual and reciprocal fellow workers through ongoing dialogue.

Lacan wrote that the psychoanalyst's journey "requires a long subjective ascesis" (Lacan, 1966/2006, p. 264). This ascetic journey—the development of knowledge— is not found in discrete techniques and manuals. This book is intended to benefit both the clinician (analyst, psychologist, or psychotherapist) and those interested in spirituality, not by providing an instruction manual of integration, but by offering a perspective that may serve to shift one's position in relationship to the real.

Note

1 The Lacanian concept of the real is much more complex than this suggests, but this is explored more extensively in Chapter 3.

References

Chaudhari, P. S. (2019). *Dynamis of healing: Patristic theology and the psyche*. New York, NY: Fordham University Press.

Cohen, M. (2008). A dialogue between psychology and religion in the work of Moshe Halevi Spero, an Orthodox Jewish psychoanalysis. *Shofar: An Interdisciplinary Journal of Jewish Studies, 26*(2), 13–41.

Davis, C., Pound, M., & Crockett, C. (Eds.). (2014b). *Theology after Lacan: Passion for the Real*. Eugene, OR: Wipf and Stock.

DeLay, T. (2015). *God is unconscious: Psychoanalysis and theology*. Eugene, OR: Wipf and Stock.

Dunlap, A. (2014). *Lacan and religion*. New York, NY: Routledge.

Fink, B. (2014). *Against understanding, volume I: Commentary and critique in a Lacanian key*. New York, NY: Routledge.

Kalinich, L. J. (1988). The Logos in Lacan. *St. Vladimir's Theological Quarterly, 32*, 367–383.

Kalinich, L. J. (1990). Psychoanalysis and the quest for truth. *St. Vladimir's Theological Quarterly, 34*, 356–360.

Lacan, J. (1998). *The seminar of Jacques Lacan, book XX: On feminine sexuality, the limits of love and knowledge, 1972–1973*. (B. Fink, Trans.). New York, NY: W. W. Norton. (Original work published 1975)

Lacan, J. (2006). *Écrits*. (B. Fink, Trans.). New York, NY: W. W. Norton. (Original work published 1966)

Lacan, J. (2013). *The triumph of religion: Preceded by discourse to Catholics*. (B. Fink, Trans.). Malden, MA: Polity Press. (Original work published 2005)

Moncayo, R. (1998a). The real and symbolic in Lacan, Zen, and Kabbalah. *The International Journal for the Psychology of Religion, 8*(3), 179–196.

Moncayo, R. (1998b). True subject is no-subject: The real, imaginary, and symbolic in psychoanalysis and Zen Buddhism. *Psychoanalysis & Contemporary Thought, 21*, 383–422.

Moncayo, R. (2003). The finger pointing at the moon: Zen practice and the practice of Lacanian psychoanalysis. In J. D. Safran (Ed.), *Psychoanalysis and Buddhism: An unfolding dialogue* (pp. 331–385). Somerville, MA: Wisdom Publications.

8 Introduction

Moncayo, R. (2012). *The signifier pointing at the moon: Psychoanalysis and Zen Buddhism*. London, UK: Karnac Books.

Parker, K. I. (1999). Mirror, mirror on the wall, must we leave Eden, once and for all? A Lacanian pleasure trip through the Garden. *Journal for the Study of the Old Testament, 83*, 19–29.

Rashkow, I. (2007). Psychology and the Bible: What hath Freud wrought? *Svensk exegetisk årsbok, 72*, 31–48.

Roudinesco, E. (1997). *Jacques Lacan: Outline of a life, history of a system of thought.* (B. Bray, Trans.). New York, NY: Columbia University Press. (Original work published 1993)

Schneider, C. (2009). The transformation of Eros: Reflections on desire in Jacques Lacan. In A. Pabst & C. Schnedier (Eds.), *Encounter between Eastern Orthodoxy and radical Orthodoxy: Transfiguring the world through the Word* (pp. 271–289). Burlington, VT: Ashgate.

Spero, M. H. (1996). Original sin, the symbolization of desire, and the development of the mind: A psychoanalytic gloss on the Garden of Eden. *Psychoanalysis and Contemporary Thought, 19*, 499–562.

Thermos, V. (2002). *In search of the person: True and false self according to Donald Winnicott and St. Gregory Palamas.* (C. Kokenes, Trans.). Montreal, Quebec, Canada: Alexander Press.

Ware, T. (1993). *The Orthodox Church*. New York, NY: Penguin.

Wyschogrod, E., Crownfield, D., & Raschke, C. A. (1989). *Lacan and theological discourse*. Albany, NY: State University of New York Press.

Yannaras, C. (1996). Psychoanalysis and Orthodox anthropology. In J. T. Chirban (Ed.), *Personhood: Orthodox Christianity and the connection between body, mind, and soul* (pp. 83–89). Westport, CT: Praeger.

Žižek, S. (2003). *The puppet and the dwarf: The perverse core of Christianity*. Cambridge, MA: MIT Press.

Chapter 2

Lacanian psychoanalysis
An overview

Anything titled "overview" necessarily overlooks; it exists as a method of overlooking and redacting. In doing so, it belies the very ideas it seeks to present, as it organizes them into a synchronic system and gives senses of completeness and understanding to the reader, so often too easily. Even so, the overview imposes itself here as a necessity. Without some review of Lacanian analysis (and later of Orthodox Christianity), what follows would be significant only to the select persons familiar with both fields rather than to members of each field. These overviews offer a recapitulation of the ideas and perspectives of each respective field as they relate to the concepts necessary for the consideration of anthropology. On the Lacanian side, we are presenting the most critical information pertaining to the formation and structure of the psyche (or more precisely, the subject).

Lacanian analysis is far more complex and less organized than our overview may suggest. As such, readers quite familiar with Lacanian analysis will find room for disagreement with the outline we construct in this chapter. We view such disagreement as a central strength of a vibrant and growing community, and we hope that the process of reading this book will nonetheless contribute to the reader's knowledge at the very least through negation.

With this in mind, this chapter is not intended to be a comprehensive introduction to Lacanian psychoanalysis and much less a comprehensive introduction to Lacan as a biographical figure. It does not map all the peaks and valleys of the known landscape, but does attempt to provide enough of a map to navigate the exploration of a ground between analysis and Orthodox theology.

Biographical and preliminary remarks

Lacanian psychoanalysis is the school of analysis descended from the theory and practice of Jacques Lacan. Lacan trained at a number of prestigious hospitals in the late 1920s and early 1930s, becoming specially trained in forensic psychiatry (Marini, 1992; Roudinesco, 1993/1997).[1] After having defended his thesis on paranoiac psychosis, he mailed the work to Freud, receiving only "a banal postcard" in return (Marini, 1992, p. 100), presaging Lacan's lifelong turbulent relationship to the psychoanalytic establishment, particularly in the form of the International

DOI: 10.4324/9781003214359-3

10 Lacanian psychoanalysis

Psychoanalytic Association (IPA). This conflict was especially severe in 1953, when Lacan and some of his colleagues left the French component of the IPA, the *Société Parisienne de Psychanalyse* (SPP), to form the *Société Française de Psychanalyse* (SFP) over disagreements of technique (Roudinesco, 1993/1997).[2] Lacan and the others did not consider that this would cause their membership in the IPA to lapse; thus, the SFP began years of negotiations with the IPA to regain membership. In 1963, the SFP members were admitted into the IPA on certain conditions, one of which was that Lacan be excluded from the list of training analysts. After this, in 1964, Lacan went on to found his *École Freudienne de Paris* (EFP), which remained operative until his dissolution of it in 1980.

In 1953, Lacan began his famous seminar, which would last from 1953 until 1980, elaborating each year upon a different topic, concept, or problem in psychoanalysis, with a break in 1963 for the "inexistent seminar" (Miller, 2011) that Lacan never delivered due to his exclusion as a training analyst. During these years, Lacan developed his ideas leaning heavily on Freud but borrowing extensively from linguistics, mathematics, and topology, among other fields (Roudinesco, 1993/1997). Even when moving beyond Freud's theories, Lacan maintained a sense of connection to Freud, maintaining even to his death that he was a Freudian rather than a Lacanian.

Lacan's personal relationship with religion was mixed throughout his life. Lacan's family was Catholic, his mother and brother devoutly so; however, in his early youth, Lacan radically rejected the Catholicism and conservatism of his family even as his brother, Marc-Francois, pursued monasticism (Roudinesco, 1993/1997). The educated but somewhat detached religion of the French university at the time appealed to Lacan, who became interested in Spinoza and later in Nietzsche and German philosophy. Lacan was displeased with his brother's choice to enter monastic life. Despite this, Lacan dedicated his thesis "to the Reverend Father Marc-Francois Lacan, Benedictine of the Congregation of France, my brother in religion" (Roazen, 1996, p. 325).

Many years later, in 1953, during the internecine conflicts within French psychiatry (in the SPP), Lacan sought support from the Catholic Church (as well as the Communist Party), writing to his brother that his teaching was certainly within the "Christian tradition" (Roudinesco, 1993/1997, p. 205). Lacan went so far as to petition his brother for a meeting with Pope Pius XII, affirming how important religion was to him and referring to his holiness as "our common father" (as cited in Roudinesco, 1993/1997, p. 205). This meeting never occurred (despite Lacan's additional request for support from the French embassy). Even so, the SFP was kinder to religion than the SPP, including openness to Christians seeking to become analysts.

Lacan's interest in religion is clear throughout his seminar and appears also in his "Discourse to Catholics" and the interview referred to as "The Triumph of Religion" (Lacan, 2005/2013). Lacan was not content to dismiss religious thought, even if he never subscribed to it himself. He noted genially to the Catholic audience of his "discourse" that, during one session in the seventh year of his seminar, he lapsed into a lengthy quote from St. Paul, a shift his students noticed only due to the different "rhythm" of the passage (Lacan, 2005/2013, p. 19).

Lacan's interest in religious and philosophical thought extended to East Asia, with an interest particularly in Daoism (Roudinesco, 1993/1997). Although Lacan himself never made the trip to China for which he had at one point longed, his interests beyond the west appear even in the first year of his seminar, which Lacan (1975/1988) began with reference to Zen Buddhism's epistemology. Some years later, his seminar is also where he expressed discomfort with "the West" as "a term that I have no particular fondness for, and that one would be wrong to see as the center of my thought" (Lacan, 1986/1992, p. 123).

Despite his inclusion, at times, of religious thought in his teaching, Lacan was an atheist until his death; although he had imagined for himself a Catholic funeral, this was not possible (Roudinesco, 1993/1997). His brother Marc celebrated mass in his honor nonetheless, affirming that Lacan's work was "steeped in Catholic culture" (p. 408).

Lacan's exposition of psychoanalytic theory transformed over time, though he never synthesized or systematized his theory from some final vantage point; instead, he utilized his evolving ideas to continue moving the field of psychoanalysis forward. Lacan's *oeuvre* is often split into periods based on general themes, with Lacan's early period focused on his idea of the imaginary, his middle period on the symbolic, and his late period on the real (Hoens & Pluth, 2002, p. 2). This division is debatable, and dates vary; rather than attempting to mark geological periods in Lacan's thought, this overview focuses on Lacanian analysis through the lens of its actual practice today. To that end, in addition to Freud and Lacan, we will refer to the works of Bruce Fink and Raul Moncayo, among others, in organizing our approach.

Lacanian psychoanalysis is a unique manifestation of psychoanalytic theory. Whereas many forms of psychoanalysis in the United Kingdom (such as object relations) and in the United States (such as ego psychology) diverged sharply from Freudian psychoanalysis over the course of the 20th century, Lacan's influential ideas were based on a return to Freud. Lacan and his followers consistently reread Freudian texts, and Lacan offered glosses on many of Freud's ideas that showed both continuity with and separation from the Freudian analysis. Specifically, Lacanian analysis foregrounds those portions of Freudian theory that were most readily placed in the background by other schools of analysis: the unconscious (rather than the ego) and the death drive. By relying on these ideas, Lacanian analysts retain strong links with Freud, his works being a constant point of reference in the clinical literature (Hughes & Malone, 2002).

In addition to this theoretical divergence from other schools more popular in the Anglophonic world, the barrier of language also slowed the access of monolingual English speakers to direct experience of Lacanian theory and clinical practice. Even in surmounting this barrier through translation, Lacan's frequent use of word play and ambiguity in French further complicated (and still complicate) the transmission of his works into English (Fink, 1998).

12 Lacanian psychoanalysis

Due to the theoretical divergence and linguistic barriers between Lacanian psychoanalysis and its peers in the Anglophonic world, analysts from other schools may be unfamiliar with and possibly disoriented by some of Lacanian psychoanalysis' tenets and terminology. Indeed, the language of Lacanian psychoanalysis retains many Freudian elements that may sound atavistic—if not objectionable— to casual readers.

Bearing these differences in mind, the following overview provides a foundation of Lacanian analysis for considering anthropology while addressing possible points of confusion for those unfamiliar with Lacanian concepts. There are several more in-depth introductions to Lacanian analysis for those interested in exploring the theory further.[3]

Conversely, those familiar with Lacanian analysis will no doubt find elisions and gaps in the concepts presented here, but will hopefully also appreciate the lack that is necessary in any articulation of Lacanian thought (or any thought, for that matter). As with many fields, especially with Lacanian analysis, the reduction of a living practice to technique or the simplification of inherently complex ideas into comprehensible overviews poses a significant hazard. Ideally, rather than reducing Lacanian concepts or rendering them violently simplified, this overview offers glimpses of a much broader theory—providing enough context to ground discussion without becoming its own introductory text.

Conceptual overview of Lacanian analysis

With anthropology as the focal point of our work, exploring a Lacanian conception of the human person is critical, and much of this overview focuses on Lacanian understandings of the subject. The order in which these ideas are presented is intended to ease the reader into more complex ideas; conveniently, this also roughly follows something of a chronology in the development of Lacanian analysis.

First, the Lacanian conception of the self is discussed. Second, the three registers (*real, symbolic, imaginary*) are explained. Third, Lacan's distinction of need, demand, desire, and drive is addressed; this is followed, fourth, by the Freudian unconscious and, fifth, a consideration of subjective structure. More complex topics, including sexuation and narcissism, will be introduced in the context of later chapters.

The self

We begin the discussion of Lacanian anthropology with a Lacanian view of the self. "Self," here, is not a theoretical term in Lacanian analysis the way it is in some schools of psychoanalyses. The self, for Lacan as for Freud, is not a unified whole but a series of divergent agencies, which will be presented here in the context of their institution. A key concept to understanding the appearance of a "self" in Lacanian analysis is deferred action. This Freudian concept will be reviewed, as will the Mirror Stage, alienation, separation, and the Oedipus complex. These

Lacanian psychoanalysis 13

ideas will be presented in a graduated fashion, but apart from the related logical moments of alienation and separation, they do not necessarily represent a linear progression. They are all interrelated concepts, however, and benefit from the proximal discussion.

Deferred action

Lacanian analysis generally avoids developmental views of the self; Lacan (1975/1998) warned against "slipping back into the rut, the rut I call 'development,' which is merely a hypothesis of mastery" (p. 55).[4] Rather than presuming the possibility of mastery or viewing a child as moving chronologically through developmental stages (such as oral, anal, phallic, and genital), any type of a "developmental" stage in Lacanian analysis should be viewed as a sequence of logical moments (Evans, 1996; see Lacan, 1975/1988, 1966/2006). These logical moments are only discovered in retrospect, as a matter of construction. This can be understood as an operation of the Freudian principle of deferred action, or *Nachträglichkeit*.

The quintessential example of deferred action is Freud's (1950/1966) case of Emma, a woman who was not "able to go into shops *alone*" (p. 353). In her work with Freud, Emma revealed a memory of going into a shop when she was 12 years old, but left in fright when she saw two shop assistants laughing. Emma believed they "were laughing at her clothes and that one of them had pleased her sexually" (p. 353). However, Freud did not see a strong connection between her compulsion (not entering shops alone) and the incident with the shop assistants. With further work, Emma produced a second memory. When she was 8 years old, she entered a shop alone, and a shopkeeper sexually molested her by groping her genitals over her clothes.

In exploring what might have associated this second scene (of the assault) with the first (of the shop assistants), Freud (1950/1966) observed three connections. First, the laughter of the shop assistants mirrored the grin of the shopkeeper during the assault; second, the shop assistants were laughing at her clothes, which were also implicated in the assault; and third, Emma's sense that one of the shop assistants was sexually pleasing related to a "*sexual release*" that the memory aroused, which the event itself "was certainly not able to at the time" (p. 354), and which Emma experienced as anxiety. What had caused this change in the experience of the memory of the second scene? Emma's undergoing of puberty between the ages of 8 and 12. The physiological changes of puberty invested the first remembered scene (at 12) with a traumatic element (sexual release) absent in the event (at 8) as it occurred. It is this form of retroactive operation that is called *deferred action*.

Lacan employed the concept of deferred action in a variety of ways, such as connecting it to the way sentences are meaningful only when the final word arrives, which then solidifies the meaning and requires the sentence to be reread (Lacan, 1966/2006). The significance of logical time for Lacanian conceptions of the self is that, rather than espousing development stages, Lacanian analysis understands logical moments or times. Thus, the following descriptions of development should

14 Lacanian psychoanalysis

not be viewed as stages through which a person moves but "moments which, while not always or easily discernible chronologically, must have occurred for the child to have reached its present clinical structure" (Fink, 1997, p. 248).

The Mirror Stage

When an infant is born, it does not have, in a psychoanalytic sense, an ego (Moncayo, 2008, p. 4). Although evidence has shown newborn infants do have a sense of self in some way (e.g., Stern, 1985), this sense of self should not be conflated with the ego in the psychoanalytic sense. The ego is not simply a neural network capable of response or adaptation, a repository of consistent behavioral patterns, or a seat of conation. The ego, rather, is reflexive and metacognitive. It is the image a person assumes through primary identification as oneself (Lacan, 1966/2006); the infant is not born with this identification or self-reflection.

Furthermore, when an infant is born, neither is it "all id," as the unconscious and desire, in Lacanian analysis, are not physiologically inherent but psychically instantiated. Initially, the infant is not a subject split into conscious and unconscious, but possesses only a fragmentary body (Lacan, 1966/2006). The infant is *infans*, "the one who does not yet speak" (Apollon, 2002a, p. 52; see Lacan, 1966/2006, p. 371). An infant has not yet assumed the image that will form the ego. However, "at the *infans* stage," the infant has some primordial sense of self (Lacan, 1966/2006, p. 76) and is able to communicate, in some sense, by crying; however, it is the Other (often, the mother)[5] who attributes a meaning to the cries rather than the infant (Fink, 1997). The infant, as an organism without an assumed image or ego, experiences physiologically based *needs*. Lacanian analysis differentiates need from drive, in that drive is a function of the unconscious and therefore only present in a subject who has undergone primal repression (Lacan, 1966/2006)—a subject split between conscious and unconscious. For this reason, an infant cannot be said to be ruled by drives or by the unconscious as this split has not occurred.

Rather, the beginning of the subjective split (conscious/unconscious) in the child comes during the Mirror Stage, the time in a child's life from about 6 to 18 months of age when it comes into contact with its reflection (Lacan, 1966/2006). When the child sees its reflection, it sees an image of wholeness and unity and makes a connection between the image and its self. When the child sees this specular image, it turns to the Other (frequently the mother) who affirms the misrecognition of the image as the self—"That's you!" (Fink, 1995, 1997). This is a misrecognition because "the image of [the child] in no way contains him" (Lacan, 2005/2013, p. 35). This affirmation from the Other leads the child to the assumption of the specular image as its self, as its ideal ego. The ideal ego is, more or less, the child's conception of how the mother (Other) sees it and is how the child strives to be. The ideal ego has a close relationship to the mother's object, and "the existence of the object [of the mother] precedes that of the ego" (Moncayo, 2008, p. 4). This is important in understanding the child always enters into a predetermined field: "A child is . . . born into a preestablished place in its parents' linguistic universe, a space often prepared many months, if not years, before the child sees the light of day" (Fink, 1995, p. 5). The mother's object informs the specular image and ideal ego that the child assumes. Lacan (2005/2013) noted "the ego is made up of identifications that are superimposed like [layers of] peels" (p. 35), of which the specular image is the first to appear.

The object that precedes the ego, that the ego is formed around, is called by Lacan the *objet petit a*.[6] The meaning of *objet a* was developed over many years and is quite dense. It is the object-cause of desire or, as Willy Apollon (2002a) aptly referred to it, "the lost cause of desire" (p. 51). This is an object of absence; it is the cause, rather than the sought after and illusory satisfaction, of desire. What it means for the ego to be formed around the *objet a* is first that the child seeks to be what the mother desires by assuming the ideal ego (Moncayo, 2008).

Regardless of who the Other is for the child (mother or another), the *objet a* will always be lacking in the image of the ideal ego (or in most cases, anyhow; see Moncayo, 2008; Waitz, 2019). In other words, the ego itself is formed around a lack or "empty core" (Moncayo, 2008, p. 24), and the subject will seek what is lacking throughout life.

Alienation

Alienation refers to the alienation of the subject from itself in its appearance in language. Although the ego might exist in some sense without alienation, alienation is necessary to the institution of the subject proper. Alienation is precipitated when the child experiences the presence and absence of the Other, which creates space for the entrance into language—indeed, forces the child to enter language.

Regarding the necessary play of presence–absence, Freud (1920/1955) recounted watching his grandson play with his toys in a game: *fort-da*. In this game, the 18-month-old child would throw his toys away while making an exclamation that Freud interpreted as *Fort!* or "Gone!" in German. When the child would bring the toy back to himself, he would exclaim *da!* or "There!" in German. Freud interpreted this as the child's response to his mother's absence and presence, making his toys present and absent in the same way. He offered multiple hypotheses regarding the function of the play, all focused on the presence–absence of the mother. Freud examined this occurrence for its significance in relation to repetition and what he would develop as the death drive, but Lacan (1966/2006) read in this example a Freudian basis for the effects of the institution of the subject within language. For Lacan, Freud recounted cases like this "in a flash of genius . . . so that we might see in them that the moment at which desire is humanized is also that at which the child is born into language" (1966/2006, p. 262).

Both desire and its counterpart lack enter through language. It is the alternating presence and absence of the mother (who is, prior to this alternation, undifferentiable from the infant itself) that will induce symbolization in the infant; if mother is always present or always absent, then there is no need for symbolizing "mother," and the mother is essentially a part of the infant or is never there.

16 Lacanian psychoanalysis

Symbolization enters the infant first in the form of crying, which is interpreted by the mother as a symbol (Fink, 1997). The institution of language is thus predicated on absence and loss, both the loss of the mother's presence and the loss of that part of the child left out of the first signifier (whatever, e.g., is missed in the mother's attribution of meaning to the infant's cry). It is what is lost when entering language that situates the desire of every speaking being—"the symbol first manifests itself as the killing of the thing, and this death results in the endless perpetuation of the subject's desire" (Lacan, 1966/2006, p. 262). Thus, the subject's desire and lack are "coextensive" (Fink, 1995, p. 54).

The entrance into language is a forced choice, which Lacan dramatized as a *vel*, borrowing from the field of logic (Lacan, 1973/1978, p. 209). Where *vel* typically refers to the inclusive logical disjunction between two terms, Lacan used the *vel* in another sense, that the choice in entering language is one that requires one to know "whether one wishes to preserve one of the parts, the other disappearing in any case" (p. 211). The example Lacan provided to explain this is the demand of a mugger, "*Your money or your life!*" (p. 212). A person responding to the demand will lose their money no matter what, but they might choose to keep their life— but a life lacking something (the money). For alienation in language, the choice is between being and meaning, which Lacan represented as a Venn diagram with "non-meaning" in the overlapping area.

As Lacan (1973/1978) described:

> If we choose being, the subject disappears, it eludes us, it falls into non-meaning. If we choose meaning, the meaning survives only deprived of that part of non-meaning that is, strictly speaking, that which constitutes in the realization of the subject, the unconscious. In other words, it is of the nature of this meaning, as it emerges in the field of the Other, to be in a large part of its field, eclipsed by the disappearance of being, induced by the very function of the signifier.
>
> (p. 211)

When the subject answers the call of the Other through language, being slips away. Lacan referred to this slippage as *aphanisis* (somewhat repurposing Ernest Jones' terminology), meaning disappearance. "If the subject appears on one side as meaning, produced by the signifier, it appears on the other as *aphanisis*" (p. 210).

Thus, just as the symbolization of the mother is tantamount to her death/ absence, the institution of language in the subject causes the loss of being. Conversely, choosing being over meaning results in the loss of both, as the subject cannot exist without the imposition of language. For most, the forced choice is resolved as choosing meaning and thus accepting the signifier of the Other—as well as the loss of being attendant. The institution of the subject in this dialectic is, for Lacanian analysis, primal repression (*Urverdrängung*), in which the first signifier (for Freud, *Vorstellungsrepräsentanz*) is repressed and which institutes the unconscious (Fink, 1990).[7]

Separation

Lacan (1973/1978) introduced another moment of subjective determination in connection with alienation: separation. In alienation, the child accepts the signifier of the Other for the subject, thus leading to a loss of part of the subject (what is lost in being). However, at a certain point, the child comes to perceive that the mother has a desire outside of the child; in other words, the child perceives the lack in the Other. The child attempts to fill this lack, to be whatever the Other desires. Lacan (1966/2006) observed, however, that the child does not actually

> fill the lack . . . he encounters in the Other, but rather, first of all, the lack that results from the constitutive loss of one of his parts, by which he turns out to be made of two parts. Therein lies the twist whereby separation represents the return of alienation.
>
> (p. 716)

The loss of that part of the child in alienation is reconstituted in the pursuit of the Other's desire, a pursuit stymied by the limit encountered by the child that forbids the lack in the child and the lack in the Other from overlapping wholly. This is also related to the *objet a*, which is the ideal overlapping lack/desire between the subject and the Other,[8] and which Lacan identified as the lost object of Freudian analysis (Fink, 1995). For Lacan (and not for Freud), the object was never possessed in the first place.

Oedipus complex

The Oedipus complex is an undeniably important part of psychoanalysis. Although Lacan initially followed the concept closely, he later distanced his ideas from the Oedipus complex in his own theoretical development, moving "Beyond the Oedipus Complex" (Lacan, 1991/2007, p. 85), calling it "Freud's dream" and suggesting its interpretation as such (p. 117).[9] Even so, the theory is still of import in Lacanian analysis, and reviewing the complex from a Lacanian standpoint is useful for explicating certain aspects of Lacanian analysis and terminology, as Lacan redefined many of Freud's terms and continued to use them in his own way.

The Oedipus complex, in Lacanian analysis, "operates as the mythical structure of that trauma which underlines the domination of the Law over the satisfaction of the drive" (Apollon, 2002b, p. 105). In other words, it is intimately related to the impositions of the paternal function and it is of practical import to Lacanian diagnostics and treatment. Lacan divided the Oedipus complex into three logical moments (Evans, 1996).

The first moment is that in which the child[10] recognizes the mother's desire for something Other than the child (Evans, 1996). The object of desire in this case is the *phallus*, which Lacan (1966/2006) distinguished from the penis. The penis is the physiological organ existing in the real. The imaginary phallus (symbolized as

18 Lacanian psychoanalysis

φ) is the object of satisfaction and presence, while the symbolic phallus (symbolized as Φ) is the object of desire, precisely that which is lacking (Evans, 1996). The mother's desire is for the phallus of the father, in Lacanian terms (though it should be noted that the term *father* also has real, imaginary, and symbolic dimensions). The child attempts to be the mother's phallus in an imaginary sense, to be her object of satisfaction and completion. However, the realization that the child does not have the imaginary phallus, coupled with the mother's omnipotence at this moment, produces anxiety in the child (Evans, 1996). In Lacanian analysis, the mother–child dyad is truly a triad (mother–phallus–child), and the relationship produces anxiety rather than satisfies desires.

The second moment of the Oedipus complex is the interdiction of the imaginary father, who causes the privation (lack in the real) of the mother by forbidding her unfettered access to the child (Evans, 1996). The imaginary father is "the composite of all the imaginary constructs that the subject [child] builds up in fantasy around the figure of the father" and "often bears little relationship to the father as he is in reality" (Evans, 1996, p. 63). As the child perceives him, the imaginary father's interdiction establishes the incest taboo, which is the "no of the father," or *le Nom-du-Père*, a phrase Lacan used to signify both the No-of-the-Father as well as the Name-of-the-Father, which are homophonous in French: *le Nom-du-Père, le Non-du-Père* (Fink, 1995). The Name-of-the-Father signifies the imposition of the Law, the essence of which is the incest taboo. It is this taboo that the child runs into during separation, that which prevents the lack in the Other from perfectly fitting with the lack in the child.

The third moment of the Oedipus complex is that in which the child realizes the real father has the phallus and competition is meaningless and impossible to win (Evans, 1996). The child then identifies symbolically with the father, producing the *ego ideal*. Whereas the ideal ego is the specular image of perfection toward which the ego strives or imagines it has attained (Moncayo, 2008), the ego ideal is the introjected view of the ego from the perspective of the Other; it is what views the ego as object (Fink, 2004).

The process of the Oedipus complex leads to the symbolic castration of the child (Evans, 1996). Broadly speaking, symbolic castration is the imposition of the Law most obviously in the incest taboo. It is the preclusion of wholeness and the satisfaction of desire. However, incompleteness and the inability to achieve plenary satisfaction are structural realities of the human psyche, and the imaginal perfection before castration is merely a fantasy. As a matter of structuration, castration in Lacanian analysis is not reserved for a few subjects but is the general rule.

The registers

Central to Lacanian analysis, and a steady theme throughout Lacan's teaching, is his introduction of three psychic registers or orders. These three registers are the real, the symbolic, and the imaginary. These registers are typically illustrated by the Borromean knot, which is a chain of three rings connected together in such a way that the cutting or removal of one ring leads to the dissolution of all three (Leupin, 2004). The knot illustrates the interconnected nature of the registers and the fact that not one exists without the other two. Each of these registers will be considered in turn.

The imaginary

The imaginary is best understood as pertaining to images rather than to imagination as such, as it is not illusory per se (Lacan, 1966/2006). Because the imaginary is based on images, imaginary perspectives do not perceive lacks or absences. Images convey a sense of wholeness, as images and sights seem to contain everything and include all there is to see. The imaginary does have linguistic components, but serves essentially the function of defense by closing gaps in understanding by presenting a gestalt.

In Lacanian analysis, the imaginary register is thoroughly connected with the ego, due to the ego's formation in the Mirror Stage, where its coming-into-being is predicated on the assumption of the specular image as the self—the child sees an image in the mirror and takes on the image as "me" (Lacan, 1966/2006; Evans, 1996; Moncayo, 2008). Due to the otherness of the ego, a person will experience ambivalence toward the ego as well as toward little "o" others whom they encounter and perceive as rivals, precisely due to their similarity to the ego (Moncayo, 2008).

For this reason, the ego is "the center of all resistances to the treatment of symptoms" (Lacan, 1966/2006, p. 118). This is seen with particular clarity in both persons who are too rigid to see from another perspective and those who are too eager to take on the perspectives of others, as both positions are founded on the importance of meaning in the ego. In this way, the ego is "the mental illness of man" (Lacan, 1975/1988, p. 16), a direct inversion of ego psychology. As Bruce Fink (1997) observed,

> Of course the patient does not really want to change! If symptoms have developed, if the patient engages in symptomatic behavior, it is because a great deal of energy has become tied up in those symptoms. . . . Although the patient may initially claim to want to be relieved of his or her symptoms, he or she is ultimately committed to not rocking the boat.
>
> (p. 3)

The captation by the specular image is thus a key feature in understanding the nature of the register of the imaginary, as this identification is the source of a person's overarching commitment not to "rock the boat," as doing so is an affront to identity.

The symbolic

The symbolic encapsulates a variety of concepts; it is the realm of words and signifiers, but also of social and cultural rubrics and rules. In essence, the symbolic

20 Lacanian psychoanalysis

(and to a lesser extent, the imaginary) is the fabric of reality—reality as distinct from *the real*. It is the framework of understanding that comprises cultural, civilized, and linguistic topographies of the human world.

Freud's (1913/1953) *Totem and Taboo* is a mythological account of the foundation of civilization and illustrates the instantiation of the symbolic order (Lacan, 1966/2006, p. 106). In Freud's myth, the first humans lived in a primal horde, where the primal father drove away all his sons to bar them from having sexual relations with any of the females of the horde. The brothers then conspired against their father and murdered him, gaining access to all of the women. In consequence of the murder, however, two issues arose: first, the brothers, out of remorse, forbid the killing of the totem animal. Second, they recognized that every brother would want to become the new father and banish all the others. In view of this, the brothers instituted the incest taboo, "by which they all alike renounced the women whom they desired" (Freud, 1913/1953, p. 144). This law preserved their newfound allegiance to one another, and therefore is the Law *par excellence*, as it guaranteed the birth of civilization and marks the difference between the human and animal realms.

Lacan (1966/2006) was not naive to the "mythical circularity that vitiates" the story of *Totem and Taboo*, "insofar as from a mythological event—the killing of the father—it derives the subjective dimension that gives this event its meaning: guilt" (p. 95). As Safouan (2004) puts it, "It was the brothers, who were still engulfed in the order of nature, who created the condition that humanized them" (p. 36). Still, Lacan extracted the important elements from the story: the role of the-Name-of-the-Father (the dead father) in regulating the libidinal economy through culture. This is seen in the brother's adoption of the totem animal as the symbolic father and the assumption of the law of the father in the practice of exogamy (not having sexual relations or marriage with those of the same totem). The incest taboo in Lacanian analysis is essential to the process of identification that occurs in separation, as it is the taboo that precipitates the realization that the subject's lack and the lack of the Other are not able to exist in perfect superimposition.

The real and jouissance

The real is most simply understood as that which escapes both the symbolic and the imaginary (Fink, 1995). Insofar as the symbolic and imaginary are the fabric of human reality, the real is that which "ex-sists," which is to say it is beyond existence within reality, within words and images, or within understanding or meaning (Fink, 1995, p. 25). Although the real is that which ex-sists outside reality, it is important to note the real is not prior to the imaginary and the symbolic in either chronological or logical senses[11]; as with the Borromean knot, the real would not hold together without the other registers. However, because it ex-sists outside the everyday reality that people experience, the real appears as trauma and provokes anxiety at a conscious level (Fink, 1995). The real is "what does not work" (Lacan, 2005/2013, p. 61), is not manageable within meaning-making systems, and is that which people tend to work hard to cover over or to explain in order to maintain their reality. Unconsciously, the rupture of the real into reality, despite being traumatic, may also be experienced as a form of excessive pleasure/pain called *jouissance*.

Indeed, the real, while not prediscursive, is fantasized by the subject as an archaic period of unlimited enjoyment, such as the supposed union with the mother—that is, prior to castration/alienation (Moncayo, 2011). The subject is bitter for having had to relinquish this enjoyment in alienation and fantasizes replacing it (Fink, 1997). This plenary enjoyment is a fantasy of an animal-like desire that is able to reach satisfaction by joining with its complement (in other words, the fantasy of genitality). This tendency can be observed in fantasies of communion with nature, the "happily ever after" of Hollywood filmmaking, or in more extreme form, in Sadean fantasies. This fantasy of a real of limitless enjoyment is predicated on (or caused by) the prohibition of the incest taboo; Lacan (1986/1992, p. 83) quoted St. Paul, who wrote that "if it had not been for the law, I should not have known sin" (Rom. 7:7, RSV). The prohibition moves the satisfaction experienced from the prohibited action from pleasure to *jouissance* (Fink, 1997).

Jouissance is a concept that entails both enjoyment—often with a sexual connotation—and pain, and is typically left untranslated in Lacanian literature to communicate these ideas together. The *jouissance* produced by prohibition is phallic *jouissance*, as it is a product of the phallic function, that is, of castration. It is a phallic *jouissance* the subject seeks from a prediscursive real, which makes the situation something of a cruel joke: because it is the prohibition that creates *jouissance*, there is no *jouissance* accessible before the Law; it is pure fantasy (Lacan, 1966/2006, pp. 682, 696). Although unlimited phallic *jouissance* from before castration is a logical impossibility, there is an Other *jouissance* that makes an appearance in Lacanian analysis (Lacan, 1975/1998). This Other *jouissance* is beyond, rather than before, the phallic function (Moncayo, 2008), and is discussed further under the Sexuation heading.

One final note of consideration regarding *jouissance* is that pleasure, as the maintenance of homeostasis through the ministrations of the pleasure principle, serves as a limit to *jouissance* (Lacan, 1966/2006). To the extent that approaching the *objet a* (in the form of the overlapping desire between the subject and Other) produces *jouissance*, the incest taboo that splits the subject from the object is a form of the pleasure principle.

Need, demand, desire, drive

Among the central pillars of Lacanian analysis rests desire, which is one of the themes Lacan is most known for developing (Bernstein, 2012). Desire in Lacanian psychoanalysis is specifically *unconscious* desire. Where Strachey translated *Wunsch* as "wish," the French translation of Freud's term is *désir*, which is then

22 Lacanian psychoanalysis

translated in English Lacanian texts as "desire" rather than the Stracheyo-Freudian "wish" (Evans, 1996; see also Lacan, 1966/2006, p. 518). Evans (1996) noted that both the English "desire" and French "*désir*" have "the implication of a continuous force, which is essential for Lacan's concept" (p. 37). For Lacanian analysis, desire is both unconscious and constant.

Lacan maintained a distinction between *Instinkt* and *Triebe* in the Freudian *oeuvre*, which is again contra Strachey, who translated both terms as "instinct" in the Standard Edition (Lacan, 1966/2006). For Lacanian analysis, the instinct is a biological need with a direct object, whereas the drive is a psychological function with no direct object (Fink, 1997; Lacan, 1973/1978). Given the place of importance both Lacan and Freud give to sexuality, this distinction is fundamental to the psychoanalytic concept of the human person, as sex is addressed as a matter of drive rather than instinct. To understand the relationship between instinct, drive, and desire, more must be said about each in relation to the others within Lacanian psychoanalysis.

Need and demand

Need, for Lacan, is a term essentially associated with instinct (e.g., Lacan, 1966/2006, p. 680); it is a physiological necessity, such as hunger. Animals and humans share the experience of need, such that both an animal and a human organism might experience hunger, eat, and be satisfied. Unique to humans,[12] however, is that when an infant experiences need, it must communicate this to the Other in the form of a demand, or request,[13] in language—and what a "mouse hole" is language into which need must squeeze (Lacan, 1998/2017, p. 78)! The demand, Lacan (1966/2006) noted, "bears on something other than the satisfactions it calls for. It is a demand for a presence or an absence" (p. 579). The demand is directed toward an Other that is alone capable of providing satisfaction of the need, and as such, the provision of the satisfaction is simultaneously a proof of love. This leads to demand's "transmuting" every satisfaction "into a proof of love" and every demand into a love demand (p. 580). There is, then, an ever-unsatisfied leftover. This leftover is desire, which is "neither the appetite for satisfaction nor the demand for love, but the difference that results from the subtraction of the first from the second, the very phenomenon of their splitting" (p. 580).

Desire

The formation of desire through need and demand can be articulated as the alienation of something of need in the articulation of demand which returns in desire (Lacan, 1966/2006). This is another way of understanding the operation of alienation. As desire is the difference of need and demand, it has no object of satisfaction, only its object-cause, the *objet a*. Because of this, desire is never satisfied and is always a "*desire for something else*" (Lacan, 1966/2006, p. 431).

Lacanian psychoanalysis   23

A subject's desire is also "the desire of the Other" (Lacan, 1973/1978, p. 235) in all senses encompassed therein. Desire is initially encountered in the Other as the mother's desire for something else, the hole constituting the lack of the Other, as discussed previously. Because desire proceeds from the lack of the Other, it is this lack the child initially tries to satisfy with the superimposition of its own lack, caused, as it was, in alienation (Lacan, 1973/1978). This is why desire is both of and for the Other. The only truly physiological phenomenon here, then, is need; desire is a product of the articulation of need in demand and is a psychological phenomenon alone, which also produces the drive.

Drive

The Freudian *Trieb*, similar to desire, is not at all related to physiological functioning (Lacan, 1973/1978, 1966/2006, p. 680). Although an animal might achieve satisfaction of instincts or physiological needs, the speaking being is barred from any such satisfaction for desire. Animal sexuality serves the purpose of reproduction, but human sexuality is bounded by the incest taboo (Leupin, 2004). Where animals might conjugate indiscriminately in order to maximize reproduction, the speaking being's sexuality is bound up with language and the prohibition of incest. Desire, being engendered by the prohibition (in alienation and separation), is solely a human phenomenon, and its object-cause (the *objet a*) is "the object around which the drive turns" (Lacan, 1973/1978, p. 243). Like desire, the drive is a psychological phenomenon and dependent upon the alienation of the subject within language.

Although Freud recognized dualism of the drives in life drives and death drives (or Eros and Thanatos), Lacanian analysis recognizes "two sides of the drive" (Lacan, 1973/1978, p. 199) or "two aspects of the drive" (p. 257), but not opposing drives. The drive might appear sexual or lethal depending on whether the drive appears in the imaginary or symbolic (Evans, 1996). Additionally, Lacan asserted that all drives are partial drives—partial in relation to their *aim* (Lacan, 1973/1978). Here, an aside to Freud may prove helpful.

Freud (1915/1957a) specified four aspects of the drive: thrust, source, object, and aim (pp. 122–123). In elaborating on Freud, Lacan (1973/1978) focused on the aim of the drive (*Triebziel*). While Freud discussed satisfaction of the drive as the achievement of its aim (i.e., genital and reproductive sex), Lacan noted the inherent contradiction in this idea of satisfaction, given satisfaction could also be obtained through aim-inhibited (*zielgehemmt*) sublimation of the drive. Lacan (1973/1978) "clear[ed] up the mystery of the *zielgehemmt*" by explaining the concept of the *Triebziel* through its French translation *but pulsionnel* (p. 179). Lacan noted *but* could be translated into English as "aim" and also as "goal":

> When you entrust someone with a mission, the *aim* is not what he brings back, but the itinerary he must take. The *aim* is the way taken. The French word *but* may be translated by another word in English, *goal*. In archery, the

24 Lacanian psychoanalysis

goal is not the *but* either, it is not the bird you shoot, it is having scored a hit and thereby attained your *but*.

(Lacan, 1973/1978, p. 179)

In this way, the *Triebziel*, or aim of the drive, is not the goal of reproduction but simply a return to its source, forming a circuit. This explains the satisfaction to be had from aim-inhibited drives—they do not achieve the reproductive goal, but do achieve the aim of return. However, it is the fact that the aim of the drive is not sexual reproduction that renders all drives partial (not reproductively aimed) and, therefore, "every drive is virtually a death drive" (Lacan, 1966/2006, p. 719).

What about the object of the drive? Earlier it was noted that the drive turns around the *objet a*, and Lacan (1973/1978) imagined the circuit of the drive leaving the source, circling around the *a*, and returning once again to the source (achieving its aim). The *objet a* is merely "a hollow, a void, which can be occupied . . . by any object" (p. 180). Thus, the complete circuit of the drive includes the orbit of the object. Where Freud (1915/1957a) saw active and passive forms of the drive (e.g., to see, to be seen), Lacan suggested this was "support, artifice, which Freud uses in order to enable us to understand the outward-return movement of the drive [in its circuit]" (p. 200). Instead of activity and passivity, Lacan asserted an essentially active and reflexive drive ("to make oneself seen," [p. 200]).

One final consideration in the discussion of the drive is the libido. Lacan relied on the concept of libido much less frequently than Freud (Evans, 1996), but his reflections are significant. In considering the libido, Lacan (1973/1978) developed the myth of the lamella. The lamella is something that "flies off" when the human fetus emerges from the egg membranes (p. 197). It is "extra-flat" and "moves like an amoeba" (p. 197). He also hinted that it "is related to what the sexed being loses in sexuality, it is, like the amoeba in relation to sexed beings, immortal—because it survives any division, any scissiparous intervention. And it can run around" (p. 197). This last bit Lacan used to add a little horror: "suppose it comes and envelopes your face while you are quietly asleep" (p. 197). This horrific, immortal, amoeba-like organ is:

> the libido, *qua* pure life instinct, that is to say, immortal life, or irrepressible life, life that has need of no organ, simplified, indestructible life. It is precisely what is subtracted from the living being by virtue of the fact that it is subject to the cycle of sexed reproduction. And it is of this that all the forms of the *objet a* that can be enumerated are the representatives, the equivalents. The *objets a* are merely its representatives, its figures. . . . The *objet a* certainly represents that part of himself that the individual loses at birth, and which may serve to symbolize the most profound lost object.
>
> (Lacan, 1973/1978, p. 198)

That is, the *objet a*, the lack around which the subject is instituted, is none other than a representative of the lamella. The *objets a* are multiform, but the lamella is

Lacanian psychoanalysis 25

singular. What's more, the lamella plays an intimate role in human sexuality—by its absence.

According to Lacan (1973/1978), human sexuality is not strictly defined by drive or physiology; rather, "sexuality is established in the field of the subject by a way that is that of lack" (p. 204). The superimposition of two lacks is relevant here again, the first lack of the subject instituted in alienation, and the second lack that occurs through the cycle of sexual reproduction. Whereas sexual reproduction guarantees the ongoing life of the living being, sexual reproduction is predicated on the eventual destruction of one's genetics as only half are ever passed on. Lacan called this second lack of sexed reproduction a real lack, "because it relates to something real, namely, that the living being, by being subject to sex, has fallen under the blow of individual death" (p. 205). This real lack is the lamella, indestructible life. Lacan noted that rather than searching for a soulmate, a person goes through life searching for "the part of himself, lost forever, that is constituted by the fact that he is only a sexed living being, and that he is no longer immortal" (p. 205). For Lacan, this loss is the origin of the drive and sexuality, and the reason the drive is "profoundly a death drive and represents in itself the portion of death in the sexed living being" (p. 205). In other words, the drive is a manifestation of the death of the subject due to sexual reproduction.

Lack in the Oedipus complex

Having differentiated the three registers and delineated need, demand, desire, and drive, a brief return to the Oedipus complex is useful to clarify Lacan's reading of the complex in greater detail. In describing the process of castration, Lacan differentiated the form that lack takes in the three registers (Lacan, 1994/2021). Each form of lack pertains to a different agent and a different object (see Table 2.1).

In the first logical moment of the Oedipus complex, the symbolic mother, the Other to whom the child addresses the demand for love, causes the frustration of the child in the imaginary (the realm of the demand for satisfaction) through the lack of the real object, the breast (Evans, 1996). This, of course, influences the child's perception of the mother as all-powerful and the child as her object.

However, in the second moment of the Oedipus complex, the imaginary father causes the privation of the mother—her lack in the real—of the child, who is for her the symbolic phallus (Evans, 1996). The frightening imaginary father here

Table 2.1 Three types of lack of object

Agent	Lack	Object
Real father	Symbolic castration	Imaginary phallus
Symbolic mother	Imaginary frustration	Real breast
Imaginary father	Real privation	Symbolic phallus

Source: Adapted from Lacan (1994/2021, p. 207).

26 Lacanian psychoanalysis

separates the child from the mother in a real sense, showing the mother (who respects the father's interdiction) does not have the phallus.

In the third moment of the Oedipus complex, the real father, as that which the mother desires, causes the castration—the lack in the symbolic—of the child, that which the child had attempted to be for the mother, namely, the imaginary phallus (Evans, 1996).

This movement of imaginary, real, and symbolic demonstrates the different dimensions of the mother, the father, and lack. Although these moments are not necessarily essential to an understanding of the Oedipus complex, they provide helpful texture in contemplating the determination of the subject from a psychoanalytic perspective.

The unconscious

Lacanian psychoanalysis is not a depth psychology, as there is no depth to plumb.[14] Rather than some primordial well, whether individual, collective, or familial in nature, the unconscious might better be conceived of as a Möbius strip (Lacan, 1966/2006; see Fink, 1995; Leupin, 2004), where what appears to be two sides are truly only one side, different only when taken at specific local points. The unconscious is always on the other side.

In explaining the unconscious, Lacanian analysis relies on one of Lacan's most famous dicta, that "*the unconscious is structured like a language*" (e.g., Lacan, 1973/1978, pp. 149, 203). Freud (1915/1957b) stipulated that affect, or emotion, is never repressed; as Lacan (1973/1978) puts it, it only "goes off somewhere else, as best it can" (p. 217). Rather, it is thoughts—or signifiers in Lacan's language[15]— that are repressed. There is a signifier (S_1) that is repressed in primal repression and around which other signifiers (S_2) build up (Fink, 1995), comparable in some ways to a plaque or to amyloidosis, forming an unconscious signifying chain. In this way, the primally repressed signifier S_1, or master signifier, is essentially devoid of meaning and yet provides order to all other S_2 signifiers. It is the master signifier that remains unspoken, but toward which parapraxes and dreams point.

Lacan's use of linguistic terminology derives in many ways from Saussurean linguistic theory (Lacan, 1966/2006; Leupin, 2004). Saussurean linguistics relies on signification as a process split between the signified and the signifier (Leupin, 2004). For Saussure, the signified, or the concept being represented, is primary; it determines the necessity of a signifier. In contrast, Lacan placed the signifier (the linguistic representative) in the primary place over the signified (Lacan, 1966/2006). Therefore, against Saussure's example of an image of a tree (signified) calling for its signifier, Lacan offered the example of identical doors with only signifiers distinguishing them.

As Moustafa Safouan (2004) explained, "there is a relation [between signifier and signified], not the relation of the tree calling for a word, but rather the word that, in its different uses, may determine different significations" (p. 13). The primacy of the signifier means where Saussure saw signifier and signified as tied

Lacanian psychoanalysis 27

together, Lacan averred the "incessant sliding of the signified under the signifier" (Lacan, 1966/2006, p. 419).

This slippage brings the discussion back to the unconscious. The slippage is displayed in two linguistic operations of the unconscious that Lacan elaborated: metaphor and metonymy. Lacan (1966/2006) equated the Freudian operation of condensation (*Verdichtung*) with metaphor and the operation of displacement (*Verschiebung*) with metonymy. These two operations represent shifts in the unconscious signifying chain, the first which has one signifier substitute for another (a synchronic operation) and the latter in which meaning slips due to the connections of signifiers (a diachronic operation).

The organized presentation here notwithstanding Lacan's discussion of psychic elements shifted over the course of his teachings. One such shift can be found in Lacan's exploration of *das Ding* during the year of his seminar in which he focused on ethics (Lacan, 1986/1992). The Thing is almost entirely absent from Lacan's work other than in this year of his seminar and a smattering of references in contemporaneous works (Evans, 1996; Lacan, 1966/2006, 2005/2013). The *objet a*, as it developed in Lacan's later formulations, assumes many characteristics of *das Ding* (Evans, 1996), but his theoretical exposition of *das Ding* is distinct from his later exposition of the *objet a*, and therefore deserves special attention.

Freud (1915/1957c) wrote that what is repressed in the unconscious is *Sachvorstellungen* (thing-presentations), whereas *Wortvorstellungen* (word-presentations) belong instead to the preconscious. Some of Lacan's critics accused him of innovation by violating this principle when he reported signifiers are repressed (Evans, 1996). Lacan (1986/1992) clarified that *Wortvorstellungen* are indeed at the level of the *Vorbewusstsein*, or preconscious, but the *Wortvorstellungen* are related to discourse rather than "an economy of words," which are indeed repressed (p. 63). At the level of the economy of words is the *Vorstellungsrepräsentanz*, or "representative of the representation" (Lacan, 1973/1978, p. 217):

> That which in the unconscious represents, in the form of a sign, representation as a function of apprehending—of the way in which every representation is represented insofar as it evokes the good that *das Ding* brings with it.
>
> (Lacan, 1986/1992, p. 72)

Lacan (1986/1992) distinguished between the level of the *Sache* and *Wort*, which "form a couple," and the level of the *Vorstellungsrepräsentanz*, maintaining the linguistic structure of the unconscious (p. 45). In relation to these levels, Lacan insisted "*das Ding* is found somewhere else" (p. 45) and "is something entirely different" (p. 52). *Das Ding* is "the beyond-of-the-signified" (p. 54).[16]

In exegeting Freud, Lacan (1986/1992) differentiated between two words for "thing" in German—"*das Ding*" and "*die Sache*" (p. 43). *Die Sache* appears in thing-presentations, *Sachvorstellungen*, as noted. *Das Ding* is not this. Lacan called *das Ding* "the prehistoric Other that it is impossible to forget" (Lacan, 1986/1992, p. 71). The Thing is "at the heart of a subjective world . . . at the center, with the

28 Lacanian psychoanalysis

subjective world of the unconscious organized in a series of signifying relations around it" (p. 71). It is this strange and alien thing "at the heart of me" that "on the level of the unconscious only a representation can represent" (p. 71). This latter comment is a reference to the *Vorstellungsrepräsentanz*. The *Vorstellungsrepräsentanz* is the site of primal repression, which covers over the absence that *das Ding* marks.

This Thing, the beyond-of-the-signified, which "at the level of *Vorstellungen* . . . is not nothing, but literally is not" (Lacan, 1986/1992, p. 63), forms the gravitational center of the subject, around which the universe of the *Vorstellungen*, the signifying chain, turns (pp. 58, 62). The Thing is "a forbidden good," a good that one may not possess (p. 70). Thus, in relation to the Thing, the subject either keeps its distance to protect *Wohl*, well-being, or else it approaches the Thing, moving beyond the pleasure principle (*Lustprinzip*) toward the *Gut*, the Good, and the subject "cannot stand the extreme good that *das Ding* may bring him" (p. 73). When approaching the Thing, "the outer extremity of pleasure is unbearable to us" (p. 80). Thus, the pleasure principle serves a "regulatory" function (p. 57), protecting the *Wohl* of the subject. The way it achieves this is by determining the structure and movement of the constellation of the *Vorstellungen*.

To maintain distance from the Thing *qua* lost object, the subject, under the regulation of the pleasure principle, seeks the lost object only through its "pleasurable associations" (Lacan, 1986/1992, p. 52). Through the pursuit of a series of objects, the subject is able to maintain a distance from the Thing. The pursuit of pleasurable associations, in this sense, provides a limit to *jouissance* (the extreme good).

In addition to this substitution of objects at the level of the *Vorstellungen*, Lacan (1986/1992) noted two ways the subject may relate to the Thing, though he leaves open the possibility of the existence of other ways. One response is to act on desire (and *das Ding* is "the place of desire," [p. 110]) in a perverse manner, and the other is "excessive object sublimation" (p. 109), which is to "raise an object . . . to the dignity of the Thing" (p. 112). De Kesel (2001/2009) noted that in the former, the subject moves to take the place of the Thing, while in the latter, the object is put in the place of the Thing. Lacan described sublimation as an imaginary process, "coloniz[ing] the field of *das Ding* with imaginary schemes," where "the object is inseparable from imaginary and especially cultural elaborations" (Lacan, 1986/1992, p. 99). Thus, while the "economy of substitution in which the repressed drive is usually satisfied" (p. 110) is the circling of the Thing, sublimation is the centering of the object as "surrounded by," rather than "slipped into," "the network of *Ziele*," that is, the network of drive aims (p. 112).

Lacan (1986/1992) elaborated a couple of weeks later that there are perhaps three general forms of sublimation, namely, art (related to hysteria), religion (related to obsession), and science (related to paranoia). In all three cases, the Thing is kept at a distance, either by emphasizing its "emptiness," its "fullness," or by disbelieving in it altogether (De Kesel, 2001/2009, p. 97).

Finally, Lacan (1986/1992) situated the entire universe of the *Vorstellungen* "between perception and consciousness"[17] (p. 61), such that the unconscious is

Lacanian psychoanalysis   29

determinative in some way of what is available to the conscious system through the discourses of the preconscious system. As noted, *das Ding* is largely absent hereafter from Lacan's *oeuvre*, many of its characteristics passing onto the *objet a*, though notably the Thing has some commonalities with the lamella, including its lack of ontological reality and presence primarily as an absence through which series of objects dance.

Clinical structure

The subject's formation in alienation and separation may or may not follow the expected course, so to speak. Whether or not the subject undergoes these moments in its relation to the Other is determinative of its clinical structure. Lacanian analysis generally recognizes three clinical structures: psychotic, perverse, and neurotic (Fink, 1997). Regarding the latter category of neurosis, two substructures appear: the obsessive and the hysteric.[18] Each structure represents a different way of relating to the Other. Because the relation to the Other is the basis of clinical structure, these structures are not nosological in the same way the categories of the DSM are nosological; they do not comprise "the phenomenology of apparent symptoms," as Cantin (2002b, p. 155) noted, and do not signify abnormal states, per se. Rather, as every person relates to the Other in some way, everyone is positioned in one of these structures, as neurotic (obsessive or hysteric), perverse, or psychotic—there is no "normal" person (Fink, 1997).[19]

Psychosis

When the subject has undergone alienation and accepted the master signifier, undergoing the splitting of the subject into conscious and unconscious, there is an accession of meaning and a fading of being. The accession of meaning in the acceptance of the master signifier leads to the establishment of a connection between signified and signifier through *points de capiton*, translated variously as "quilting points," "anchoring points," or "button ties" (Evans, 1996; Fink, 1997). The *point de capiton* is a term borrowed from upholstery, and it describes the link between a button and the fabric of a couch or chair to prevent the movement of the stuffing. In the linking of the signified and signifier, the signifier is represented by the fabric and the button; signifiers relate only to one another, but the *points de capiton* secure the signified (stuffing) with the upholstery of the signifiers (Nobus, 2000). Thus, as noted earlier, the master signifier introduces order by organizing all other signifiers; Fink (1995) argues that "in accordance with Lacan's later usage, the Name-of-the-Father thus seems to be correlated with the S_1, the master signifier" (p. 75). Again, Lacan's terminology shifts over time, but the matter of crucial importance, whether one refers to the master signifier, the Name-of-the-Father, or the paternal function, is that the subject's acceptance of undergoing this experience is key to determining subjective structure.

Alienation is a *vel*, a forced choice in which the subject chooses between being and meaning, but always loses being regardless of the choice. A binary option

30 Lacanian psychoanalysis

exists, and in responding to the Other in the *vel* of alienation, the subject might accept meaning, or else it might defend itself through *foreclosure*, by foreclosing the Name-of-the-Father and ostensibly choosing being over meaning (see Lacan, 1973/1978). This foreclosure precludes the interdiction of the Name-of-the-Father and results in the absence of *points de capiton*, such that the psychotic is not constituted in language as a subject. Because of this, the psychotic subject experiences a lack of structure and a tenuous relationship to language. Worthy of note here is that psychosis from a Lacanian standpoint is not the same as psychosis in the sense of descriptive psychiatry. Because clinical structure is not related in a direct fashion to symptomatology, a person who has never had a "psychotic episode" may have a psychotic structure, a sort of latent psychosis (Fink, 2007). In fact, a major reason for the importance of determining clinical structure in Lacanian analysis is to avoid triggering a psychotic break in someone with a psychotic structure (Fink, 1997).

The interdiction of the Name-of-the-Father in alienation prevents the mother's access to "the imaginary of a possible *jouissance*," requiring the mother to recognize her own lack that is not able to be satisfied, which is her own desire (Cantin, 2002c, p. 42). This is where the clinical import of the incest taboo is clear:

> The law of the Father limits the jouissance demanded by the Other in the imaginary of the child; it states that the Other is not to be satisfied; that the lack it signifies refers to something that is beyond any relationship with others.
>
> (p. 42)

Thus, the foreclosure of the Name-of-the-Father does not inscribe a lack in the mother that results in the child's status as object of *jouissance* rather than object of desire (Cantin, 2002a). The lack of imposition of the Name-of-the-Father is very specifically the failure of the symbolic father rather than the imaginary father (Evans, 1996). This failure leads to the primacy of the imaginary for someone with a psychotic structure (Fink, 1997). Thus, as the imaginary is the realm of the mirror image and rivalry, relations with the father are competitive and aggressive. Bergeron (2002) noted that a psychotic person "experiences every relation as an imaginary one of strength and power" (p. 77). The psychotic person is thus one who experiences profound consequences of the lack of an interdiction on the Other's demands.

Perversion

Perversion, in its Lacanian sense, should not be confused with sexual deviancy (Evans, 1996); while a subject with a perverse structure may engage in sexual acts that are deviant from sociocultural norms, the acts do not make a person perverse. Perversion is a designation of subjective structure, thus, is a term that describes a subjective position in relation to the Other.

Whereas the psychotic subject has foreclosed the Name-of-the-Father and avoided in some way the primal repression of alienation, the perverse subject has undergone alienation (Fink, 1997). Unlike the neurotic subject, however, the perverse subject has not fully undergone separation. The defense common to the perverse structure is *disavowal*. Disavowal entails a simultaneous affirmation and denial, not of anything that arises, but specifically of castration of the maternal phallus (Cantin, 2002b; Fink, 1997). The pervert disavows the castration of the mother (and himself) by the intervention of the symbolic father, without which "the mother produces a fixation to the omnipotent mother and the primal father" (Moncayo, 2008, p. 56). The mother is the imaginary mother, whole and without lack or desire. Because the pervert does not thoroughly experience the mother's desire, he cannot attempt to be her object-cause of desire (*objet a*), and instead, he assumes the role of object-cause of her *jouissance* (Swales, 2012). However, as disavowal is also predicated on a fundamental affirmation of the mother's lack, perverse symptoms betray the perception of a lack, which distinguishes disavowal from repression (Fink, 1997).

Another way of expressing the disavowal of the mother's lack is the denial of the phallus (Cantin, 2002b). In this sense, the phallus as *Vorstellungsrepräsentanz* is disavowed, rendering the origin of the drive-in language disavowed for the perverse subject. The pervert instead conflates *Trieb* with *Instinkt*, attempting to collapse desire into needs capable of satisfaction.

The failure of the Law to fully instantiate in the perverse subject leads the subject to attempt to support or prop up the Law himself (Fink, 1997; Swales, 2012). The perverse subject's attempts to prop up the Law or to bring it into existence might assume a number of forms, including fetishism, sadism, and masochism, among others (Fink, 1997). For example, Fink (1997) discussed a case of fetishism in which the perverse subject was horrified by an object that represented the mother's phallus and was sexually aroused by the fetish object that reminded him of her lack.

Neurosis

The neurotic structure is defined by the subject having undergone both alienation and separation (Fink, 1997). The primary defense of the neurotic is repression, in which unacceptable thoughts are kept out of conscious awareness. Fink (1997) noted that "once a thought is repressed, it does not lie dormant" (p. 114). Rather, "it proliferates in the dark, as it were" (Freud, 1915/1957b, p. 149). The repressed thought is linked with associated thoughts (signifiers), developing a signifying chain. These signifiers will return in the form of parapraxes, dreams, and psychosomatic symptoms (Fink, 1997). For Lacanian psychoanalysis, free association and dream analysis are still key to the work.

Although neurosis is generally characterized by repression as a defense mechanism, two substructures within neurosis are delineated in Lacanian analysis: obsessional neurosis and hysterical neurosis. As with the other structures, these

32 Lacanian psychoanalysis

are distinguished not by symptomatology but by "subject position" (Fink, 1997, p. 115). The two can be differentiated in a number of ways, only some of which are explored here.

The obsessive's position of relation to the Other is only toward the object (Fink, 1997). The obsessive attempts to demean the Other to the *objet a* since, if he has the *objet a* (an imaginary proposition), then he is whole. An example of this is the man who objectifies women—reduces women to whatever object interests him. Fink (1997) borrows from Soler (1996) the example of a man who arranged to receive a phone call from another woman during sex, thereby reducing his partner and guaranteeing his continued subjectivity without fading (Fink, 1997, p. 123). Ultimately, the obsessive's desire is a desire for an "impossible desire" (Lacan, 1991/2015, p. 366), which Fink (1997) suggested may manifest as unattainable standards for partners or in constantly becoming infatuated with unavailable others.

The hysteric, in contrast, relates to the Other as the Other's object-cause of desire (Fink, 1997). (Note that this is similar to, yet different from, the perverse subject's position as object-cause of *jouissance*.) As such, the hysteric relates to the Other from the position of object rather than subject. This is a clear distinction from obsession, which relates to the object and not to the Other. The hysteric's desire is a desire for an "unsatisfied desire" (Lacan, 1991/2015, p. 366), such that the hysteric seeks to perpetuate desire rather than to fulfill it. By identifying with the *objet a*, the hysteric serves to "repress the lack of the Other as the hysteric's own" (Cantin, 2002b, p. 163). Ultimately, the hysteric's purpose in relating to desire in this way is to maintain their position as the *objet a*. As Fink (1997) noted,

> The Other as desiring subject here is but a puppet: it is the Other whose desire is kept unsatisfied by the hysteric in order for the hysteric to be able to maintain her role as desired object, as desire's lack.
>
> (p. 123)

Conclusion

This brief recapitulation of important components of Lacanian psychoanalysis by no means does justice to the complexity of either Lacan's original corpus or the work of analysts who followed him. While this introduction leaves so much aside, the primary aim will hopefully have been reached—to prepare the reader by providing the frame of reference for the body of the work to follow.

Notes

1 This biographical sketch relies heavily on Roudinesco's (1993/1997) landmark work.
2 The reasons, of course, varied for each analyst. The primary reason for Lacan's departure was the IPA and SPP's disapproval of his use of the variable length session (Roudinesco, 1993/1997). The practice of the variable length session, or "scanding," per Fink's (1997, p. 229) neologism, is predicated on a Lacanian understanding of the

unconscious. The technique was especially controversial when Lacan began experimenting with and propounding it, and those opposed to it pejoratively termed it "short sessions"—but not necessarily inaccurately, as Lacan's sessions at the time averaged about 20 minutes (Roudinesco, 1993/1997, p. 204)

3 Bruce Fink's (1995) theoretical introduction is inclusive of a wide breadth of Lacanian concepts for those interested in theory. His clinical introduction (Fink, 1997) is directed toward practicing clinicians and shares a helpful balance of theory and practice. Joel Dor (1998) also offers an introduction, and those more whimsically inclined may appreciate Leader's (2005) introduction in the style of a graphic novel.

4 It should be noted that while Lacan objected to developmentalism, he also rebutted the more puzzling analytic insistences on the psychical condition of the infant:

> Analysts have concluded from this [Freud's attribution of auto-erotism to the *Real-Ich*] – as it must be situated somewhere in what is called development, and since what Freud says is gospel—the infant must regard everything around him as indifferent. One wonders how things can go on, in a field of observers for whom articles of faith have such overwhelming value in relation to observation.
>
> (Lacan, 1973/1978, p. 190)

He also noted that

> personally, I have never looked at a baby and had the sense that there was no outside world for him. It is plain to see that a baby looks at nothing but that, that it excites him, and that that is the case precisely to the extent that he does not yet speak.
>
> (Lacan, 1975/1998, p. 56)

Lacanian analysts still tend to avoid developmental approaches, even when discussing what might be easily confused as such (see, e.g., Cantin, 2010; Fink, 1997).

5 The language in this chapter will rely on "the mother" when referring to the first Other. While any figure can wear the clothes of the Other, this language is used for ease of reference and continuity with existent analytic literature.

6 Lacan wished this French term to remain untranslated to maintain its meaning as a "sign" (Sheridan, 1977, p. xiv). In general, this book uses the French, either "*objet a*" or "*objet petit a.*"

7 Fink (1990) addressed the issue of reconciling (more or less) Freud's (1915/1957b) concept of *Urverdrängung*, or primal repression, with Lacan's. In short, Fink appealed to Freud's lack of clarity regarding *Vorstellungsrepräsentanz*, the ideational representative of the drive subject to primal repression, and Lacan's (1973/1978) equation of *Vorstellungsrepräsentanzen* with signifiers.

8 This is admittedly a condensation. Lacan's teachings do not usually shake out into nifty, corresponding bits of information. Even so, Fink (1995) appears to consider the Mirror Stage as an earlier antecedent to alienation. Though it does not form a significant argument in this book, we do generally treat the Mirror Stage and alienation as well as separation and the interdiction of the paternal function (also in line with Fink [1995]) as distinct but highly related phenomena. Similarly, the moments of the Oedipus complex discussed subsequently overlap with these ideas as well.

9 Russell Grigg (2008) discussed in detail Lacan's reasons on abandonment of the complex.

10 Lacan's exposition of the Oedipus complex espouses the asymmetrical progression of both boys and girls; that is, both boys and girls desire the mother (Evans, 1996). In other words, there is no Electra complex in the Lacanian analytic tradition.

34 Lacanian psychoanalysis

11 Leupin (2004) noted that with the Borromean knot, "none of the orders logically prevails" (p. 27). However, in the next sentence, he noted that "their ordering is only logical and temporal" (p. 27). It seems more sensible to note that they are logically equivalent, even if chronological progression is affirmed. Fink (1995) described two sorts of real—a "presymbolic real" and "a real after the letter" (p. 27). Fink was careful to note, however, that this presymbolic real is "in the final analysis, but our own hypothesis" (p. 27).

12 A reader might question the relevance of Harlow and Zimmermann's (1959) famous monkey experiment here. In this experiment, researchers provided infant rhesus monkeys with two artificial mothers: one made of wire mesh and one covered in cloth. In one condition, only the wire mesh mother provided milk for the infant, while in another, only the cloth mother provided milk. Notably, the monkeys consistently preferred the cloth mother in both conditions. This landmark research supported what virtually everyone but a psychologist could already say: there is more to the infant–mother bond than milk. Cormac Gallagher (1986) noted the Harlow study, in relation to Lacanian analysis, focused on the commonalities of human and animal bonds rather than their distinctions. As a further comment, it seems worth noting that infant–mother bonding is not what is at stake in Lacan's discussion of the demand—of course animals experience bonding. Rather, it is the linguistic nature of the demand at stake, both through the mother's imputation of meaning to cries and to the child's development of language to make specific demands. Reference can be made to so-called feral children to illustrate the importance of the linguistic component.

13 The French *demande* is widely translated into English (in Lacanian texts specifically) as "demand," however, Leupin (2004, p. 11) objected to this translate and noted that "request" is more appropriate in English. Fink (2004) also noted that "request" is appropriate, and Evans (1996) noted that the French term lacks "the connotations of imperativeness and urgency conveyed by the English word 'demand'" (p. 35). Even so, "demand" is used throughout this book to promote consistency with other literature in the field.

14 Lacan (1966/2006) noted that "depth psychology" acquired its name "no doubt because of the utterly superficial scope of what it replaced" (p. 105). He also noted somewhat more obliquely that "psychoanalysis involves allowing the analysand to elaborate the unconscious knowledge that is in him not in the form of a depth, but in the form of a cancer" (as cited in Fink, 2007, p. 30).

15 Lacan (1986/1992, pp. 57–70) equated Freud's *Vorstellungsrepräsentanz* with the signifier. See also Lacan's discussion immediately following regarding *Wortvorstellungen*.

16 In fairness to critics, Lacan (1986/1992) stated that "Freud speaks of *Sachvorstellung* and not *Dingvorstellung*" (p. 45), whereas the editorial comments in the Standard Edition of Freud note that Freud used "*Dingvorstellung*" at times, including as early as the *Traumdeutung* (Strachey, 1957, p. 201n1).

17 This is in reference to the *Project for a Scientific Psychology* (Freud, 1950/1966) with relation to the φ and ψ systems.

18 This is setting Lacan's conception of phobia aside; phobia will be revisited later in this book, but for simplicity is not included here.

19 The discussion of clinical structures here draws significantly from Fink's (1997) discussion of the structures.

References

Apollon, W. (2002a). The jouissance of the Other and the sexual division in psychoanalysis. In R. Hughes & K. R. Malone (Eds.), *After Lacan: Clinical practice and the subject of the unconscious* (pp. 49–58). Albany, NY: State University of New York Press.

Apollon, W. (2002b). The letter of the body. In R. Hughes & K. R. Malone (Eds.), *After Lacan: Clinical practice and the subject of the unconscious* (pp. 103–115). Albany, NY: State University of New York Press.

Bergeron, D. (2002). The work of the dream and jouissance in the treatment of the psychotic. In R. Hughes & K. R. Malone (Eds.), *After Lacan: Clinical practice and the subject of the unconscious* (pp. 71–85). Albany, NY: State University of New York Press.

Bernstein, J. W. (2012). Jacques Lacan. In G. O. Gabbard, B. E. Litowitz, & P. Williams (Eds.), *Textbook of psychoanalysis* (2nd ed., pp. 225–237). Arlington, VA: American Psychiatric Publishing.

Cantin, L. (2002a). From delusion to dream. In R. Hughes & K. R. Malone (Eds.), *After Lacan: Clinical practice and the subject of the unconscious* (pp. 87–102). Albany, NY: State University of New York Press.

Cantin, L. (2002b). Perversion and hysteria. In R. Hughes & K. R. Malone (Eds.), *After Lacan: Clinical practice and the subject of the unconscious* (pp. 155–165). Albany, NY: State University of New York Press.

Cantin, L. (2002c). The trauma of language. In R. Hughes & K. R. Malone (Eds.), *After Lacan: Clinical practice and the subject of the unconscious* (pp. 35–47). Albany, NY: State University of New York Press.

Cantin, L. (2010). The borderline, or the impossibility of producing a negotiable form in the social bond for the return of the censored. *Konturen, 3*(1), 186–201.

De Kesel, M. (2009). *Eros and ethics: Reading Jacques Lacan's Seminar VII.* (S. Jöttkandt, Trans.). New York, NY: SUNY Press. (Original work published 2001)

Dor, J. (1998). *Introduction to the reading of Lacan: The unconscious structured like a language.* New York, NY: Other Press.

Evans, D. (1996). *An introductory dictionary of Lacanian psychoanalysis.* New York, NY: Routledge.

Fink, B. (1990). Alienation and separation: Logical moments of Lacan's dialectic of desire. *Newsletter of the Freudian Field, 4*(1–2), 78–119.

Fink, B. (1995). *The Lacanian subject: Between language and jouissance.* Princeton, NJ: Princeton University Press.

Fink, B. (1997). *A clinical introduction to Lacanian psychoanalysis: Theory and technique.* Cambridge, MA: Harvard University Press.

Fink, B. (1998). Preface. In J. A. Miller (Ed.), *The seminar of Jacques Lacan, book XX: On feminine sexuality, the limits of love and knowledge, 1972–1973* (pp. vii–ix). New York, NY: W. W. Norton.

Fink, B. (2004). *Lacan to the letter: Reading Ecrits closely.* Minneapolis, MN: University of Minnesota Press.

Fink, B. (2007). *Fundamentals of psychoanalytic technique: A Lacanian approach for practitioners.* New York, NY: W. W. Norton.

Freud, S. (1953). Totem and taboo. In J. Strachey (Ed. & Trans.), *The standard edition of the complete psychological works of Sigmund Freud: Volume XIII (1913–1914)* (pp. 1–162). London, UK: Hogarth Press Limited. (Original work published 1913)

Freud, S. (1955). Beyond the pleasure principle. In J. Strachey (Ed. & Trans.), *The standard edition of the complete psychological works of Sigmund Freud: Volume XVIII (1920–1922)* (pp. 7–64). London, UK: Hogarth Press Limited. (Original work published 1920)

Freud, S. (1957a). Instincts and their vicissitudes. In J. Strachey (Ed. & Trans.), *The standard edition of the complete psychological works of Sigmund Freud: Volume XIV (1914–1916)* (pp. 117–140). London, UK: Hogarth Press Limited. (Original work published 1915)

36 Lacanian psychoanalysis

Freud, S. (1957b). Repression. In J. Strachey (Ed. & Trans.), *The standard edition of the complete psychological works of Sigmund Freud: Volume XIV (1914–1916)* (pp. 146–158). London, UK: Hogarth Press Limited. (Original work published 1915)

Freud, S. (1957c). The unconscious. In *The standard edition of the complete psychological works of Sigmund Freud: Volume XIV (1914–1916)* (pp. 159–215). London, UK: Hogarth Press Limited. (Original work published 1915)

Freud, S. (1966). Project for a scientific psychology. In J. Strachey (Ed. & Trans.), *The standard edition of the complete psychological works of Sigmund Freud: Volume I (1886–99)* (pp. 295–397). London, UK: Hogarth Press Limited. (Original work published 1950)

Gallagher, C. (1986). The function of the father in the contemporary family: Psychoanalytic notes. *Studies, 75,* 130–138.

Grigg, R. (2008). *Lacan, language, and philosophy.* Albany, NY: State University of New York Press.

Harlow, H. F., & Zimmermann, R. R. (1959). Affectional responses in the infant monkey. *Science, 130,* 421–432.

Hoens, D., & Pluth, E. (2002). The sinthome: A new way of writing an old problem? In L. Thurston (Ed.), *Re-inventing the symptom: Essays on the final Lacan* (pp. 1–18). New York, NY: Other Press.

Hughes, R., & Malone, K. R. (2002). Introduction. In R. Hughes & K. R. Malone (Eds.), *After Lacan: Clinical practice and the subject of the unconscious* (pp. 1–34). Albany, NY: State University of New York Press.

Lacan, J. (1978). *The seminar of Jacques Lacan, book XI: The four fundamental concepts of psychoanalysis.* (A. Sheridan, Trans.). New York, NY: W. W. Norton. (Original work published 1973)

Lacan, J. (1988). *The seminar of Jacques Lacan: Book 1: Freud's papers on technique, 1953–1954.* (J. Forrester, Trans.). New York, NY: Cambridge University Press. (Original work published 1975)

Lacan, J. (1992). *The seminar of Jacques Lacan: Book VII: The ethics of psychoanalysis 1959–1960.* (D. Porter, Trans.). New York, NY: W. W. Norton. (Original work published 1986)

Lacan, J. (1998). *The seminar of Jacques Lacan, book XX: On feminine sexuality, the limits of love and knowledge, 1972–1973.* (B. Fink, Trans.). New York, NY: W. W. Norton. (Original work published 1975)

Lacan, J. (2006). *Écrits.* (B. Fink, Trans.). New York, NY: W. W. Norton. (Original work published 1966)

Lacan, J. (2007). *The seminar of Jacques Lacan: Book XVII: The other side of psychoanalysis.* (R. Grigg, Trans.). New York, NY: W. W. Norton. (Original work published 1991)

Lacan, J. (2013). *The triumph of religion: Preceded by discourse to Catholics.* (B. Fink, Trans.). Malden, MA: Polity Press. (Original work published 2005)

Lacan, J. (2015). *Transference: The seminar of Jacques Lacan, book VIII.* (B. Fink, Trans.). Malden, MA: Polity Press. (Original work published 1991)

Lacan, J. (2017). *Formations of the unconscious: The seminar of Jacques Lacan, book V.* (R. Grigg, Trans.). Malden, MA: Polity Press. (Original work published 1998)

Lacan, J. (2021). *The object relation: The seminar of Jacques Lacan, book IV.* (A. Price, Trans.). Malden, MA: Polity Press. (Original work published 1994)

Leader, D. (2005). *Introducing Lacan.* Cambridge, UK: Totem Books.

Leupin, A. (2004). *Lacan today: Psychoanalysis, science, religion.* New York, NY: Other Press.

Marini, M. (1992). *Jacques Lacan: The French context.* (A. Tomiche, Trans.). New Brunswick, NJ: Rutgers University Press.

Miller, J. A. (2011). The non-existent seminar. *The Symptom, 12.* Retrieved from www.lacan.com/symptom12/the-non.html

Moncayo, R. (2008). *Evolving Lacanian perspectives for clinical psychoanalysis: On narcissism, sexuation, and the phases of analysis in contemporary culture.* London, UK: Karnac Books.

Moncayo, R. (2011). *The emptiness of Oedipus: Identification and non-identification in Lacanian psychoanalysis.* New York, NY: Routledge.

Nobus, D. (2000). *Jacques Lacan and the Freudian practice of psychoanalysis.* Philadelphia, PA: Taylor & Francis.

Roazen, P. (1996). Lacan's first disciple. *Journal of Religion and Health, 35,* 321–336.

Roudinesco, E. (1997). *Jacques Lacan: Outline of a life, history of a system of thought.* (B. Bray, Trans.). New York, NY: Columbia University Press. (Original work published 1993)

Safouan, M. (2004). *Four lessons of psychoanalysis.* (A. Shane, Ed.). New York, NY: Other Press.

Sheridan, A. (1977). Translator's note. In J. Lacan (Ed.), *Ecrits: A selection* (pp. ix–xiv). New York, NY: Tavistock/Routledge.

Soler, C. (1996). Hysteria and obsession. In R. Feldstein, B. Fink, & M. Jaanus (Eds.), *Reading seminars I and II: Lacan's return to Freud* (pp. 248–282). Albany, NY: State University of New York Press.

Stern, D. N. (1985). *The interpersonal world of the infant: A view from psychoanalysis and developmental psychology.* New York, NY: Basic Books.

Strachey, J. (1957). Editorial comment. In *The standard edition of the complete psychological works of Sigmund Freud: Volume XIV (1914–1916).* London, UK: Hogarth Press Limited.

Swales, S. S. (2012). *Perversion: A Lacanian approach to the subject.* New York, NY: Routledge.

Waitz, C. (2019). Immersion in the mother: Lacanian perspectives on borderline states. *Psychoanalytic Review, 106*(1), 29–47.

Chapter 3

Eastern Orthodox Christian theology

An overview

Christianity is often categorized, at least in the U.S. context, as a Western religion. This is understandable, as the largest forms of Christianity in the United States—Catholicism and Protestantism in all its varieties—share the same historically Western European backdrop. "All alike . . . have been profoundly influenced by the same events: by the Papal centralization and Scholasticism of the Middle Ages, by the Renaissance, by the Reformation and Counter-Reformation" (Ware, 1993, p. 1). However, the Church was originally constituted as a singular religious body comprising five independently governed Patriarchates, the highest form of episcopal see. These Patriarchates included those of Rome, Constantinople, Alexandria, Antioch, and Jerusalem.

A myriad of political, cultural, and religious concerns played out in these Churches over the 700 years following the Edict of Milan, which granted religious tolerance to Christianity in AD 313. Politically, the bifurcation of the Roman Empire into its Latin-speaking West and Greek-speaking East had far-reaching consequences for the unity of these half-empires, each identifying itself as the legitimate successor of the Roman Empire. The subsequent fall of the Western Roman Empire led to dramatically different circumstances for the Church in the West and the East. While the Roman Church in the West dealt with the fallout of the Empire's dissolution, the Eastern Empire persisted for another 1,000 years, though admittedly with diminishing borders and power. Ultimately, the differences between the Eastern Churches and the Roman Church culminated in the Great Schism of 1054, leaving in its wake the Roman Catholic Church (the Roman Patriarchate) and the Eastern Orthodox Church (the remaining Patriarchates). Thus, while Christianity is a Western religion in some senses, it is also true that this classification is only part of the story.

The communion of Churches remaining in the East after the Schism is collectively referred to today as the Eastern Orthodox Church.[1] The Orthodox Church has some similarities with Catholic and Protestant forms of Christianity, such as its focus upon the person of Jesus Christ. However, in contrast to the Scholasticism of the West, the Orthodox Church is mystical through and through. The mysticism of the Church is not maintained only in cloisters of monastics separated from the world; it is an inherent and important part of its very being (see

DOI: 10.4324/9781003214359-4

Eastern Orthodox Christian theology 39

Lossky, 1944/1957) and part of the experience of each Orthodox Christian. This mysticism, maintained in the Church for millennia, contributes to a quite different understanding of God and humanity than that obtained in Scholasticism or even in Western mysticism. To facilitate some conception of the distinctions between Eastern Orthodox theology and Western Christian theology, this overview will highlight some critical differences between these Traditions. This overview will highlight these differences while also introducing unique aspects of Orthodox theology relevant to the dialogue with Lacanian psychoanalysis.

The differences between Western Christianity and the Eastern Orthodox Church will be found most readily in the central notions of soteriology in each Church. Therefore, this chapter will begin with a discussion of salvation and atonement, first by considering some common theories of atonement, then by describing Orthodox theology about creation. This orientation will introduce the reader to the Orthodox belief in deification. After this, we will describe the differences between the *apophaticism* of the East and the *via negativa* of the West. A review of the Orthodox understanding of God's freedom will follow, as will a discussion of three areas central to anthropology: the Orthodox conception of the human person, the fate of humanity, and human sexuality.

Nature of salvation

Soteriology is perhaps the clearest point of distinction between the Orthodox Church and its Western counterpart. There are several strands of atonement theory across different forms of Christianity. For simplicity, and not to rehearse well-trodden ground in theological literature, we will simply summarize three common theories of atonement: Satisfaction theory (associated with Anselm of Canterbury), Penal Substitution theory (associated with Thomas Aquinas), and Ransom theory. Following an elaboration of the Orthodox understanding of creation, Orthodoxy's soteriological conception of *theosis* will be described.

One of the most common conceptions of salvation in Western Christianity is the satisfaction theory proposed by Anselm of Canterbury shortly after the Great Schism (*Cur Deus Homo?*; see Finlan, 2005). In brief, the Satisfaction theory proposed by Anselm rests upon the idea that humanity dishonored God through sin and is, therefore, subject to God's wrath and condemnation. This theory essentially mirrors the feudal world from which it sprung, with God filling the role of an offended lord (Finlan, 2005). Aulen (1931) characterized this as an objective view of atonement because the person undergoing change is God. Satisfaction theory can be formulated as follows: The threat from which humanity must be saved is the wrath of God; the intervention is the suffering of Christ, which placates God; and the resolution is the satisfaction or restitution of God's honor. Critically, God is the one from whom humanity must be saved and the one who undergoes change.

Satisfaction theory was further developed in the Reformation into Penal Substitution theory, which has a prominent role among Protestants including John

40   Eastern Orthodox Christian theology

Calvin (e.g., *Institutes of Christian Religion* 2:16:10) and John Wesley (e.g., *Justification by Faith*), and finds a foothold in Evangelicalism as well.[2] In Penal Substitution theory, atonement is viewed through a juridical lens. Humanity broke God's law and suffered punishment from God as a result, specifically death and eternal damnation in hell. Christ's sacrifice is the fulfillment of a legal obligation toward God through the legal fiction of the sin imputed to Christ (in turn resulting in the imputation of righteousness to the Christian, at least in Reformed theology). A recent popular book defending the concept of penal substitution summarizes the doctrine thus: "God gave himself in the person of his Son to suffer instead of us the death, punishment and curse due to fallen humanity as the penalty for sin" (Jeffery et al., 2007, p. 21). This theory could be formulated with the threat to humanity being posed by Divine Justice due to humanity's legal infraction; Christ's legal fulfillment of the sentence of death as the intervention; and the subsequent transitive distribution of Christ's innocence to the human person as the resolution. Whether in the form of Satisfaction theory or Penal Substitution theory, these models assume God is the source of death (Romanides, 1998).

Meyendorff (1974) referred to the law in penal substitution as "transcendent Justice" (p. 161). The idea that God cannot operate outside his own law is naturally puzzling.[3] Similar problems arise for Ransom theory, which predates the Satisfaction and Penal Substitution theories. Ransom theory casts Satan as the adversary of humanity and of God (Finlan, 2005). However, this theory rests upon the idea that Satan has a legitimate claim over humanity that God would be unjust to violate. As a result, God must perform as a trickster, setting a trap for Satan to free humanity through an unwitting exchange. While the threat in this theory is not God but Satan, the question of why an omnipotent God must operate within certain legal bounds remains.

Regarding Satisfaction and Penal Substitution theories, these sound to an Orthodox Christian virtually pagan in nature (Romanides, 1998). Humanity's adversary in these models is God himself, either through offense to his honor or through a Law that he himself is apparently unable to abrogate. Ransom theory, though less problematic in this sense, retains some contortions of reasoning with respect to why Satan's claims must be respected (but respected with enough authenticity to avoid trickery). The Orthodox understanding of salvation is quite distinct from these perspectives, and is predicated on the Orthodox view of creation and the *fall*; we will first turn to these two topics before returning to a discussion of salvation.

Creation of humanity

In the Orthodox tradition, humanity is "the center of creation" and "his free self-determination defines the ultimate destiny of the universe" (Meyendorff, 1974, p. 138). Humanity, created in the image and likeness of God, is a microcosm of the universe, "lord of creation" (p. 142), "priest of the natural creation" (Yannaras, 1979/1984, p. 99). As a microcosm, humanity's vocation is to bring together creation and the Divine (Romanides, 1998). Uniting created and Uncreated is a movement and thus requires progression; as such, and in contrast to Western

Eastern Orthodox Christian theology   41

understandings, Adam and Eve were not created immortal and in a perfect state from which they fell. Instead, they were created perfect in an unrealized or "potential sense" (Ware, 1993, p. 219; see Lossky, 1967/1974, p. 126; Romanides, 1998, p. 122), and were created "neither necessarily mortal nor necessarily immortal" (Lossky, 1978, p. 77). Rather than being the pinnacle of human perfection, St. Irenaeus (*On the Apostolic Preaching* 12; 1997) noted that Adam was "a young child" (p. 47), and Lossky (1978) described humanity's vocation as "to emerge from an infantile unawareness by agreeing, through love, to obey God" (p. 78).

Humanity was meant to grow and mature into union with God (Lossky, 1944/1957). Indeed, echoing Theophilus of Antioch (*To Autolycus*, 2.25), Romanides (1998) noted:

> God did not forbid them [Adam and Eve] to eat from the tree because it was bad in itself and fatal for man but because man was as yet unperfected and incapable of properly assimilating the knowledge gained from the tree.
>
> (p. 125)

Similarly, Lossky (1978) explained:

> The fruit was good in itself, but everything hinges on the personal relationship of man and God. And when Eve sees that the tree is beautiful, a value outside of God appears. 'You will be like God,' says the serpent. He does not altogether deceive man: for the latter is called to deification. But here 'like' signifies an equality, through resentment, of him who stands up to God: autonomous god against God, god by himself, god of the earthly cosmos isolated from God.
>
> (p. 82)

The significance here is that humanity was created to grow, and godlikeness was not forbidden humanity. Rather, to be truly in God's likeness (i.e., to attain godlikeness), growth through moral action and exercise of free will is necessary.

Because of Orthodoxy's perspective on creation, the fall in Orthodoxy is somewhat less dire, and humanity is not totally corrupted (Ware, 1993), in contrast to some Protestant views on the total depravity of humanity (e.g., *The Westminster Confession of Faith*, 1647, sec. 9.3). Even so, because humanity is a microcosm, the fall causes a change so fundamental that the state of the universe is no longer natural: Death is "the outcome of that fallenness which precipitates man into an anti-natural state where the will of man, contaminating the cosmos, gives to non-being a paradoxical and tragic reality" (Lossky, 1978, p. 84). "By turning away from God, who is immortality and life, humans put themselves in a state that was contrary to nature" (Ware, 1993, p. 223). It is salvation that "restores it [humanity] to its 'natural' state" (Meyendorff, 1974, p. 146).

Although the world is not entirely fallen and still retains revelatory value, it must be viewed through the light of special revelation (Staniloae, 1978/1994). Another way of stating this would be to say Orthodoxy relies upon retroaction (in

42 Eastern Orthodox Christian theology

the sense of *Nachträglichkeit*) to understand the fall: "Although God did not actually create the human race *in* this condition, there was, nevertheless, no period of time before which human beings were not engulfed: there is, for St. Irenaeus, no lost golden age of primordial perfection" (Behr, 2006, p. 102).

The Orthodox Church differs not only in the understanding of creation and the fall but also of the consequences of the fall. For much of Western Christianity, there is usually some version of the doctrine of *original sin*, or heritable guilt and *sin nature*. These doctrines are not found in the Orthodox Church (Meyendorff, 1974). Guilt is not heritable, nor is there a nature of sinfulness, per se, though Orthodoxy does admit of a will weakened by "what the Greeks call 'desire'" (Ware, 1993, p. 223). Instead of guilt or dishonor in the eyes of God, what is transmitted from what the Orthodox call the *ancestral sin* is death (Romanides, 1998). Death came into the world through sin (Rom. 5:12), and "through fear of death," humanity has been "subject to lifelong bondage" (Heb. 2:15). Death is the last enemy (1 Cor. 15:26), and it is death Christ came to destroy.

Regarding death, Mantzaridis (1984) noted "Death is not a kind of divine judgment but the natural consequence of man's separation from God" (p. 24). This is because God himself is life, and separating oneself from life is necessarily death; it is precipitated through the free will of humanity itself (Romanides, 1998). This form of death is spiritual death and is a consequence of sin. Physical death, however, "is a benevolent concession on God's part, since by means of it the course of sin is interrupted and evil is not perpetuated" (Mantzaridis, 1984, p. 25). Similarly, God permits death "not out of a punitive divine decision as Augustine imagined but out of divine compassion. Otherwise, the righteous would be under the rule of sin eternally" (Romanides, 1998, p. 99) and "better that man dies, that is to say, be excluded from the tree of life, than that his monstrous condition be made eternal" (Lossky, 1978, p. 83). The expulsion from the Garden to prevent man from eating from the Tree of Life was similarly a sign of compassion, as physical death is a limit to sin (Irenaeus, n.d., *Against Heresies*, 3.23.6).

Thus, humanity was not created for death. The notion humanity was also not created immortal requires further comment. As noted, the union of created and Uncreated requires growth, and the teleological end of an only potentially perfect humanity, already being in the image of God, is to attain his likeness. In contrast to many more recent expositors (Mantzaridis, 1984), Orthodoxy distinguishes between the *image* and the *likeness* of God (Lossky, 1944/1957). Every human is always in the image of God, but the likeness must be pursued. Lossky (1944/1957) recounted various theologians' attempts to localize the image of God to some aspect of humanity, but asserted:

> The image of God in man, in so far as it is perfect, is necessarily unknowable . . . for as it reflects the fullness of its archetype, it must also possess the unknowable character of the divine Being.
>
> (p. 118)

Eastern Orthodox Christian theology   43

The mystery of humanity is the mystery of God, and it is God's radical unknowability in essence (Being) that constitutes the image in man. The image is indestructible and present in all humanity, but it takes the will of the human person (in addition to that of God, the two being fellow workers in *synergia*) to achieve the likeness (Lossky, 1944/1957). The likeness is the moral choice of humanity and "is destroyed by sin" (Ware, 1993, p. 219). Pursuing the likeness of God through *synergia* is the goal of humanity; in Orthodoxy, the end of likeness is *theosis*, or deification.

Theosis is, as St. Peter wrote, becoming "partakers of the divine nature" (2 Pt. 1:4; all Scriptures are quoted from the RSV). "To acquire the likeness [of God] is to be deified, it is to become a 'second god,' a 'god by grace'" (Ware, 1993, p. 219). It is a reciprocal movement, in which "God made Himself man, that man might become God," as a number of early Fathers wrote (Lossky, 1967/1974, p. 97). This concept will be discussed further, but one more point here is relevant: In addition to the conception of salvation as union with God in the pursuit of his likeness, a complementary point is that, for the Orthodox, God did not create death.

Orthodoxy is adamant that God is not the source of death (Romanides, 1998), "because God did not make death, and he does not delight in the death of the living" (Wis. 1:13). This means death is not a punishment from God (Romanides, 1998) and cannot be viewed as such. In considering the Orthodox view of salvation, this is key to understanding. God is not the source of threat to humanity. Death is not a punishment from God.

By way of summary, Theophilus of Antioch (n.d./1885) penned many of the foregoing points quite succinctly:

> Was man made by nature mortal? Certainly not. Was he, then, immortal? Neither do we affirm this. But one will say, Was he, then, nothing? Not even this hits the mark. He was by nature neither mortal nor immortal. For if He had made him immortal from the beginning, He would have made him God. Again, if He had made him mortal, God would seem to be the cause of his death. Neither, then, immortal nor yet mortal did He make him, but, as we have said above, capable of both; so that if he should incline to the things of immortality, keeping the commandment of God, he should receive as reward from Him immortality, and should become God; but if, on the other hand, he should turn to the things of death, disobeying God, he should himself be the cause of death to himself.
>
> (2.27)

Salvation in the Eastern Church

With this understanding, we now return to the distinct conception of salvation in the Eastern Orthodox Church. Where Adam and Eve strayed from the vocation of union with God, Christ came to fulfill this mission, becoming "the first true human being" (Behr, 2006, p. 111). Salvation is not based on the death of

44 Eastern Orthodox Christian theology

Christ alone, but on his whole Incarnation as well as the Resurrection (Mantzaridis, 1984; Romanides, 1998). As Lossky (1967/1974) wrote, "If this union has been accomplished in the divine person of the Son, who is God become man, it is necessary that each human person, in turn, should become god by grace" (p. 98). Salvation in the Orthodox Church, as sung in the Paschal troparion, is precisely Christ's "trampling down death by death, and upon those in the tombs bestowing life." The restoration of Christ's action is not simply a mechanism to transfer a limited portion of humanity from the juridical category of "guilty" to "not guilty" (and certainly not "innocent"!); it is "a cosmic event . . . man's restoration in Christ is a restoration of the cosmos to its original beauty" (Meyendorff, 1974, p. 152).

To clarify what theosis means, what it means to becoming god by grace, one must also consider the Orthodox distinction between *essence* and *energies*. This distinction developed in the 14th century during a controversy that arose regarding a certain practice called *hesychasm* (Meyendorff, 1974).

St. Gregory Palamas (1296–1359) was a monk of Mount Athos—the "Holy Mountain," as it is called, is revered in Orthodoxy because of the long history of monasticism there (Ware, 1993, p. 39). St. Gregory, also the archbishop of Thessaloniki, engaged in a significant dispute with Barlaam of Calabria, an Italian theologian, regarding hesychasm, which was a method of prayer practiced by the monks of Mt. Athos (Mantzaridis, 1984). Hesychastic prayer is a form of contemplative prayer with the purpose of *theoria*, an experience or vision of God as Uncreated light (Ware, 1993). St. Gregory maintained the divine light experienced by monks engaged in hesychastic prayer was not created grace but Uncreated grace (Mantzaridis, 1984), which is to say, God himself. In St. Gregory's account, humanity may have direct communion with God in this manner. To Barlaam, this direct communion with God appeared to be communion in God's essence, which would endanger God's transcendence. Therefore, Barlaam insisted that God does not directly commune with humanity. To maintain God's transcendence as well as his direct communion with humanity, St. Gregory argued for a distinction between God in his essence and God in his energies. God in his essence is entirely transcendent, radically unknown and unknowable; it is only in his energies, his active engagement or revelation in the world, that God can be known (Lossky, 1944/1957). It is his energies that St. Gregory argued were present in the Uncreated light (Mantzaridis, 1984) the monks would experience. Barlaam attacked these ideas, arguing the light experienced by the Hesychasts was created, steadfastly refusing the possibility of direct communion with God. Ultimately, St. Gregory Palamas's arguments prevailed over Barlaam, thus solidifying the essence/energies distinction in Orthodox doctrine.

This distinction is fundamentally important to theosis. To become God by *grace* what he is by *nature* is to experience profound union with God in his energies (grace), while his essence (nature) remains unknowable. This maintains both God's transcendence and his immanence (Ware, 1993), and it distinguishes what would be polytheism (becoming by nature what God is by nature) from true mystical union with God.

Eastern Orthodox Christian theology   45

It is also significant to note that in the Orthodox Church, regardless of the fall, there is no disjunction in the fate of humanity—it has always been deification (Lossky, 1978). As Fr. John Behr (2006) argued:

> Creation and salvation are not two distinct actions, but the continual process of God's activity in his handiwork, bringing the creature, when he allows himself to be skillfully fashioned, to the stature of the Savior, by whom and for whom all creation has come into being.
>
> (p. 86)

When the first Adam did not pursue the likeness of God, the second Adam did; Christ fulfilled the fate of humanity and, for the Orthodox, calls the rest of humanity to follow. A simple formulation of the story of salvation in Orthodoxy would be difficult, but it would be reasonable to say the threat in Orthodoxy is death, unleashed upon all creation; the intervention is the entire Incarnation event—the life, death, and resurrection of the Word of God; and the result is the "glorification of man, which is also the glorification of the whole of creation" (Meyendorff, 1974, p. 153).

Apophaticism

Because of the distinction between God's essence and energies, and God's unknowability in his essence, the Orthodox Church adheres primarily to negative, or *apophatic*, theology. Negative theology is called negative in the sense it is predicated on negation: God is not this, or God is not that. However, it is more than simple negation. Lossky (1944/1957), one of the 20th-century Orthodox theologians most focused on mysticism and apophaticism, described apophaticism as, "above all, an attitude of mind which refuses to form concepts about God" (pp. 38–39). This is because "the concepts which we form in accordance with the understanding and the judgment which are natural to us, basing ourselves on an intelligible representation, create idols of God instead of revealing to us God Himself" (p. 33). Yannaras (1967/2005) similarly noted that:

> The apophaticism of the Greek East is not confined to negations, it presupposes both affirmative natural knowledge and, at the same time, its denial, that is to say, the *abandonment* of any claim to consolidate and objectify the truth in conceptual definitions.
>
> (p. 71)

The emphasis here is twofold: (a) natural theology is insufficient for independently informing faith (see Knight, 2013)[4] and (b) that God is primarily to be approached through *experience* rather than through *conceptual knowledge*. "Christianity is not a philosophical school for speculating about abstract concepts, but is essentially a communion with the living God" (Lossky, 1944/1957, p. 42).

46 Eastern Orthodox Christian theology

Although apophatic theology may be as simple as the statements "God is not stone, He is not fire," it also reaches complexity at "the heights of contemplation," causing one to abolish all idols of God: "God is not being, He is not the good" (p. 40). Lossky (1978) even argued that God is beyond Hegel's being and nothingness: "One must evoke God beyond all that can be known as being" (p. 22), and "one cannot fix God with a concept, even that of essence" (p. 23); quite simply, "He 'is not'" (p. 32). Yannaras (2004/2011) also took apophasis to its conclusion: "Within the limits set by the semantics of our language, the limits of our world, it makes better sense to say *God does not exist* than to say *God exists*" (p. 57).

Lossky (1944/1957) was careful not to associate this radically Unknown God with "the God of the philosophers" (p. 43). The apophatic approach does not terminate in an impersonal nothingness (or everythingness), either in the philosophical sense or in the sense of reabsorption into some cosmic All (Lossky, 1978; Yannaras, 1967/2005). Rather, apophasis leads to the antinomy and mystery of the Holy Trinity (Lossky, 1944/1957). Thus, the aim of apophaticism is an experience of a personal God.

Yannaras (1967/2005) distinguished "*apophaticism of essence*" from "*apophaticism of the person*" (p. 29). The apophaticism of the West, in the *via negativa*, is characterized by apophaticism of essence, which has as its starting point rational conceptions of entities in their essences. Apophaticism in this sense is the acknowledgment that, in relation to "uncreated, transcendent and supernatural" essence (i.e., God), "I grant that I may *conceive* the existence of such a being, but I *do not know* its reality" (Yannaras, 1967/2005, p. 29). In other words, apophasis of essence is focused on rational conceptions *about* God in the absence of personal experience *of* God. This undergirds the Western use of apophaticism as a method of delimiting rational, analogical, cataphatic suppositions rather than as something unique to itself. In other words, it emphasizes God in his essence as something unknowable, and without the distinction between essence and energies, God becomes an impersonal absolute.

Yannaras (1967/2005) included Western mysticism in the strain of theology that reduces God to an impersonal absolute, and which he argued ultimately culminated in the ossification of God as a philosophical necessity that is eventually revealed by Nietzsche's (1887/2006) madman to be dead—"and we have killed him" (p. 90). Yannaras implicated by name several Western saints, including Teresa of Avila and John of the Cross (p. 119) (whom Lacan [1975/1998] himself called to mind in his own discussion of mysticism). Yannaras objected that, although these individuals pursued Christ, they did so precisely as individuals within the constraints of the Western categories of essence that preclude the possibility of any direct relationship with God. As such, Yannaras found their mystical experiences to be "a one-sided, psychological appeal on the subject's behalf to a *substantially* inaccessible object of desire—it is a matter of erotic self-hedonism" (p. 119) and "affective contemplation . . . of the absolute" (p. 86). Yannaras' assessment is harsher than ours is, but he raises two important considerations. First, to the extent anyone has a direct experience of God (and not with

Eastern Orthodox Christian theology 47

created grace), it is generally in contravention of the Western theological context that maintains God's transcendence. Second, Yannaras noted that in the Western approach, because it precludes the possibility of direct communion with God in both mystical and rational modes, "we relate to an unknown, inaccessible 'object' of thought or consciousness" (p. 120)—a point that will become relevant when bringing Orthodoxy into direct dialogue with Lacan's psychoanalysis.

In contrast to this, Yannaras (1967/2005) explicated the apophaticism of the East as apophaticism of the person. In this case, the starting point is not an apprehension of entities in their essence but "the *way* I exist and the *way* that I know . . . are facts of accomplished relationships" (p. 29). Relationship, for Yannaras, is primary and is experienced through the senses as well as various other critical and imaginative faculties. Coming into contact with an other in a relational way occurs prior to any conception of essences or rational conclusions. God is known and experienced as a person rather than an essence. In the language of Orthodox theology, this places emphasis on the *hypostasis*, or persons of God, rather than his *ousia*, or essence.

The distinction Yannaras (1967/2005) made is important because the apophaticism of essence is still restricted to rational, informational knowledge, whereas apophaticism of the person is predicated on direct relationship and is therefore not a simple methodology but the opening of true personhood through the experience of God.[5] This delineation clarifies the substantive differences between apophaticism as it is often understood in Western theology and its Eastern counterpart.

Apophasis is critical to the Orthodox faith and understanding of God. Predicated on the distinction between God's essence and energies, apophasis is the pathway to the experience of God rather than to idolatrous "knowledge" of God that constrains in human ideals a God beyond all categories. As such, it is not simply an approach to theology but the path to the illumination by God of the human person in theosis.

The freedom of god

Creation in Orthodoxy is from nothing, or *ex nihilo*. That creation is from nothing preserves two important points in Orthodox theology: (a) the radical freedom of God and (b) the contingency of creation (Romanides, 1998).

Regarding the freedom of God, Romanides (1998) argued vehemently that creation is not reflective of the essence of God, nor based on archetypes or forms (which would necessarily be coeternal with God and therefore be God). Here, the essence/energies distinction is again vital, as God creates in his uncreated energies, not by his essence and not through created energies. "In His essence, God is not the creator, foreknower, judge, and savior. He is these things but only by His will and His energy" (Romanides, 1998, p. 54). The creation through the energies of God means that the world is not a copy of eternal thoughts in the mind of God, nor is the material world some product of evil (as with Gnosticism's demiurge).

Regarding the contingency of creation, it is clear: "God might not have created" (Lossky, 1978, p. 53). Nothing in the essence of God necessitates creation.

48 Eastern Orthodox Christian theology

Rather, "creation is a free act of His will, and this free act is the sole foundation of the existence of all beings" (Lossky, 1944/1957, p. 93). The Church Fathers also made this distinction, particularly in rejecting cosmologies such as Origen's, which included a belief in the pre-existence of souls (Meyendorff, 1974).

These two stipulations—the freedom of God and the contingency of creation—are particularly important in considering the Greek philosophical idea of *eudaemonia* (εὐδαιμονία; roughly, happiness). Romanides (1998) explained the concept of *eudaemonia*:

> The *eudaemonia* of philosophy is attained according to the degree to which one approaches the good and acquires it. Full happiness is achieved through the ultimate vision of, or union with, the highest good. Throughout the world of reality there is a scale of values, and through them all things are drawn to the supreme being, which is not drawn to anything itself because it is perfect. At best, there could be within it a movement only toward itself because outside itself there exists nothing that is more perfect.
>
> (pp. 43–44)

Romanides (1998) argued this conception of the universe is predicated on "self-seeking love" (p. 104); for Western theologians who did not distinguish God's essence and energies, they were compelled to protect God's essence from pantheism by denying his interaction with the world at all, leading to a form of *eudaemonism*: "God does not love things outside of the divine essence but loves their beginningless, everlasting, and changeless archetypes within the divine essence" (Romanides, 1998, p. 104). For the Orthodox, understanding the freedom of God and the contingency of creation, the problem of potential pantheism simply does not present itself. Romanides clearly stated that this idea of God the *eudaemon* is "completely untenable" (p. 105). God has no need of creation whatsoever; he created not out of his essence and by necessity, but out of his energies and by absolute freedom. "God's love for the world is above every selfishness and necessity because true love 'seeketh not its own'" (p. 105). The end of man in pursuing the likeness of God lies not in *eudaemonia* but in becoming "perfect as the God of Holy Scripture and the Greek Fathers, Who is free of all necessity and selfishness" (Romanides, 1998, p. 106).

The creation from nothing, therefore, is a central tenet of Orthodoxy. The *ex nihilo* demonstrates God's complete freedom; God has no need of anything and is completely selfless. Creation could have as easily never existed. Even so, God acts freely in love through his energies and chose freely to create the world.

Human sexuality in the Orthodox Church

The Orthodox Church, much like in the Catholic and (many) Protestant Churches, maintains traditional sexual practices, such as the ban on premarital sex (Ware, 1993).[6] This is because the Church views sexuality quite highly and marriage as

Eastern Orthodox Christian theology 49

no less a commitment than monasticism. Understanding the Orthodox theology of sexuality is important in grasping Orthodox anthropology, as the two go hand-in-hand. Indeed, Yannaras (1979/1984) noted:

> Sexual love . . . is the central axis for the formation of personality and its conscious, subconscious, and unconscious layers . . . Many centuries before Freud discovered the significance of the libido, or psychoanalysis 'liberated' sexual life from its 'social restraints' and made it a separate area of man's life insulated from the whole—showing it as an end in itself, tragic and unfulfilled—the Greek church fathers had connected man's existential problem with the orientation of his natural sexual impulse: whether it turns towards sensual pleasure or towards giving life a hypostatic reality as communion and relationship. . . . Through the thought of the fathers, it become [sic] clear that the Church recognizes in sexual love man's existential identity, but does not equate it exclusively with the reproductive process. Or, at the very least, she does not restrict *eros* to its natural starting point, the distinction between the sexes.
>
> (pp. 164–165)

For the Church, in Yannaras' reading, as too for psychoanalysis, sexuality is at the core of the human person. This sexual love is coterminous with neither reproduction nor "institutional marriage" (p. 165), but is found most truly in asceticism (including in the mystery of marriage).

Lossky (1978), in considering human sexuality and Christian anthropology, discussed the view of some Church Fathers that sexuality was a result of the fall and that sexual reproduction was something of a safeguard against death. Lossky rightly noted the meagerness of this argument in that not only sex, but all of creation was affected by the fall—sex is not a special result. Furthermore, "human love, the absolute passion of lovers, has never ceased harbouring, in the very fatality of its failure, a paradisiacal nostalgia where heroism and art are rooted" (p. 77).

However, in balance to this, Lossky (1978) also noted the story of creation must be read backward: "The narrative of creation . . . is expressed in the categories of the fallen world" (p. 67). He explained regarding the narrative:

> The Fall has changed the very meaning of the words. Sexuality, this 'multiplying' that God orders and blesses, appears in our universe as irremediably linked to separation and death. This is because the condition of man has known, at least in his biological reality, a catastrophic mutation. But human love would not be pregnant with such a paradisiacal nostalgia if there did not remain painfully within it the memory of a first condition where the other and the world were known from the *inside*, where, accordingly, death did not exist.
>
> (p. 67)

The eros of humanity—the sexual drive—appears after the fall dressed up in death and separation. Lossky's awareness that the creation story must be read

50 Eastern Orthodox Christian theology

backward allows him to affirm both the Church Fathers' difficulty in accepting sexuality as we know it existing in paradise while also affirming the goodness of sexuality generally. In considering what it is about the fall that affected sexuality in this way, Lossky (1978) expounded further:

> Paradisiacal sexuality, stemming completely from consubstantial interiority and whose marvelous multiplication, which should fill everything, would certainly have demanded neither multiplicity nor death, is almost entirely unknown to us; for sin, by objectifying bodies ('they saw that they were naked'), made the first two human persons two separate natures, two individual beings, having between them external relations.
>
> (p. 77)

The *consubstantial interiority* Lossky noted is of the same sort as God; just as God is three persons in one essence, so humanity was in one essence at creation with more than one person (Lossky, 1944/1957). This is the knowing from inside that Lossky associated with paradisiacal nostalgia. Notably, Lossky here placed sin prior to sexuality as we know it ("sin, by objectifying"). It is only through sin that human nature is damaged and fragmented into *individuals* rather than *persons*.

Indeed, Yannaras (1979/1984) argued similarly to Lossky that "at each natural birth the inevitable fragmentation of nature into individual entities is put into effect, and with it the condemnation of human existence to confine its life to individual survival and to be subject to corruption" (p. 185). Sexuality, while good in itself, is subjected to the necessity of the fallen world, such that it perpetuates "nature through a succession of mortal individuals, and they perpetuate the subjection of nature to corruption and death" (p. 186).

This may seem a rather bleak way to view sexuality, especially as "sexual intercourse is a gift from God" (Ware, 1993, p. 296), but we are interested in viewing human sexuality beyond the "positive" or "negative" aspects some may attribute to various characteristics. Instead, sexuality and the human person are viewed with respect to the erotic communion with God and each other. Yannaras (1979/1984), as the Orthodox Church does in general, stressed the nonreproductive aspects of sexuality because of this perspective. Yannaras distinguished "true *eros*" as that which is capable, through asceticism,[7] of becoming "like the love of Christ," selfless and without exclusivity (p. 165). The goal of human sexuality in Orthodoxy is to transcend the natural relationship (the relationship subject to natural necessity) to become the "eucharistic relationship," which is possible to share "with all the members of Christ's body" (p. 167).[8]

Human sexuality, at its heights in true eros, is connected to freedom from necessity, as the person is in theosis and as God is in creation. True eros is always an ecstasy. Eros must be purified through asceticism and self-emptying, or *kenosis* (κένωσις); kenosis in this respect is accomplished, according to Yannaras (1979/1984), "through a love which is not of the order of social 'altruism' but an existential change, a process whereby individuality is 'emptied' of

Eastern Orthodox Christian theology 51

self-determination in its conduct and relinquishes its autonomous resistances" (p. 164). Mantzarides (1973) confirmed the same point:

> True love demands the mortification of individuality and self-serving and the acceptance of this mortification as life. Life for the Christian is not the maintenance of the biological function of individuality, but rather its surpassing and its reference to the source of imperishable personal life, God.
>
> (p. 173)

Notes

1 This is an oversimplification; strictly speaking, it is accurate that the Great Schism resulted in the separation of the Patriarch of Rome (becoming the Catholic Church) from the Patriarchs of Constantinople, Alexandria, Antioch, and Jerusalem (the Eastern Orthodox Church). It is also true; however, that other Eastern Churches exist and were already independent from the larger Church before the Great Schism, including the Oriental Orthodox Church and the Church of the East. See Ware (1993).

2 See the National Association of Evangelicals' (NAE) Statement of Faith: "We believe in the deity of our Lord Jesus Christ . . . [and] in His vicarious and atoning death through His shed blood" (NAE, n.d., para. 3). This could be interpreted as satisfaction rather than penal substitution, which may be the purpose (providing a big tent); the Southern Baptist Convention (2000) makes explicit reference to penal substitution, stating that Christ "honored the divine law by His personal obedience . . . in His substitutionary death on the cross" (sec. II.b) and that God provides "gracious and full acquittal . . . of all sinners who repent and believe in Christ" (sec. IV.b). Anecdotally, having attending or worked at many Evangelical churches, study groups, non-profits, camps, and other events, I (CW) feel comfortable noting that there is a fair amount of penal substitution in at least parts of the Evangelical world.

3 The inability of God to operate outside his own Justice is not universally held, it should be noted. Aquinas explicitly states this himself (*Summa Theologica* III, Q46, Art2, ad3).

4 The status of natural theology in Orthodoxy varies to a notable degree, as Knight (2013) noted, though he specified that for some Orthodox, "natural theology can only be valid when integrated into a mystical knowledge of God and of his creation—a knowledge that transcends any cataphatic [positive theological] affirmation" (p. 218). The matter of natural theology is far from peripheral to Orthodoxy; Romanides's (1998) refutation of *analogia entis* is predicated on the *ex nihilo* creation and the distinction between essence and energies. This point is relevant to anthropology as "the correct understanding of the destiny of man essentially depends on the correct understanding of God," and the condition of humanity prior to the fall cannot be obtained "by following fallen man's philosophical theories, as Western theologians generally do" (p. 38). In other words, while some theological information might follow from the world, it must be understood as it is through special revelation that it can be read (Staniloae, 1978/1994), as the world is currently in a "defective state" (Meyendorff, 1974, p. 134). See Davydov (2017) for further discussion.

5 Some readers may note that this sounds, from a Lacanian standpoint, like a prediscursive reality. However, Yannaras (1967/2005) is clear the faculties of relationship include "the sensory, the critical, the abstractive, the analytic, the imaginative, the emotional, the intuitive, the visionary and probably others" (p. 29). Of this list, critical, abstractive, and analytic faculties are all predicated on linguistic reasoning. Yannaras is not rejecting language or rational thought, or arguing for something prior to language per se, but is advocating the apophatic methods that "refuse to absolutize the effectiveness of their semantics" (p. 71), that is, that refuse to "realize the symbolic of the imaginary" (Fink,

52 Eastern Orthodox Christian theology

1995, p. 143). While differences between Yannaras' view and Lacanian analysis exist, this particular issue does not reflect significant conflict given Lacan's own vehement refusal of systematized or reified thought.

6 One notable exception is that Orthodox Christians are permitted divorce and up to three marriages (Ware, 1993).

7 Asceticism, it should be noted, is not the vocation solely of the monastic in Orthodoxy (Ware, 1986). As the struggle against the passions, asceticism is the endeavor of all Orthodox Christians. Asceticism in the Orthodox context should not be confused with self-abuse; for a lay Orthodox, it might be as simple as following a rule of prayer and participating in the Church's fasts.

8 This should not be confused with polyamory; Yannaras's (1979/1984) vision here is focused on eschatological eros. He argued that in the fallen world, reproduction is inextricably tied up with death, to the degree that "no 'ethics of sexuality' can remove the subjugation of the sexual impulse to the natural necessity of perpetuating death" (p. 160). In other words, no organization of sexuality—whether monogamy or polyamory—can overcome the continuance of human mortality.

References

Aulen, G. (1931). *Christus victor.* (A. G. Hebert, Trans.). Eugene, OR: Wipf & Stock.

Behr, J. (2006). *The mystery of Christ: Life in death.* Crestwood, NY: St. Vladimir's Seminary Press.

Davydov, O. (2017). Reception of analogy of being in contemporary Eastern Orthodox theology. *Dialog, 56*(3), 290–297.

Fink, B. (1995). *The Lacanian subject: Between language and jouissance.* Princeton, NJ: Princeton University Press.

Finlan, S. (2005). *Problems with atonement.* Collegeville, MN: Liturgical Press.

Irenaeus of Lyons. (1997). *On the Apostolic preaching.* (J. Behr, Trans.). Crestwood, NY: St. Vladimir's Seminary Press.

Jeffery, S., Ovey, M., & Sach, A. (2007). *Pierced for our transgression.* Wheaton, IL: Crossway Books.

Knight, C. C. (2013). Natural theology and the Eastern Orthodox tradition. In R. R. Manning (Ed.), *The Oxford handbook of natural theology* (pp. 213–226). Oxford, UK: Oxford University Press.

Lacan, J. (1998). *The seminar of Jacques Lacan, book XX: On feminine sexuality, the limits of love and knowledge, 1972–1973.* (B. Fink, Trans.). New York, NY: W. W. Norton. (Original work published 1975)

Lossky, V. (1957). *The mystical theology of the Eastern Church.* (Fellowship of St. Alban & St. Sergius, Trans.). Crestwood, NY: St. Vladimir's Seminary Press. (Original work published 1944)

Lossky, V. (1974). *In the image and likeness of God.* (J. H. Erickson & T. E. Bird, Eds.). Crestwood, NY: St. Vladimir's Seminary Press. (Original work published 1967)

Lossky, V. (1978). *Orthodox theology: An introduction.* (I. [Ian] Kesarcodi-Watson & I. [Ihita] Kesarcodi-Watson, Trans.). Crestwood, NY: St. Vladimir's Seminary Press.

Mantzarides, G. (1973). The witness of Orthodox to the contemporary world. *St. Vladimir's Theological Quarterly, 17,* 170–180.

Mantzaridis, G. I. (1984). *The deification of man: Saint Gregory Palamas and the Orthodox tradition.* (L. Sherrard, Trans.). Crestwood, NY: St. Vladimir's Seminary Press.

Meyendorff, J. (1974). *Byzantine theology: Historical trends and doctrinal themes.* New York, NY: Fordham University Press.

Eastern Orthodox Christian theology   53

National Association of Evangelicals. (n.d.). *Statement of faith*. NAE. Retrieved from www.nae.net/statement-of-faith/

Nietzsche, F. (2006). *The gay science*. (T. Common, Trans.). Mineola, NY: Dover. (Original work published 1887)

Romanides, J. S. (1998). *The ancestral sin*. (G. S. Gabriel, Trans.). Ridgewood, NJ: Zephyr.

Southern Baptist Convention. (2000). *Baptist faith and message 2000*. Retrieved from https://bfm.sbc.net/bfm2000/

Staniloae, D. (1994). *Orthodox dogmatic theology: The experience of God*. (I. Ionita & R. Barringer, Eds. & Trans.). Brookline, MA: Holy Cross Orthodox Press. (Original work published 1978)

Theophilus of Antioch. (n.d.). To Autolycus. In A. Roberts, J. Donaldson, & A. Cleveland Cox (Eds.), *Ante-Nicene Fathers vol. II*. (M. Dods, Trans.). Buffalo, NY: Christian Literature Publishing Co. Retrieved from www.newadvent.org/fathers/0204.htm

Ware, K. (1986). *The Orthodox way*. Crestwood, NY: St. Vladimir's Seminary Press.

Ware, T. (1993). *The Orthodox Church*. New York, NY: Penguin.

The Westminster Confession of Faith. (1647). Retrieved from www.pcaac.org/wp-content/uploads/2019/11/WCFScriptureProofs.pdf

Yannaras, C. (1984). *The freedom of morality*. (E. Briere, Trans.). Crestwood, NY: St. Vladimir's Seminary Press. (Original work published 1979)

Yannaras, C. (2005). *On the absence and unknowability of God: Heidegger and the Areopagite*. (H. Ventis, Trans.). New York, NY: T&T Clark International. (Original work published 1967)

Yannaras, C. (2011). *Relational ontology*. (N. Russell, Trans.). Brookline, MA: Holy Cross Orthodox Press. (Original work published 2004)

Chapter 4

Lacanian psychoanalysis and Christianity

The literature at the intersection of Eastern Orthodoxy and Lacanian psychoanalysis is quite limited; Dunlap (2014) included a single paper at this intersection in his review of writings on Lacan and religion, noting that "it is a rare example of an Eastern Orthodox reading of Lacan" (p. 137). Eastern Orthodox writers (theologians and authors of spiritual writings) do discuss psychology[1] at times (e.g., Chrysostomos, 2004a, 2004b; Morelli, 2006; Thermos, 2010; Thermos, 2011), and even psychoanalysis in Winnicottian and Jungian forms (Chaudhari, 2013, 2019; Chrysostomos, 2004a; Thermos, 2002). Direct engagement with Lacanian analysis is exceedingly rare. For their part, Lacanian authors (analysts as well as theologians) have not addressed Eastern Orthodoxy despite addressing other forms of religion and Christianity.

Although the body of literature relating to Orthodoxy and Lacanian analysis is limited, we have nevertheless devoted this chapter to interacting with any material that seemed relevant to the topic of the book in general and to this chapter in particular. First, we turn to Lacan's comments on God and religion to see what may be gleaned directly from him. Second, some recent theological writings engaging Western Christian traditions (Catholicism, Protestantism) and Lacanian analysis are examined, both for guidance and for important points of divergence from Eastern Orthodoxy. Third, we will evaluate what literature does exist at the intersection of Orthodoxy and Lacanian analysis.

Lacan's comments on religion

Lacan was quite genial at times toward religion—at least when it was relevant for his purposes—and addressed religion both directly and indirectly throughout his *oeuvre*. Just as Lacan did not engage in the systematic construction of theory, Lacan never expressed a systematic analysis of religion. Therefore, rather than attempting to construct a synthetic scaffold or comprehensive review, this sketch of Lacan's thoughts on religion emphasizes his most salient contributions to the subject. The information in this sketch is presented thematically, focusing on the function of religion, God and the unconscious, creation *ex nihilo*, and mysticism and sexuality. The primary sources for these discussions are Seminar VII: *The Ethics of Psychoanalysis* (Lacan, 1986/1992), Seminar XX: *Encore*[2] (Lacan,

DOI: 10.4324/9781003214359-5

1975/1998), and the volume containing both the "Discourse to Catholics" and "The Triumph of Religion" interview (Lacan, 2005/2013). Although the purpose of this section is the review of Lacan's work in relation to religion, Yannaras (2005) is included in the discussion at certain points because of important and relevant clarifications his writings yield.

The function of religion

Lacan (2005/2013) viewed religion, in its "truest" form (the Roman Catholic Church), as a sort of defense against the real. Much like the ego, religion functions to develop meaning to explain what is entirely outside of human systems of meaning. In Lacan's discussion of the Thing in the seventh year of his seminar, he suggested that where the Thing appears as an absence or an emptiness, religion appears to cover it over—"religion in all its forms consists of avoiding this emptiness" (Lacan, 1986/1992, p. 130). This is a perspective Lacan voiced numerous times that year, and he even extended the logic to evolutionism, which is "a form of defense, of clinging to religious ideals, which prevents you from seeing what is happening in the world around you" (p. 126). Lacan's consideration of religion did stop at the same place as Freud, however, and he suggested that, in addition to avoidance, "a phrase like 'respecting this emptiness' perhaps goes further" (p. 130). During this year of his seminar, Lacan formulated sublimation in relation to the Thing, stating that sublimation "raises an object . . . to the dignity of the Thing" (p. 112), and it is this role that Lacan saw religion playing at the time.

Given sublimation's role as an imaginary process wherein "the object is inseparable from imaginary and especially cultural elaborations" (Lacan, 1986/1992, p. 99), this is significant, as it places religion generally on the side of the imaginary and positioned as a defense against the real. This essentially places religion in opposition to psychoanalysis with respect to the real.

In contrasting psychoanalysis and religion in this way, Lacan (2005/2013) provided a structural formulation in which the two are at cross-purposes. However, Yannaras's (1967/2005) critique of Western theology and philosophy distinguishes Orthodoxy from this conception of religion as imaginary, as Yannaras, too, recognized that conceptual understandings of God comprise "the first obstacle to the 'knowledge of god,' the obstacle which is anthropocentric self-assurance of natural knowledge" (p. 75). Apophaticism, one of the core distinctions of Orthodoxy, consists in the "denial of the psychological props of egocentric assurance and the sentimental protection offered by conceptual certainties" (Yannaras, 1967/2005, p. 17). For Yannaras, the "place of the absence of God" in philosophical nihilism (Heidegger and Nietzsche are his primary points of reference) is a recognition of the results of cataphatic theology (p. 52). He noted the proclamation of the "death of God" (or more accurately of his murder)[3]

> is a fact only for those who have not given up seeking him: for people who seek God persistently, but who, within the constraints of western rationalist theology—its individualistic fideism or mysticism, its utilitarian ethics, the

56 Lacanian psychoanalysis and Christianity

authoritarian institutionalism of the Churches—can ascertain nothing else than his absence.

(pp. 50–51)

For Yannaras, then, as well as Lacan, (Western) Christianity seeks, insofar as possible, to cover over the place of the absence of God.[4] Yannaras and Lacan hold similar views of the function of religion, even if they show differentiation in their views of God. Even so, this difference is not as great as it first appears when one considers that Lacan also offered some comments in the direction of a beyond of the absence of God in *Encore*, to which we will return later.

God and the unconscious

In addition to commenting on religion generally, Lacan also engages the question of God specifically at numerous points. Lacan's consideration of God shifts somewhat over the years, largely in line with his overall shift from emphasis on structuralism to a poststructuralist approach. Here we will consider three primary points of Lacan's reflections on God: his comments in *The Ethics of Psychoanalysis*, a particular note in *The Four Fundamental Concepts of Psychoanalysis*, and Lacan's views in the much later *Encore*.

God and ethics

In pursuit of his exploration of ethics in the seventh year of his seminar, Lacan (1986/1992) spent significant time exegeting Freud's *Totem and Taboo* (Freud, 1913/1953b) and *Moses and Monotheism* (Freud, 1939/1964). Analyzing God's appearance to Moses[5] in the burning bush, Lacan (Lacan, 1986/1992) suggested the expression of God's identification, "I am what I am," shows "a God who introduces himself as essentially a hidden God" (p. 173). Lacan derived this hiddenness from the contrast between the Greek and Hebrew versions of the passage,[6] with the Greek, for Lacan, representing an ontological entanglement, while the Hebrew (and English) translation avoids this altogether. The rendering of the Greek that Lacan provided is "he who is" (p. 81), which is taken from the phrase "ἐγώ εἰμι ὁ ὤν" in the Greek (Exodus 3:14, LXX). The more complete rendering would be something similar to "I am he who is." The emphasis admittedly seems to be on the latter portion of the statement, *he who is*, but Orthodox Christianity does not venture into the "Greek metaphysics" about which Lacan seems to be concerned (p. 81). For example, Christ's reference to this passage in John 8:58 is, in English, "Jesus said to them, 'Truly, truly, I say to you, before Abraham was, I am" (RSV). In Greek, Jesus's words are "ἐγώ εἰμι," not "ὁ ὤν," suggesting some emphasis is placed on the phenomenological sense communicated in the Hebrew rather than the ontological sense.

Furthermore, the most significant appearance of ὁ ὤν in the Orthodox Church is in the inscription of the letters found in Christ's halo in iconography (Steffler,

2002). In other words, the supposedly ontologically entangled "he who is" primarily refers to Christ, who is revealed in the Incarnation—thus, He Who Is specifically in his phenomenological presence. This is further reinforced by the fact that, generally, icons are not made of God the Father, who is unseen, but only of Christ, who was incarnated (Ware, 1993). Although Lacan's (1986/1992) concerns about problems of ontology still have some substance to them, the Orthodox expression of "he who is" should offer some balance to Lacan's rejection of the Greek altogether. Lacan's conclusion remains accurate, however: God introduces himself as hidden. The essence/energies distinction offers a pathway, unavailable in Western theology, which embraces both ontology and hiddenness.

Moreover, for Lacan (1986/1992) at this time, God is relevant to psychoanalysis most essentially in his death. Lacan built his formulation of the death of God on a certain equivocation between God and the Freudian father. He noted in interpreting *Moses and Monotheism* (Freud, 1939/1964) that "this myth is nothing other than something that is inscribed in the clearest terms in the spiritual reality of our time, namely, the death of God" (Lacan, 1986/1992, p. 143). This death of God is traced by Lacan through successive modes, from "the animal totem, then a more-or-less powerful and jealous god, and, finally, the single God, God the Father. The myth of the murder of the father is the myth of a time for which God is dead" (p. 177). The death of God, then, is found in *Totem and Taboo, Moses and Monotheism*, and finally within Christianity itself, which is the only religion that "through the drama of the passion, gives a full content to the naturalness of the truth we have called the death of God. . . . Christianity, in effect, offers a drama that literally incarnates the death of God" (Lacan, 1986/1992, p. 193). It is at the moment of the murder of God, who has always been dead, that Lacan locates the advent of the Law, as did Freud. The dead father guarantees the symbolic order. Although Christianity insists on the resurrection, for Lacan, "that's simply a promise" (p. 193).

Despite his death, "God himself doesn't know" he is dead (Lacan, 1986/1992, p. 184). Because of this, "*jouissance* still remains forbidden as it was before, before we knew that God was dead" (p. 184). The Law continues. Indeed, in Lacan's reading of Christianity, the Law is not dismissed, but undergoes *Aufhebung*, "the conservation of something destroyed at a different level"; it ascends to the command "Thou shalt love thy neighbor as thyself" (Lacan, 1986/1992, p. 193). Lacan employed his own well-known reading of St. Paul's own words to clarify that, without the Law, *jouissance* is not possible (p. 177).

Lacan (1986/1992) discovered in the religious formulations of God a "Symptom-God" or "Totem-God or taboo" that only demonstrates "the God of truth," or more precisely, "the truth about God . . . namely, that God was really killed by men" (p. 181).[7] This Symptom-God, or God who orders, hides the dead God "as a child reveals the place of the object that he or she wants to hide by standing in front of it," to borrow Cantin's (2002, p. 87) description of dreamwork.

The death of God—and ultimately his absence—is related to "the field of the Thing" (Lacan, 1986/1992, p. 214), which is:

58 Lacanian psychoanalysis and Christianity

this field onto which is projected something beyond, something at the point of origin of the signifying chain, this place in which doubt is cast on all that is the place of being, on the chosen place in which sublimation occurs.

(p. 214)

The field of the Thing, then, where sublimation occurs, is the field where religion typically places God, where evolution places its own teleological principle (natural selection or consciousness), and where courtly love places the beloved. It is significant to note that Lacan (1986/1992) recognized a range of "solutions to the perspective of the field of the Thing," including Sade's "Supreme-Being-in-Evil" (p. 215). This is at the level of sublimation, the raising of the object to the dignity of the Thing. The Thing is only "the emptiness at the center of the real" (p. 121), a place where one might pursue pleasurable associations in repetition, raise the object to the dignity of the Thing in sublimation, or else engage in perverse acts.

In an incisive moment near the end of the seminar on *Ethics*, Lacan (1986/1992) revisited the concept of the Oedipus complex to make sense of the appearance of the superego in relation to the father (and, in some sense, to God). Lacan reminded his audience of his formulated distinctions between privation, frustration, and castration. Here, Lacan elaborated that the "imaginary father and not the real one . . . is the basis of the providential image of God" (p. 308). That is, having experienced the castration of the real father, the child takes the real father to be the imaginary father, "the father who has fucked up the kid" (p. 308), the one who has the power that is godlike. The imaginary father is not the superego; rather, the superego is a response to the imaginary father, and it is "hatred for God, the reproach that God has handled things so badly" (p. 308). Understanding the Oedipus complex in this way, one's image of God—especially at the level of imaginary cultural elaborations—reflects in part the experience of the resolution of the Oedipal crisis and is intimately related not only to God *qua* God but also to a person's unconscious self-conception.

God is unconscious

One of Lacan's (1973/1978) most well-known statements about God is that "the true formula of atheism is not *God is dead* . . . the true formula of atheism is *God is unconscious*" (p. 59). This comment is left largely without elaboration, but its context is key. Specifically, Lacan mentioned this while interpreting the dream of the burning child, which Freud (1900/1953a) recounts in *The Interpretation of Dreams*:

> The preliminary conditions of this typical dream were as follows: A father had been watching day and night beside the sick-bed of his child. After the child died, he retired to rest in an adjoining room, but left the door ajar so that he could look from his room into the next, where the child's body lay surrounded by tall candles. An old man, who had been installed as a watcher, sat

beside the body, murmuring prayers. After sleeping for a few hours the father dreamed that the child was standing by his bed, clasping his arm and crying reproachfully: 'Father, can't you see that I am burning?' The father woke up and noticed a bright light coming from the adjoining room. Rushing in, he found that the old man had fallen asleep, and the sheets and one arm of the beloved body were burnt by a fallen candle.

(p. 509)

As the dreamer did not dream of the child having never died but instead of the child returned to life, Lacan (1973/1978) located in this dream some unconscious belief in or desire for some part of life to follow after death. In the middle of Lacan's assertion of the true formula of atheism, he interjected "even by basing the origin of the function of the father upon his murder, Freud protects the father" (p. 59). In other words, Freud himself cannot escape the pull of the father. As Žižek (2009b) noted, "The modern atheist thinks he knows that God is dead; what he doesn't know is that, unconsciously, he continues to believe in God" (para. 4).

This insistence on the continued belief in God at the unconscious level is perhaps a continuation or outgrowth of Lacan's (1986/1992) thoughts in *The Ethics of Psychoanalysis* regarding the death of God. God, for Lacan, is still operable—he does not know he is dead—even for the atheist in secular society. However, this should not be confused for a support or argument in favor of religion; it is simply a clinical reality. This statement, though brief, plays an important role in the intersection of psychoanalysis and religion and will be revisited.

Mysticism and sexuality

In Seminar XX, *Encore*, Lacan (1975/1998) again spent significant effort addressing the notion of God psychoanalytically, but in a very different way than his earlier years. The *Ethics of Psychoanalysis* primarily addressed God in a structural manner in relation to the Oedipus complex and the father in the imaginary and symbolic. In *Encore*, Lacan maintained some of these structural ideas; however, he spent much of *Encore* addressing God in relation to the real.

Importantly, Lacan (1975/1998) clarified in this year of his seminar the relationship of three separate but connected terms. Lacan first distinguished a as "what is related to the imaginary," the imaginary object (p. 83), and A (the Other) as "what is related to the symbolic," and "it is indubitable that the symbolic is the basis of what was made into God" (p. 83). Finally, from these two, Lacan distinguished S($Å$), the signifier of the lack in the Other. S($Å$) is often confused with a, as Lacan noted, which occurs especially in psychology, and it is the separation of a and S($Å$) that makes psychoanalysis unique in its project. This is a crucial distinction. Lacan noted that the *Lustprinzip* is, "in effect, based only on the coalescence of a with S($Å$)" and that "if by S($Å$) I designate nothing other than woman's *jouissance*, it is assuredly because it is with that that I am indicating that God has not yet made his exit" (p. 84). It is in the Other *jouissance* ("woman's *jouissance*")

60 Lacanian psychoanalysis and Christianity

that Lacan located the Supreme Being—Aristotle's unmoved mover—and thus Aristotle's formulation of the Good is that every speaking being "must orient itself toward the greatest being by confounding its good, its own good, with that with which the Supreme Being shines" (pp. 84–85). In other words, the pleasure principle strives for and operates only in relation to the superimposition of *a* over S(Å). Significantly, this is also the same point of reference (the *eudaemonism* of Greek philosophy) that Romanides (1998) took in critiquing Western Christian theology's secular influence. As he noted about *eudaemonia*, "the successful satisfaction of human thirst is found only in ingenerate and unchangeable things in which the soul's unstable condition of unfulfilled quests ceases" (p. 43). This could as easily be an apt definition of the pleasure principle.

Given that S(Å) designates the location of the Other *jouissance*, beyond the phallic function, its mystics of both anatomical sexes are feminine in structure as they relate to the beyond of the phallic function. Lacan (1975/1998) identified the experience of this Other *jouissance* with the mystical experiences of, among others, John of the Cross and Teresa of Avila. It is insofar as there is something lacking in the Other through which one can experience the Other *jouissance* that Lacan can almost be found to say God exists.[8]

Lacan's (1975/1998) discussion of God in *Encore* is located precisely in the context of differentiating levels of *jouissance* and in distinguishing *a*, A, and S(Å). Although Lacan did not avow belief in God, he acknowledges something outside the phallic function and beyond language. The relationship between the subject and the S(Å) in mysticism is primary in understanding Lacanian conceptions of mysticism and forms a part of the basis of the discussion to follow.

Perspectives on Christian theology and Lacanian psychoanalysis

Moving on to the consideration of works addressing Christian theology from a Lacanian perspective, there are a number of edited collections and monographs to examine. These works engage almost exclusively with Western Christian theology. Rather than interacting with each volume, we will note those that are most relevant to our topic. We do so with the specific intent of highlighting the contrasts between Western and Eastern perspectives and considering the ways these authors make use of Lacanian analysis in their views of God. This interactive engagement will provide important scaffolding for the developments we propose in the following chapters.

Among the edited collections that address (mostly) Christian theology from a Lacanian perspective are Wyschogrod et al.'s (1989) *Lacan and Theological Discourse*; Davis et al.'s (2014b) *Theology After Lacan: Passion for the Real*; and Skomra's (2005) religiously oriented issue of *Umbr(a)*, *The Dark God*.[9] The essays in these collections are generally more philosophical in their approach to God than religiously minded. Given the goals in mind noted previously, our discussion here will engage Davis et al.'s (2014b) anthology in order to highlight

Lacanian psychoanalysis and Christianity   61

how Lacanian engagements with Christian theology to date miss the mark from an Orthodox perspective.

Davis et al.'s (2014b) anthology is solidly in the Western tradition, including chapters that focus on, among others, Aquinas (Beattie, 2014) (in concert, puzzlingly, with the rock band Queen) and Luther (Raschke, 2014). Many contributions are both entertaining and insightful, but ultimately distal to Orthodox belief.

Furthermore, in what one comes to expect from the more academic corners of Lacanian literature, Davis et al. (2014a) informed readers in their introduction that the collection "reworks Lacan in theological terms that deform our understanding of theology and reconfigure our understanding of Lacan" (p. 14). The iconoclastic[10] glee that is so common in academic publications in the humanities is sharply discontinuous with the Orthodox Church's value of the "understanding of theology" that has been passed down through the Fathers and Mothers of the Church. Continuity and respect for tradition are important in Orthodox life, and the tenor of academic theology is often in contrast with these values. Although disagreement should not preclude discussion, the radically different *Weltanschauungen* and values involved here considerably reduce the possibility of engaging in dialogue that fully values both perspectives. Indeed, to the extent that a dialogue exists, it must take into account the place from which each field begins without forcing the one or the other to divest itself of such foundational values.

Additionally, Davis et al.'s (2014b) collection takes a different object (Western theology and philosophy) than the present discussion, and it is similarly sustained by a different source and goal, which is first to reveal the "fake god, the big Other" (Davis et al., 2014a, p. 1) and then to traverse the fundamental theological fantasy the editors see implied therein. In their conception, they are exposing "traditional theology" as responsible for trauma caused by "the impossible demands of the Superego, The Paternal Father, the Big Other, God, etc." (p. 2). This trauma "needs to be drained into the symbolic order so that desire once again flows through contingency, otherness, difference, and ultimately love" (p. 2).

There is a basis for this understanding, of which Fink's (1995) theoretical introduction forms the foundation for these authors. However, it seems to be an essentially academic proposition to suggest well-done theology forms obstinately (in reaction formation, as it were) to what are called "traditional" beliefs about God. This type of theology is still founded on an in/out dichotomy and relies—just as much as what it seeks to replace—on a whimsical and angry God who imposes arbitrary rules that traumatize. This is because it is necessary for this "new" theology to have a "fake god" to reveal. On closer inspection, the itemized theological complaints of Davis et al. (2014a), particularly against the Paternal Father, are primarily symbolic complaints against an imaginary conception of a rivalrous God. In this way, even in trying to counteract "traditional" (Western) theology's dour and punitive (imaginary) nature with a lighter, more playful tone, the function served by Davis et al.'s updated theology is essentially the same as that of the one they denounce—"[realizing] the symbolic of the imaginary" (Fink, 1995, p. 143).[11] Perhaps the fact that this same structure underlies both "traditional"

62 Lacanian psychoanalysis and Christianity

and "new" beliefs about God is simply theology repeating itself, "first as tragedy, then as farce" (Žižek, 2009a).[12] Regardless, this is the appearance of the very formula of atheism Lacan espoused; as we see, "the sons kill the fathers" (Green, as recorded in Lacan, 1973/1978, p. 215).

The differences between Davis et al.'s (2014b) project and Orthodox theology are quite large, and the project's own reliance on tropes about angry gods is a noteworthy limitation. Orthodoxy does not seek to perpetuate the story of the angry, imaginary God nor does it seek to symbolically kill such a pagan god. Instead, it emphasizes the rupture of the real. Orthodoxy also reveals a fake god, but only incidentally, by fixing its gaze on what *cannot* be seen of God. The Unknown God is the source of the rupture at the center of Orthodoxy, not the slights of the imaginary God. The project of Davis et al. is exemplary of the philosophical theology that currently holds the highest page count of Lacanian engagement with religion; while all theology is philosophical to some extent; the efforts are generally in the direction of interesting iconoclasm rather than dialogue or mutual enhancement of experience. The goal in reviewing Davis et al. is not to single out the anthology but to take it as an example of the work that has been done already and the distance that must still be traveled in this nascent dialogue.

In addition to edited collections, several notable monographs have also been released, including Leupin's (2004) *Lacan Today: Psychoanalysis, Science, and Religion*; Pound's (2007) *Theology, Psychoanalysis, and Trauma*; Crockett's (2007) *Interstices of the Sublime: Theology and Psychoanalytic Theory*; Dunlap's (2014) *Lacan and Religion*; and DeLay's (2015) *God is Unconscious: Psychoanalysis & Theology*. While these writings are often more evidently informed by faith and religion than the noted edited collections, they also pursue their respective projects from a Western Christian perspective. To continue building the scaffolding for the following chapters, Pound's (2007) and DeLay's (2015) works will be considered in more detail.

Pound's (2007) *Theology, Psychoanalysis and Trauma* is an impressive collection of essays largely revolving around engagement between Lacan, Kierkegaard, and Roman Catholic theology. We share some theoretical concerns with Pound regarding the interface of theology and psychoanalysis. For example, Pound noted that the conclusions of Lacanian secular theology are changing the field into a "very private and liberal theology" (p. 12). He also argued that "because religion is now under the private jurisdiction of the believer, despite their concern for Otherness, it would seem that a hidden form of mastery is smuggled in" (p. 12). This move additionally cuts the authors of such theology off from actual communities of belief.

Beyond these theoretical concerns, some of Pound's arguments are helpful to consider in relation to Lacanian psychoanalysis' position toward religion. Three major areas are important here: the premise of Pound's project, his exposition of the analytic and theological view of God, and the logical outcome of his project given his vision of the relationship between faith and analysis.

Pound (2007) sought in his collection to show "psychoanalysis is already a theology," theology is "already psychology," and liturgy should be considered *"as* psychoanalysis" (p. 5). This project is quite ambitious, and his goal places this text in the stream of literature seeking identification of one field with the other (or in this case, each for the other). This aim is counter to ours, which seeks as much as possible to maintain the integrity of both fields. The importance of such integrity seems to be shared among Orthodox writers, with Chaudhari (2019) insisting that "each field is to be taken on their own terms of experience and self-identification" (p. 11) and Cazacu (2013) referring with admiration to Thermos' ability to balance "the mutual inviolability" of these fields (p. 14).

Another important aspect of Pound's (2007) discussion is that, for Pound, "ultimately theology surpasses psychoanalysis because whereas postmodern psychoanalysis assigns the subject a despairing lack, eucharistic devotion points the subject towards the divine plenitude of God's love" (p. 28). The logic undergirding this conception of theology's surpassing of analysis seems to be that plenitude is inherently truer or better than lack, and seems to rest on a sort of primal optimism more than explicit theological or analytic tenets. The challenge here is that this perspective is at risk of conflating whether an idea is pleasing with whether it is valid, and is also suggestive of the *Lustprinzip*, as it coalesces the imaginary object with the signifier of the lack in the Other. Theology may well surpass psychoanalysis but not because it is more pleasing. This subtle point inflects some of Pound's later arguments, including his interpretation of the analytic view of God.

Pound (2007) implicitly identified God and *das Ding*, citing Lacan's (1986/1992) comment that "religion in all its forms consists of avoiding this emptiness" (p. 130) to suggest Lacan "offers little advance on Freud's thesis" regarding religion as a product of obsessional neurosis (Pound, 2007, p. 71). Discontent with the antinomy between analysis and theology, Pound affirmed Kierkegaard's view of faith as creative transformation over against Lacan's view. Without irony, Pound argued that taking Kierkegaard's position in combination with Lacan's analytic theory allows one to

> not only affirm Lacan, but also in that moment reinvite God back into the discourse, the lost object, to be rediscovered through the labour of repetition *and* as he who gives himself freely, thereby replacing resignation to loss with hopeful expectancy.
>
> (p. 72)

By identifying God with the lost object and noting that the lost object will be found again, Pound made the common move of divesting Lacanian analysis of its content in favor of filling it with one's preferred theology. This subtle privileging of theology over psychoanalysis allows analysis to have its perspective only where it already agrees with theology. The implicit demand for conformity results in a theology that assumes analytic terminology in the manner of a substitution cipher rather than as part of a productive dialogue. Lacan (1986/1992) was unequivocal when he said *das Ding* "cannot be found again. It is in its nature that the object as such is lost. It will never be found again" (p. 52). Insofar as Pound

64 Lacanian psychoanalysis and Christianity

(2007) asserted theology allows the finding of the object, he proves Lacan correct in his estimation that religion seeks to avoid the emptiness.

Pound (2007) also reflected on God in relation to the *Non-du-Père*, noting (in Kierkegaard's reading of the story) the interdiction of God at Babel was not a refusal of an original *jouissance* (or "adamic language," p. 85) but a recognition of the fact there already is no original *jouissance*. No "pure mediation of God," direct communion through an original language, is possible (p. 85). Pound used this premise to argue that God is "the very principle *of* difference" rather than a defense against difference (p. 85). This suggests a symbolic God (at the level of difference) rather than an imaginary God (at the level of similarity), but seems to stop short of returning to God as *das Ding*, "beyond-of-the-signified" (Lacan, 1986/1992, p. 54), or a real God, as Pound previously suggested. It also demonstrates the absence in Western theology of an essence and energies distinction—there is only God in his absence (without direct communion) as the principle of difference.

Pound (2007) pointedly credited apophaticism with "curtailing the idolatry of direct relations with God" (p. 137). This is clearly a reference to the apophaticism of essence that Yannaras (1967/2005) outlined in Western thought. Referring to direct relationship with God as "idolatry" (Pound, 2007, p. 137) is the most direct contradiction of apophaticism when the latter is understood as apophaticism of the person. Pound's theology is circumscribed within the same "insurmountable limits" that would—if true—prevent anyone, even the Western mystics, from any experience of God (Yannaras, 1967/2005, p. 119). By affirming the absence of a direct relationship with God, Pound followed Barlaam of Calabria and continued to maintain God as existing outside of direct relationship and identified by difference. This suggests God as the symbolic God of the big Other and guarantor of the Law. Although the object—whether identified with God or not—exists at the level of the imaginary and the symbolic, Pound did not address its appearance in the real. Restricting God to the symbolic is a necessary outcome of the affirmation of the absolute difference of God without the essence/energies distinction.

Indeed, the initial chapters of Yannaras' (1967/2005) *On the Absence and Unknowability of God* outline the progression in Western thought from the cataphaticism of Augustine and Aquinas, to the Reformation, to German idealism, and, finally, to the death of God and to nihilism. Yannaras rebuked cataphatic theology not for failing to prevent the death of God but for actively contributing to it. By restricting ourselves to what can be said about God, by reducing God to a prime mover or absolute (i.e., to the symbolic) upon which reality is founded, the Church removed God from life in much the way, as we will see, DeLay (2015) decries. The dead God is the only possible outcome of this process, as God becomes inaccessible, and faith loses the ability to espouse a direct relationship with God. The essence/energies distinction arose from a dispute about this very issue—whether prayer could lead to a direct experience of God (Mantzaridis, 1984). As for Pound (2007), he used the difference of God to explore the Thomistic doctrine of participation,[13] but for the Orthodox faith, no true theology can progress from a position that precludes direct relationship with God.

Lacanian psychoanalysis and Christianity   65

Following Pound's (2007) original premise, he concluded his work with an essay arguing that the Eucharist is a form of analytic intervention. Pound viewed "the liturgical setting" as a protection "against psychoanalysis becoming a mere 'emptying of oneself into nothingness'" (p. 155). Pound achieved this by renouncing the Eucharist as "an imaginary phallus to satiate the gap of the real," instead insisting the Eucharist is based in desire rather than truth and the lack found in the Catholic faith is not an ontological lack but a divine plenitude:

> It is as if through Christ's work the truth of God now shines so brightly in an ever unfolding and increasing measure that one needs the sacraments as a filter, like a pair of sunglasses, to funnel the divine radiance lest one should burn one's eyes. Here, lack is a product of plenitude of God's truth; it is not that there is not enough, it is that there is too much! And herein is the difference between the respective goals of analysis and worship: in the former, one must be reconciled to an ontological lack; in the latter lack is a sign of God's excessive love in which we share.
>
> (p. 169)

As is the case for many theological uses of Lacan, here too appears the insistence on filling lack in some way, while insisting one is not doing so. To consider theology and psychoanalysis as so intertwined that the Eucharist is an analytic intervention misses the unique contributions of each field. Whereas the academic works of Davis et al. (2014b) tend to ignore the tenets of faith in favor of iconoclastic analysis, Pound (2007) veers in the opposite direction, placing faith in the position of primary importance, succumbing to the impulse to avoid the emptiness of the lack in the progression of his essays. The challenge of a rigorous engagement of Lacan's psychoanalysis and theology rests on whether the two can possibly both retain their major premises without mayhem.

Clayton Crockett, prior to coediting Davis et al.'s (2014b) collection, produced his own work on theology and psychoanalysis (Crockett, 2007). This volume largely follows the tenor of Davis et al.'s collection regarding its academic interest and perspective. This volume is also not specifically Lacanian; it emphasizes a variety of related theorists (such as Kristeva and Žižek) and philosophers (such as Heidegger), but several chapters rely heavily on Lacan (1986/1992, 1975/1998). Crockett's (2007) work is avowedly "against orthodoxy" (p. 6), though this is not a reference to Eastern Orthodoxy, and is intended to "unsettle both theology and psychoanalysis" (pp. 9–10). The natural academic push for theoretical individuation appears again here, but in this case, Crockett's "unsettling" arguments are relevant to the extent they unsettle the Orthodoxy of the West.

First and foremost, Crockett (2007) rightly divined the connection in Lacan (1986/1992) between God and *das Ding*; unlike Pound (2007), however, Crockett was careful to distinguish that "the Thing is not God" (p. 58). This is an important point for both analysis and (Orthodox) theology, though Crockett's explication of the difference leaves room for further development: "The Thing is not God,

66 Lacanian psychoanalysis and Christianity

but God can also be a thing. God can metonymically represent the Real, which resists symbolization, which must be present as an absence to symbolize or represent anything" (p. 58). Crockett viewed this "radical dislocation of theology" as a "profound challenge for ethics and for theology" (p. 58), which is true only to the degree one views ethics and theology through the constricted aperture of cataphaticism.

Taking this further, Crockett (2007) argued that "original desire is for God as Thing, a metonym for the Real beyond signification" (p. 60). "Original desire" here seems to refer to the desire Crockett located in the subject (such as it is) prior to alienation (see p. 57). In other words, Crockett viewed God as a representation (though he does not use this word) of the Thing, which itself refers to the real.

To consider God to be a metonym is essentially to reduce God to a signifier, which may or may not be problematic. From an Orthodox perspective, this understanding of God would itself be a metaphor, as it hides something more true about God that cannot be fully said, namely, his unknowability in essence. As a metonym for the real, God is essentially a concept formed to avoid the real, though Crockett views the location of God in relation to the real as an improvement on Western ontology (and undoubtedly it is). Thus, the metonymic God is one that fulfills a strikingly similar function as the Western God's cataphatic essence. For the Orthodox, God cannot be the Thing, as this would locate God's presence in some finite concept. However, the Thing itself might be a metaphor for the "place of the absence of God" (Yannaras, 1967/2005, p. 52). The Thing in this sense is no scandal for theology. Rather, it accounts for the unique way every person might experience the absence of God (e.g., how the burning bush was "Moses's Thing" [Lacan, 1986/1992, p. 174]). It also accounts for the necessity of apophaticism to avoid the reification of the sublimated object that has been raised to the dignity of the Thing.

Crockett (2007) later goes even further in the direction of an Eastern conception of God, concluding "God is not good, at least in terms of human symbolic discourse" (p. 146). Christian ethics cannot be determined by utilitarian principles, just as Lacan (1986/1992) argued the ethics of psychoanalysis is not so determined. Ethical implications and ramifications of this are discussed in Chapter 8.

Crockett's (2007) contribution to Lacanian thought on theology is admirable and even approaches Orthodox ideas, though likely without knowing it. Interestingly, Crockett's discussion, particularly of God and *das Ding*, comes the closest to an Orthodox perspective on the subject because of his emphasis on Lacan's teaching.

DeLay's (2015) *God is Unconscious* is somewhat more intellectualized in its approach to theology, especially when compared to Pound (2007). This book is primarily "a theological meditation on the life's work of Jacques Lacan" (DeLay, 2015, p. xix). In lieu of a thesis or central argument, DeLay offered the following: "This book does not attempt a constructive theology or even attempt to answer many questions at all. Instead, as any analyst worth listening to should do, it attempts to speak indirectly against postulation at its synchronic origin" (p. xxiii).

Lacanian psychoanalysis and Christianity 67

DeLay took aim at what he perceived as fundamentalism in American Christianity and occasionally commented on the political realm as well, seeming to hew closely to the radical Orthodox strain of theology.[14] His project serves as a laudable introduction to Lacan's (and, in many ways, Žižek's) thoughts on religion, but largely his work is not relevant to an Orthodox approach to the subject. However, one topic DeLay addressed that is important to review here is the relationship between God and *das Ding*.

In contrast to Pound (2007), DeLay (2015) emphasized that God is not *das Ding*.[15] Indeed, DeLay argued the idea that God is the Thing is a move to place God "purely in the Real," in a place where—in DeLay's reading—he is able to be controlled and is non-threatening. This is a God who would be

> more like Aristotle's unmoved mover than the God with which Abraham can barter. A God purely in the Real would not be a God that Moses could persuade to change. A God purely in the Real, unsullied by the world, is a lifeless statue.
>
> (p. 37)

DeLay moved on quite quickly from this point despite its significance.

Regarding this point, DeLay (2015) is, in many ways, accurate to characterize a lifeless God as a defense against anxiety, but it is unusual to consider the real a source of something that calms anxieties. Indeed, it is striking he chose to describe a God "purely in the Real" as a statue, a figure that is both imaginary and symbolic. What DeLay seems to be describing is far more similar to the dead father, that is, the symbolic father whose murder by the primal horde undergirds the self-imposed incest taboo. The dead father fits well DeLay's description of the method of alleviating anxiety by appealing to a predictable God, the Unmoved Mover, the one who can guarantee the social order.

The God DeLay (2015) contrasts with this "lifeless statue" (p. 37) is one who is passible and liable to persuasion. This God seems correspondent to the imaginary father; the example of Moses's persuasion is especially reminiscent of this, as the prophet had to remind God to abide by his word (to submit to the paternal function) rather than arbitrarily and omnipotently massacre his people.[16] This does not contradict DeLay's contrasting of dead and passible Gods, but rather shows he is contrasting symbolic and imaginary forms of God rather than addressing the real.

God in the real, even if not purely in the real, would be one about whom nothing could be said. It is here again that psychoanalysis seems to have more in common with Eastern Christianity than Western. Because Orthodoxy acknowledges the distinction between God's essence and his energies—both God—it is possible to recognize that God appears at different levels (such as imaginary, symbolic, and real). God in the real, or as connected with *das Ding*, is not problematic for the reasons DeLay (2015) suggested as this would not be a dead God by any means, but perhaps a hidden one. The possibility of a God hidden in essence, the Unknown God, is not problematic for Orthodoxy.

68 Lacanian psychoanalysis and Christianity

DeLay's (2015) text is important to illustrate, his objections withal, that connecting God and *das Ding* is not inherently problematic. The connection between God and *das Ding* is explored further in Chapter 6, which builds on this framework.

Lacanian analysis from an Orthodox perspective

Despite the interest Lacanian authors have shown in Western Christianity, none seem to have turned their attention to the mystical theology of the Eastern Orthodox Church. However, three Orthodox writers[17] have noted the affinity that Orthodox theology and Lacanian psychoanalysis seem to share. Although none have presented extensive engagement, the remarks of these authors assist in providing guidance to our work in the following chapters. First, two articles by Lila Kalinich (1988, 1990) on Orthodoxy and Freudian/Lacanian psychoanalysis are thematically grounding for this study. Second, Yannaras' discussions of subjectivity and eros provide orientation to how an anthropology informed by both fields might look. Third, the most recent and most discretely focused contribution to the discussion between Orthodoxy and Lacanian analysis by Christoph Schneider (2009) is also reviewed. Furthermore, just as Yannaras was brought into dialogue with Lacan's comments on religion where appropriate, so Lacanian analysis will appear here, also as appropriate, to further develop the scaffolding for following chapters.

Lila Kalinich

Two of the earliest explorations of Lacanian psychoanalysis and Orthodox Christianity in English come from Orthodox psychiatrist Lila Kalinich (1988, 1990). Kalinich's (1988) earlier article proffers a brief but insightful consideration of the relationship, exploring the significance of a variety of Lacanian concepts in the context of the Orthodox faith, such as Logos, the phallus, Lacanian epistemology, and *jouissance*.

Kalinich (1988) discussed the centrality of Logos to Lacan's psychoanalytic theory, focused as it was on language and the universe of signifiers. Kalinich interrogated Lacan's multiple references to the Johannine Gospel, but rather than engaging the content of his references, Kalinich explored the "rhetorical function" of his use of the Logos (p. 370). Kalinich suggested that Lacan referred to the Logos, an enormously complex and polyvalent concept, as a way of pointing to a mystery that he himself did not have greater recourse to explain. Kalinich highlighted the potential that such a use of the term might place Lacan adjacent to apophatic theologians, who "regard all positive assertions about God's nature as imaginary" (p. 371).

Regarding this use of theological language, Kalinich (1988) examined Vergote's (1983) argument that Lacan maintained the symbolic structure of philosophy and theology "while reducing their content and intention to a surface mirroring—in a word—to the imaginary" (p. 212).[18] Kalinich (1988) countered

Lacanian psychoanalysis and Christianity   69

that the subversion Vergote sees in Lacan "is only an apparent one" (p. 371). For Kalinich, Lacan's efforts against Cartesian thought reflect a concern similar to that of apophaticism. Even though Lacan did not posit a theology, Kalinich noted that his ideas are not merely structurally related to theology, but they even reflect theological content:

> Within that content [of Lacan's psychoanalysis] lurkes [sic] a human subject who is radically separated from himself, in a world that he can know only in part, finding his desire for being in his *manque*, his lack, yearning only to be desired by the Other, castrated in his contingency by death, through which language, the Logos, speaks its own Truth through him, revealing itself at moments of disclosure only to fade quickly behind the curtain of the unconscious. What better picture of Man, having committed the ultimate sin of narcissism, of self-assertion, now banished from his Eden, could be found?
>
> (pp. 371–372)

Here, Kalinich provided a lucid and clear arrangement of Lacanian concepts in a way that is relevant to the existential reality of the fall in Eastern Orthodoxy. The ability of the Orthodox faith to embrace the aspects of Lacanian analysis that are the most difficult for the broader analytic community to accept,[19] the ones most threatening to the ego, reveals the anthropological similarities between Orthodox Christianity and Lacanian psychoanalysis. The Orthodox Church is well positioned to appreciate the absence of true sexual relationship, the universality of the death drive, the insecurity of the ego, and the unconscious.

Kalinich (1988) further suggested that the phallus became the Signifier of the first sin, citing Lacan's (1966/2006) description of the phallus as "the privileged signifier of this mark in which the role . . . of Logos is wedded to the advent of desire" (p. 581). This is a somewhat creative reading of Lacan, but Kalinich wisely connected the phallus as the Signifier of sin with the first parents' decision to cover over themselves (i.e., to cover over the phallus). Kalinich also connects God's subsequent separation from humanity to desire, suggesting God's absence created desire (similar to Yannaras, 1996).

Drawing on similarities between the Areopagite, Lossky, and Lacan, Kalinich (1988) noted that the epistemological approach of Orthodoxy pursues truth over knowledge—not truth in the affirmative (and imaginary sense, as in cataphatic theology), but apophatic truth that "proceeds only by negations and leads to total ignorance, yet to *Truth*" (p. 372).[20] On this basis, Kalinich asserted Lacan's theory is more consonant with the Areopagite than Aquinas, and more consistent with apophasis than cataphasis and its Cartesian attendants. In this way, Orthodoxy and Lacanian psychoanalysis share similar epistemologies in addition to similar anthropologies.

Kalinich (1988) also made a direct connection between *jouissance* and theosis. Just as *jouissance* is connected to the death drive and goes beyond the pleasure principle, so, too, theosis requires kenosis, a self-emptying, going beyond the self.

70 Lacanian psychoanalysis and Christianity

Sexual orgasm, "the little death," is an icon of deification through their similar self-emptying (Kalinich, 1988, p. 378). Theosis is a form of *jouissance* for Kalinich and results in the emptying of "the narcissistic ego" rather than "the loss of ego boundaries" (p. 378). The connection here between *jouissance* and theosis, as well as Kalinich's comments on the role of the ego in theosis, is key and is revisited in Chapter 9.

Kalinich's (1988) conclusion after presenting her arguments on the subject was that "Lacan's move away from the West took him to the East" (p. 382). This might not surprise those familiar with Lacan's interest in Chinese thought and reticence toward Descartes. Even though Lacan was neither a theist nor a theologian (in the common sense anyhow), his challenge to Cartesian thought and turn toward negation-based and non-dualistic epistemologies place his work in close proximity to the experience of the Church that never underwent the Cartesian turn.

Subsequently, in an address at St. Vladimir's Theological Seminary, Kalinich (1990) also discussed the broad relationship between psychoanalysis and the Orthodox Church. The text of her remarks focuses solely on Freudian analysis, and she seems to assert her own sort of return to Freud. In this context, Kalinich noted that the center of psychoanalysis is the "quest for truth" (p. 356),[21] which is key for her in understanding the affinity between Orthodoxy and psychoanalysis. However, Kalinich noted, the quest for truth became lost in the language of contemporary psychotherapy: that of emotions and self-actualization, or "any number of narcissistic clichés capable of evoking something resembling nausea in people of any seriousness" (p. 357). Indeed, Kalinich attributed the Church's hesitance toward the psychoanalytic and psychotherapeutic fields to the turn of these fields toward such clichés (in addition, of course, to Freud's hostility toward religion).

In contrast to the hesitance of the Church overall, Kalinich (1990) argued that, when stripped of this clichéd narcissism and of the reductionism of the medical model, psychoanalysis is thoroughly compatible with Orthodoxy. In one striking claim, Kalinich asserted that "basically all of the principles of psychological work outlined in Freud's twenty-five volumes is contained in pure form in the spiritual exercises of the early Fathers of the Church" (p. 358). Although this language may be somewhat overstated,[22] the point is clear: Psychoanalysis (in its Freudian form) is acceptable and useful to Orthodoxy. For Kalinich, this compatibility goes beyond a lack of conflict; the Church ought to "redeem" psychoanalysis and psychiatry by shedding the Light of Truth on clinical practice (p. 358). This effort by Kalinich extends past our ambitions in visiting the intersection of Orthodoxy and psychoanalysis. Even so, Kalinich recognized the similarity of trajectories in both psychoanalysis and the Orthodox Church with respect to something of Truth.

Kalinich's (1988, 1990) comments on Lacanian psychoanalysis and Orthodoxy provide an excellent foundation for the development in the second part of this book. The emphasis of her writings on thematic connections rather than fine-grain detail is befitting of the beginning of such a large undertaking, and we look forward to continuing the work she began.

Christos Yannaras

Christos Yannaras is an eminent Greek Orthodox theologian and philosopher whose work has already been partially introduced in Chapter 3 and earlier. Whereas Kalinich is an Orthodox Christian from the field of psychiatry, Yannaras is from the field of theology. He has written prolifically on Orthodox theology, and Lacan had a clear influence on some of his writings (e.g., Yannaras, 2004/2011, 2008/2012). For our purposes, we focus on two of his works (Yannaras, 1996, 1967/2005) which are conceptually critical to the connections between Lacanian psychoanalysis and Eastern Orthodox Christian anthropology.

Psychoanalysis, subjectivity, and Orthodox anthropology

Accordingly, the first writing of Yannaras' to be considered is his book chapter "Psychoanalysis and Orthodox Anthropology," wherein Yannaras (1996) noted the primary place of desire in the constitution of the subject in French psychoanalytic thought.[23] Yannaras characterized desire as libido and as inherently relational, the aim of desire being a "fulfilling relationship" (p. 84). Following psychoanalysis, he placed the advent of the subject in the field of desire. Because, for Yannaras, desire instantiates the subject, the "presence absence" of God is a necessary condition for the institution of the "logical human," as only His absence creates desire (p. 86). This comment is similar to Spero's (1996) suggestion that God expelled Adam and Eve from the Garden as a protection against psychosis. For Yannaras (1996), God's absence in essence is necessary to allow the subject, constituted around desire, to come into being.

Where Lacan (1973/1978) described the subject in terms of a forced choice between Being and Meaning, Yannaras (1996) searched for a third term, denying the neither/nor offer. Yannaras paraphrased the Church's "answer" to the question of "self-definition of the subject" as "My beginning and hypostasis has been your creative command" (p. 86). Yannaras viewed the "hypostasis of the subject" as "the summons from non-being to being," the creative act of God (p. 86). The subject in this account is a realization of the potentialities of God's summons. The subject is not an ontological individual who desires, but is itself a phenomenological desire for relationship. Because the subject is not merely conscious, God's relationship to a subject must be inclusive of the unconscious. Yannaras proffered the ascetic practices of the Orthodox Church to demonstrate the difference between engagement with a whole subject (through asceticism) and only with the conscious principle (through morality). Yannaras also argued that the subject called into existence by God has the existential freedom to accept a relationship or reject it, and the only possibilities in the case of rejection are the annihilation of God in His Uncreated loving energies or the eternalization of the subject as rejecting—a self-imposed punishment from the subject. For Yannaras, only the latter option is tenable.

72 Lacanian psychoanalysis and Christianity

Yannaras' (1996) text on Orthodox anthropology and psychoanalysis offers important "hints" about avenues of relationship between the two fields with respect to the human subject (p. 83). Yannaras' account of psychoanalytic anthropology and its fit with Orthodox anthropology is well-founded. His conception of the presence–absence of God as necessary for the constitution of the subject is of special importance in understanding the connection between Orthodoxy and psychoanalysis. One area for clarification is Yannaras' characterization of "transcendent fulfillment" as "the aim of desire" (p. 85); Yannaras seems to recognize that desire is predicated on "forever deficient fulfillment" (p. 85), but this leaves open the question of *theosis*. Georgios Mantzaridis (1984), in explicating the writings of St. Gregory Palamas, described *theosis*: "The saints, communing in the grace of God and rendered through this communion more and more able to contain the divine radiance, will receive grace upon grace from God Himself, its infinite and unfailing source" (p. 125). The process of deification is endless, as the grace of God enlarges communion with his saints eternally—*theosis* is always, in this sense, unfulfilled, but not unfulfilling. This offers a tentative understanding of how union with God can be both achieved and at the same time never fulfilled in an ultimate sense.

Yannaras and eros

Eros is a recurring concept in Yannaras' work; it has already received significant review herein with regard to anthropology and personhood, so only a few additional words are necessary here. Eros, for Yannaras (1967/2005), is a self-transcending yearning and a mode of existence: "Human beings correspond to their creation 'in the image of God' to the extent that they realize their existence as erotic self-transcendence in the *personal* mode of existence" (p. 101). The recourse to the language of eros is necessary due to the inadequacy of "the name of love (αγαπη)" (p. 99), which is

> often charged with a 'minimal' conceptual content, reduced to the narrow confines of a social virtue, or equated with altruism, benevolence and natural affection—that is to say, with particular patterns of behavior that preserve and support the egocentric self-sufficiency of the subject.
>
> (pp. 99–100)

Love as agape (αγαπη) places a limit on personal relationship with God, which is characterized not as the gathering of information about God but "is a passion, in the literal sense of something suffered" (Yannaras, 1967/2005, p. 99). Love stops short of this passion, opting instead for self-satisfying pleasure. In this sense, agape serves for Yannaras the same purpose as the pleasure principle does for Lacan—as a limit to excess.

Yannaras (1967/2005) was also careful to delineate eros in the sense of yearning and passion—yearning to undergo the passion of the knowledge of God—and eros in the more colloquial, sexual sense. Eros in this latter sense "serves the existential self-sufficiency of individual entities, each individual desire for pleasure" (p. 101). This level of eros is a consequence of the fall and mired in self-gratifying pleasure and the drive for procreation. Even so, Yannaras followed the Areopagite in affirming that even a "licentious life" bears the marks (the "faint echo of goodness") of the yearning for true eros (p. 103). Therefore, the fallen implications of eros are not separated by some categorical difference from the yearning for union with God.

Yannaras (1967/2005) also commented that desire "always involves a reference, and therefore preserves, more or less, the dynamic of personal ec-stasy out of the existential self-sufficiency of nature" (p. 104), *ec-stasy* here referring to the leaving of oneself. Desire contains reference to something outside of the self, and for Yannaras, always points to personal relationship, "even if it is unattainable" (p. 104). This conception of desire is closely aligned with the psychoanalytic conception of desire. Desire recognizes the lack in the subject by reference to an Other, though for Yannaras, there is a person (a personal God) beyond the Other of the subject.

Christoph Schneider

Christoph Schneider (2009) has contributed perhaps the most direct and recent addition to this growing area in a book chapter titled "The Transformation of Eros: Reflections on Desire in Jacques Lacan." Schneider provided a reading of desire through the lenses of Lacan and of St. Maximus the Confessor, comparing and contrasting their views.

Schneider's (2009) reflections all circulate around desire in Lacan, considering roughly three areas: comparing Lacan's "protology" to Origenism and the nature-culture divide, discussing the mediation of desire through the Other, and considering the role of the divine energies in relation to these. Schneider's text focuses primarily on relating Lacan to St. Maximus and does so skillfully. Because the second half of this book addresses many of the same areas Schneider does, though from a different perspective, this discussion will focus primarily on two points that require consideration in this chapter.

The first point to consider is the opposition Schneider (2009) found in Lacanian analysis between nature and culture that is incompatible with Orthodoxy. This antimony certainly can be found in Lacan (e.g., Leupin, 2004), but it deserves further explication. Primarily, Schneider noted that desire for the Orthodox is not the result of cultural imposition upon nature but that desire "is grounded *in* nature," and that "it is co-primordial with being created and always already directed toward the divine" (p. 276). This led Schneider to rightful skepticism toward the view that the fall is therefore a form of salvation (which multiple authors suggest in their expositions of the Genesis narrative, as will be seen later). The perceived antinomy here between desire in Orthodoxy and desire in psychoanalysis rests upon the assumption that the word "desire" refers in both cases to

74 Lacanian psychoanalysis and Christianity

the same concept. If this antinomy is truly impassable, then either desire does not signify what Lacanian analysis says it signifies (viz., lack), or else sin and the fall are necessary conditions of a relationship with God, as it is bound up with desire. This forced choice is latent in Yannaras's (2004/2011) work but is brought to the foreground in Schneider's incisive text. Regarding the semantic range of "desire," however, Lacan did not leave things so muddled.

"Desire," from an analytic perspective, has a narrower definition than in its colloquial use.[24] Analytically, desire is the lack caused through symbolic castration. This is distinct from love and, additionally, what the Orthodox call Eros (which is itself not identical to its analytic counterpart).

Fink (2015) noted the linguistic contortions involved in defining "love" and "desire." In his efforts to clarify the matter, he organized his review of love in psychoanalysis in relation to the three registers of the real, symbolic, and imaginary.[25] Desire and love both exist within the symbolic and both are forms of interaction with the lack at the center of being. Desire in the analytic sense is the pursuit of compensation for what is lacking in the subject. The metonymy of desire operates in this way, taking various fungible objects to staunch the implicit feeling of incompleteness.

The second way of relating to the lack is through love: "Love is giving what you don't have" (Lacan, 1991/2015, p. 34). As Fink explained, a person's assumption of their lack and the "giving" of the lack to another is distinct from the metonymy of desire. As a practical example, he suggested that wealthy parents lavishing material goods (what they do have) on their children is not so much a sign of love as busy parents lavishing time (what they do not have) upon their children. This recalls the lesson of the widow's mite:

> Jesus looked up and saw the rich putting their gifts into the treasury; and he saw a poor widow put in two copper coins. And he said, "Truly I tell you, this poor widow has put in more than all of them; for they all contributed out of their abundance, but she out of her poverty put in all the living that she had."
> (Lk. 21:1–4)

The gift of the widow was not what she did have, but what she did not have. In this way, desire seeks compensation for the loss imposed by castration, while love relies on the assumption of the loss and the loss's distinction as precisely what one has to give.

To further elaborate the diction of love, Fink (2015) added "passion" as the appearance of love in the imaginary. Passion, in Fink's sense, is predicated on the similarity of the other and the ideal ego. This is the sort of love Fink understood Lacan (1975/1998) to be discussing when he wrote that love "is but the desire to be One" (p. 6), that is, "it aims at the annihilation of difference (Fink, 2015, p. 83). Imaginary passion seeks the primordial, oceanic feeling of prediscursive reality, "to return to a moment before alienation and separation" (p. 83), or in this context, to a time before the fall. The apparent forced choice between desire in Orthodoxy

Lacanian psychoanalysis and Christianity 75

and desire in psychoanalysis seems to have more to do with the choice between love (with its assumption of lack) and desire or passion.

Returning to Schneider's (2009) work, his argument that desire is "co-primordial with being created" (p. 276) does not run into problems against a psychoanalytic accounting of desire provided it is understood in relation to *love* rather than *desire* in Fink's (2015) terminology. Schneider (2009) seems to approach this point, noting later in his chapter that "divine grace and love . . . can only be actively and creatively received" (p. 286). In other words, the assumption of lack that occurs in love is an active engagement. Although the lack assumed in love is the product of a linguistic or cultural incision, there is no reason to imagine this is in contrast to an Orthodox perspective. However, metaphorically one reads the story of creation and the fall; humanity was created from the beginning to grow in union with God, specifically in his energies. With respect to his essence, humanity has always lacked, and this lack is neither contradictory to Orthodox theology nor problematic to a Lacanian understanding of language. Because the fall is only understood within the terms of its own consequences—that is, because we can only speak of the fall from the postlapsarian situation—no challenge seems to arise here.

The second point to consider in Schneider's (2009) chapter is the mediation of desire through the Other and the apparently antagonistic way the subject comes into being in relation to the Other. This is important as the antagonism between subject and Other is only problematic within Orthodoxy if the Other is considered the best understanding of God within Lacanian psychoanalysis. The placement of God in the role of the Other—and the subjugation of the subject that Schneider sees corresponding to this—are witnessed in the deontological fervor of the non-mystical traditions of many religions, Christianity included. We hope to illustrate in the second part of this book that the Other comports with the cataphatic elaborations of God while, in contrast, the Orthodox understanding of the essence/energies distinction allows for a broader understanding of the ways in which God interacts with humanity. Schneider rightfully places this idea at the center of his argument, suggesting that it is through God's energies that the subject–Other opposition is overcome. From a Lacanian perspective, a God who is unknowable and absent in his essence raises questions about whether God could be said to be the Other. Although Schneider is skeptical of the subject's move from desire to enjoyment (*jouissance*) through analysis, the consideration of God's essential absence as connected to that other great absence, the Thing, provides a greater understanding of how it is *jouissance* appears for an Orthodox Christian. Each of these threads will be taken up in the second half of this book, and the ways this shift in understanding regarding the essence/energies distinction will offer a new pathway forward.

Schneider's (2009) text is, as Aron Dunlap (2014) noted, "a rare example of an Eastern Orthodox reading of Lacan" (p. 137). Indeed, Schneider's (2009) work is the most direct literature, to our knowledge, at the intersection of Lacanian psychoanalysis and Eastern Orthodox theology. We hope to build on Schneider's

76 Lacanian psychoanalysis and Christianity

developments and to demonstrate a way to bring further engagement between these two fields, which will be evident as we turn to Lacanian interpretations of the narrative of creation and the fall in Genesis.

Lacanian interpretations of the Genesis narrative

The stories of creation and the fall are an important basis of anthropology in the Orthodox tradition. Given the limited engagement of Lacanian analysis with Eastern Orthodoxy, we seek to build connection with prior works through a similar focus on these narratives. While the interpretations of the Genesis narratives we will discuss are from non-Eastern Orthodox perspectives, the distinctions we draw here will lay the foundation for the interpretations we offer in the following chapter. The previous work in this area includes Piskorowski's (1992) brief Lacanian review, Rashkow's (1993, 2000) subversive reading of the narrative of the fall, Spero's (1996) explication from an Orthodox Jewish perspective, and Parker's (1999) interpretation of the fall.

Piskorowski

Anna Piskorowski's (1992) discussion seems to be the first explicitly Lacanian interpretation of the creation and fall narratives (at least in English). Her reading of the second and third chapters of Genesis is, in short, that "the first man and woman are subjects who accept their pre-given social and sexual roles by negotiating their own passage through the Oedipus complex" (p. 310), though Piskorowski immediately clarified that Oedipus and Electra complexes are both applied to the text.

Given when Piskorowski (1992) wrote this article, it is understandable that her reading of Genesis suffers from the relative paucity of Lacanian literature available in English at the time—a few secondary sources were used in addition to the selection of *Écrits* that Sheridan translated (Lacan, 1966/1977). This resulted in some theoretical blurriness that assumes a decidedly developmental form (which appears also in Parker, 1999). For example, the imaginary and symbolic are explained in the absence of the real, leaving Piskorowski's account with a child in imaginary union with the mother, which the father then obliterates by moving the child into the symbolic (Parker, 1999, also followed her argument here). This is not without merit, but represents a concretization of analytic concepts.

Piskorowski (1992) interpreted God as both mother/creator and father/lawgiver. Eve's desire is for God the father and is expressed in her attempting to access the knowledge of him through the eating of the Tree of Knowledge of Good and Evil. For Adam, Piskorowski viewed God the mother as "the ground," the Garden itself (p. 316). Adam's eating of the fruit is not specifically accounted for, but in the pronouncement of God that follows, Adam is separated from his "mother" by the work in which he must now engage to produce food.

Piskorowski's (1992) text is unfortunately quite brief (at about eight-and-a-half pages), but is notable both for its emphasis on Eve and for its inaugural Lacanian review of the narrative. The frame of the Genesis narrative as a form of the Lacanian interpretation of the Oedipus complex persists in future works and provides a balance to the focus on Adam in later literature.

Rashkow

Ilona Rashkow (1993) wrote a brief, feminist commentary on the fall narrative, primarily viewing it through the lens of Freud's historical formulation and abandonment of seduction theory. For Rashkow, God is the father who elicits Eve's transgression while simultaneously forbidding it, displacing responsibility from the father to the daughter. Reading the serpent as a symbol of masculinity, Rashkow viewed Eve as daughter being enticed to attempt to seize the paternal phallus (the Tree), yet, in doing so, she is banished as a daughter, becoming only a mother.

At a later point, Rashkow (2000) revisited the story of the fall to argue that the serpent, as feminine, represents a displaced mother deity that was censored from the story. Rashkow still viewed responsibility in the narrative as displaced from father to daughter, and she perceived the story as beginning the lengthy history of religion in which "the problem revolves around women" (p. 73).

Rashkow's (1993, 2000) interpretation of the fall was primarily influenced by Freudian theory, though her work overall (Rashkow, 1993, 2000, 2007) includes Lacanian influence. Her interpretation of the fall is creative and unique, but not overtly relevant to this project, and, as such, her interpretations are not significantly utilized herein.

Spero

In his article on the Garden of Eden, Moshe Halevi Spero (1996) analyzed the narrative of the Garden and the fall from a psychoanalytic perspective. Relying heavily on Lacan, Bion, and Kristeva, Spero outlined the significance of the myth in the origin of the subject. Significantly, Spero separated his rereading of the myth from moral theology, eschewing typical conceptualizations of sin in regard to the narrative—especially dismissed here is the Western concept of inherited guilt. Spero interpreted *original sin* simply to mean *first sin*.

Spero (1996) contextualized the Genesis narrative as myth, which he discussed in Lacanian terms as the subject's making sense of the space between the real and the first beginnings of imaginary identifications. As such, Spero located the myth of the Garden in a quasi-prelinguistic world. Prior to language, "one can only speak in terms of painful vacuity, of an unrepressed primary unconscious" (p. 514). Lacan's *Nom-du-Pere* is the process through which a subject emerges from this unrepressed unconscious as the Name-of-the-Father signifies the separation of a child from its mother in some meaningful away, allowing the symbolization of the mother.

78 Lacanian psychoanalysis and Christianity

Spero (1996) explicated Kristeva's notion of semiotic *chora*, a period of development that is "precognitive" and "presign" (p. 518). This stage is comprised of "minimal linguistic *ordering*" (p. 518). That is, primordial symbiosis is maintained, but ongoing sensations create impressions (which are imperceptibly different from the actual sensations and therefore not representations). Full symbolization, conversely, occurs in the process of the Mirror and Oedipal stages.

The phallus is the "symbol of negation" (Spero, 1996, p. 521) and represents the lack of the mother, meaning both her absence and what she herself lacks and desires. How the subject relates to this lack is a significant part of subjective structure. For Spero, the Tree of Knowledge is a phallic symbol, a symbol of negation. The whole process of creation, naming of the animals, and the creation of Lilith and Eve reflect progress in becoming a subject emerging from the *chora*. The Tree, as phallic symbol, is attractive to Adam[26] who lacks symbols for "sexual difference or lack" (p. 532), two functions of the phallus (in different registers). The Tree, as phallus, is the object of Adam's aggression as he consumes it, attempting to destroy the symbol of sexual differentiation and return to the primordial unity with the lost object. Adam's sin, then, is not transgressing God's command, but attempting to return to the prelinguistic world of the lost object—akin to psychotic foreclosure. This attempted foreclosure is what prompts God to expulse Adam and Eve from the Garden. By expelling them, God creates a deeper lack that can be symbolized and understood by Adam. Spero related the eating from the Tree to the process of alienation and primary repression and the expulsion from the Garden to the Oedipus complex, separation, and secondary repression.[27]

Overall, Spero's (1996) reading of the Garden of Eden myth is highly instructive. His association of the fall and expulsion with primary and secondary repression is creative and productive. However, Spero read the story of the Garden as a developmental account of the subject, for example, writing throughout the essay of "the Adam/infant." The challenge with this is that by elaborating on the prelinguistic *chora*, Spero was effectively attempting to view the past without accounting for the gravitational lensing of deferred action. This is not an internal inconsistency in Spero's work, as he clearly relied on Kristeva insofar as the prelinguistic readings. Even so, considering retroaction would (and will) produce a decidedly different reading of the narrative.

In terms of its relevance here, Spero's (1996) conclusion is limited. This is due to Spero's own religious influences—though his interpretation is quite thorough and persuasive with respect to Judaism, Orthodox Christianity's basic tenets conflict with some of Spero's discussion. For instance, Spero regarded the formation of the ego as a necessity and the defiance of the ego (in eating of the Tree) as a sin on Adam's part only insofar as it impedes nonpsychotic development.[28] This renders the fall as therefore "necessary" for the development of subjectivity (p. 536). As a corollary, then, God is either the author of evil insofar as he impels Adam to sin (for his own good) or else the author of evil in preventing Adam from sin (against his own good), and in either case, the assertion is untenable for Orthodoxy.

Parker

Parker (1999) offered an analysis of Genesis 2–3 from a Lacanian perspective in the context of postmodern biblical studies. Parker, aware of the relative absence of Lacanian analysis from biblical studies at the time of his writing, proposed to analyze whether the creation and fall narratives could be illustrative of Lacanian principles. He undertook this task as both the Genesis narrative and Lacanian analysis address the origins of human thought and development. As his central thesis, and similar to Spero (1996), Parker draws a parallel between the expulsion and the Oedipus complex.

Parker's (1999) article is a relatively lighthearted discussion (its expressive subtitle is "A Lacanian Pleasure Trip through the Garden") accompanied by a somewhat lighter Lacanian framework,[29] which may be due, in part, to translational availability—only Sheridan's 1977 selection from *Écrits* (Lacan, 1966/1977) and translation of Seminar XI (Lacan, 1973/1978) are cited, in addition to Fink's (1995) theoretical introduction and assorted other sources.

Parker (1999) provided a broad overview of Freud's conception of the Oedipus complex in boys and girls, noting the process of identification with the same-sex parent that occurs. Parker outlined that, for boys, the process of castration anxiety leads to identification with the father and the development of the reality principle, socializing the child. For girls, who discover that they are already "castrated," the process involves a turn to the father to provide in childbirth a substitute penis. This is, of course, quite similar to Piskorowski's (1992) account.

Parker (1999) described castration as the function of the acquisition of language the child experiences. Armed with this understanding, Parker ventured into a "postmodern" reading of Genesis using Lacanian psychoanalysis, noting it as a project "to discover what the text itself 'neglected' to say" (Parker, 1999, p. 24). This is a complicated goal from a Lacanian position, as it attributes some underlying, true meaning to the text the same way some depth psychologists attribute substance to the unconscious.

Parker (1999) recognized in Eve's presentation to Adam a type of the Mirror Stage. Adam identifies himself with Eve, forming, as it were, his specular image; Parker found evidence for this both in Adam's recognition of Eve as "woman" and in the movement of "two becoming one flesh" (p. 25). Parker read Adam's naming of Eve as a parapraxis, his identification with her being a misidentification because even the name he chooses is not identical to his own.

Adam, conflated now for Parker (1999) with the child ("Adam as child," p. 26), also encounters the Name-of-the-Father in the form of the prohibition against eating from the Tree of Knowledge of Good and Evil. Due to language acquisition and the prohibition, "all is definitely not well" (p. 27) for the primordial couple. Adam and Eve's eventual fall in the pursuit of a "god-like status" (p. 28) is something "God wants . . . to happen in the first place, restricting them from what they cannot have and creating sexual differentiation" (p. 29), lest Adam (and presumably Eve) should "fail to grow up" (p. 28).

80 Lacanian psychoanalysis and Christianity

From an Orthodox perspective, two immediate problems arise with Parker's (1999) interpretation. First, the fall is not the restriction of Adam and Eve from what they cannot have, namely, god-like status, as deification is the reinstatement of the same, never-altered original purpose—God offers a god-like status to humanity out of love. Second, God's complicity in sin, in Parker's reading, is untenable in Orthodoxy, the same as in Spero's (1996) account. Additionally, from a Lacanian perspective, Parker's discussion falls into similar problems as Spero's in relation to development as he made the same move as Spero in conflating Adam with the child or infant.[30]

Parker (1999) offered two critical pieces of information in his reading: first, he noted the connection of sex to the fall as it is in the text (rather than the subtext that many have traditionally read in the narrative). That is, he noted that sexual differentiation follows from the eating of the fruit, the covering of their sex organs subsequently representing an effort to "obliterate their sexual differentiation" (p. 28), or, phrased differently, to repress or disavow the knowledge of the phallus. Parker secondly noted the significance of God's words to Adam and Eve when he approaches them after they eat: God "focuses the woman's desire on the man, while further differentiating men and women to positions of ruler and ruled" (p. 28). Parker's words are focused especially on sex, but it reflects another possible way of interpreting the consequences of the fall: the institution of hysteria and obsession.

Summary of interpretations

These reviews all reflect strengths and challenges both in their theoretical Lacanian influences and in their relatability to Orthodox theology. The strengths of these reviews provide a solid foundation for further development. Parker's (1999) discussions of sexual differentiation and the role of the consequences of the fall especially warrant further consideration.

Regarding challenges with respect to Lacanian theoretical formulations, not only has the clinical literature in English advanced significantly since many of these reviews were written but also the availability of Lacan's own work in English has continued to increase. Some of the challenges found in these works include the fact that Spero (1996) and Parker (1999) explicitly conflated Adam with the infant or child, expositing the narrative as essentially a developmental progression. This presents two related complications; first, this lends an historical tone to the Genesis text, reading it as an account of events as they unfolded. Of course, this neglects the retroaction involved in any storytelling. Second, and stemming from this first, are the complications this brings, such as attempting to sort out the moment of (typically) Adam entering the Mirror Stage or the Oedipus complex. This is complex because Adam and Eve both speak prior to the expulsion (associated with separation), which the authors explained in different ways without presenting a coherent interpretive method for making sense of anachronistic linguistic components.

Lacanian psychoanalysis and Christianity 81

From an Orthodox perspective, the primary challenge raised by these interpretations is the way the interpretations necessitate God's complicity in sin in order for the subject to appear. Although this is certainly acceptable in an analytic sense (and laudable, perhaps, when considering Rashkow's [1993, 2000] objections), the attribution to God of sin is a problematic factor for Orthodoxy. Any further work requires some accounting for separation and sin without compromising the fundamental tenets of either Lacanian psychoanalysis or Orthodox Christianity.

Notes

1 A number of primarily theological works are couched in psychotherapeutic terms due to Greek underpinnings of "Ψυχοθεραπεία" (*psychotherapia*). For example, Met. Hierotheos of Nafpaktos (2005) has written of Orthodox "psychotherapy" from a spiritual perspective. Regarding Met. Hierotheos's well-known book on the subject, the (noncanonical) Abp. Chrysostomos of Etna praises Met. Hierotheos's work but cautions that the use of psychotherapeutic language may give the false impression that Orthodox spirituality replaces the treatment of psychopathology through scientifically validated methods (which is, of course, not necessarily the same as psychoanalysis' own conception of psychology and pathology). Lapin (2007) offered a brief review of the dual meaning of psychotherapy in Orthodox literature.
2 The English volume translated by Bruce Fink is utilized here. The chosen English title seems to be *On Feminine Sexuality, the Limits of Love and Knowledge, 1972–1973*; however, it is also identified on its front cover and title page as "Encore" and "Book XX." To maintain consistency with other literature and to avoid confusion regarding what might be meant by references to "feminine sexuality," the French title is used here: *Encore*.
3 "We have killed him,—you and I! We are all his murderers!" (Nietzsche, 1887/2006, p. 90). Lacan (1986/1992) also noted in discussing the death of God that Freud's myths highlighted "the truth about God . . . namely, that God was really killed by men" (p. 181).
4 Yannaras (2006/2013) offered another, more in-depth of critique of the "religionization" of Christianity in his aptly titled work *Against Religion*.
5 Moses the Midianite, not the Egyptian, for those familiar with *Moses and Monotheism*.
6 These are presumably the Septuagint and the Masoretic Text, respectively. In privileging the Hebrew—a text dated somewhere around a 1,000 years later than the Greek—Lacan places himself alongside Protestant tradition.
7 Lacan also viewed the Incarnation and death of Christ as an admission of "the human nature of the Father" (p. 181), which is a surprisingly unacknowledged lapse into Sabellianism (see Damick, 2011), given Lacan's (1986/1992) studious attention to other heterodox theologies elsewhere in his seminar (p. 215).
8 In addressing his own comments, Lacan (1975/1998) wryly noted that "naturally, you are all going to be convinced that I believe in God. I believe in the *jouissance* of woman insofar as it is extra (*en plus*), as long as you put a screen in front of this 'extra' until I have been able to properly explain it" (pp. 76–77).
9 There is also an issue of *Umbr(a)* dedicated specifically to Islam, but is not particularly relevant here; see Copjec et al. (2009).
10 The iconoclasts, historically, were those members of the Church who banned the veneration of icons (Ware, 1993). Iconoclasm was condemned as heretical in the seventh Ecumenical Council, and the Church annually celebrates the Triumph of Orthodoxy to commemorate the event. Because of this historical period, the term "iconoclast"

82 Lacanian psychoanalysis and Christianity

descended into modern usage as a description of a person who seeks to destroy traditions or institutions. In typical American fashion, iconoclasm in vernacular usage seems to be neutral to positive in connotation, coming to be indicative of individualism and independence. The term remains negatively inflected for the Orthodox Church; the word is used here to emphasize the tension between a Church dedicated to Tradition and an academic environment dedicated to innovation (another word often used pejoratively in Orthodoxy).

11 Fink (1995) made this comment while discussing Lacan's (Seminar XXI, as yet unpublished) formulations of discourses based on the Borromean knot of real, symbolic, and imaginary. Fink noted that Lacan provided the possibility of six discourses, moving around the knot either clockwise or counterclockwise: the clockwise combinations being Real–Symbolic–Imaginary (RSI), SIR, and IRS, and the counterclockwise being RIS, ISR, and SRI. Lacan elaborated only two of these, RSI and IRS, which he characterized as religious discourse in the former case and psychoanalytic in the latter (Fink, 1995). In the context of discussing the RSI discourse of religion, Fink commented this discourse "realizes the symbolic of the imaginary" (p. 143).

12 This is a reference to Žižek's (2009a) book by this title, *First as Tragedy, Then as Farce*. The title is itself a reference to Marx's essay "The Eighteenth Brumaire of Louis Napoleon," in which he commented "Hegel remarks somewhere that all great events and characters of world history occur, so to speak, twice. He forgot to add: the first time as tragedy, the second time as farce" (Marx as cited in Žižek, 2009a, p. 1).

13 The discussion is well worth reading, but it should be noted that Aquinas's participation is not the same as the Orthodox understanding of theosis (Hallonsten, 2007).

14 DeLay (2015) did not focus significantly on authors often associated with radical Orthodoxy, but did note feeling drawn to theology "particularly in its less confessional and more radical forms" (p. 47) and acknowledged "[entering] the tradition of radical theology through Caputo's introduction" (p. xviii). The intent of noting radical Orthodoxy here is not to place DeLay in a taxonomy with exactitude but to indicate the general position of his work in relation to Eastern Orthodox theology.

15 Appropriately, an ambiguous turn of phrase renders initially unclear whether DeLay (2015) said this or its opposite: "God is the beyond of the Symbolic or the Thing coextensive with the creation of the Symbolic" (p. 31). This could be read as identifying God with the Thing (interpolating a comma between "Symbolic" and "or" would render such a meaning) or saying God is the beyond of both the Symbolic and the Thing. The immediate context is suggestive of the former, but five pages later, DeLay clearly states "the Thing and the sense of uncanny (like the big Other) are not God, but they instantiate a theology" (p. 36).

16 It should be noted here that this reading is to highlight DeLay's (2015) framework. Eastern Orthodoxy recognizes the impassibility of God and Orthodox Christians would likely not view this story as one of an arbitrary God overcome with uncontrollable emotions (see Lossky, 1944/1957).

17 Given the extensive Orthodox literature in Greek, Russian, and French, as well as the extensive Lacanian literature in French and Spanish, there may well be authors who have addressed Lacanian analysis and Orthodox theology of whom we are unaware.

18 This is strikingly similar to Leupin's (2004) consideration of "homonymization" (p. 110), though Leupin did not include Vergote in his discussion.

19 For example, Moncayo (2012) noted that "within North American relational psychoanalysis, analysts don't like the negative principle associated with frustration, renunciation, or castration" (p. 208) and "Anglo-Americans view frustration as optional and would rather concentrate their efforts towards positive psychologies and the creation of non-frustrating and gratifying environments" (pp. 208–209).

Lacanian psychoanalysis and Christianity 83

20 One is reminded here of the book Nobus and Quinn (2005) composed that pertains to psychoanalytic epistemology, which they aptly titled *Knowing Nothing, Staying Stupid*. Of course, this approach is also characteristic of Zen Buddhism, a connection Lacan (1975/1988) makes and that is explored by Nobus and Quinn (2005) and more specifically by Raul Moncayo (2012).

21 Although Kalinich was not addressing specifically Lacan's views of truth, it seems relevant to note that Lacan (1986/1992) stated, "One can say right off that the search for a way, for truth, is not absent from our experience. For what else are we seeking in analysis if not a liberating truth?" (p. 24). However, he further noted the truth for analysis is particular rather than universal, found in each person's *Wunsch*—though the *Wunsch* "is to be found in every human being" (p. 24).

22 One wonders whether her audience of seminarians may have been more inclined to psychoanalysis in these terms. It is worth considering, however, that Lacan (1986/1992) made comments not dissimilar to this, noting (without necessarily approving) that one finds a "strange Christocentrism in Freud's writings" (p. 176) and even asserted that a review of Martin Luther's work is necessary to make sense of Freud's discussion of the father (p. 97).

23 Yannaras (1996) mentioned Lacan by name when citing those whose work he used in this chapter, as well as "Françoise Dolto, Denis Vasse, Gérard Séverin and Daniel Lagache" (p. 54).

24 Freud's (1912/1957) discussion of objects of affection and sensuousness already reflects a cleaving of the objects of love and desire. For Freud, the psychical impotence found in certain men was related to the incest taboo causing the split of love and desire, the treatment of which was to reintegrate the two into genital organization. Lacan himself was extremely skeptical of the concept of genital sexuality (see, e.g., Lacan, 1986/1992, p. 293), a sympathetic position when one considers, for example, the extraordinary ideas of Wilhelm Reich (1927/1980) regarding orgastic potency. In any case, the distinction between love and desire is present in Freud's work and simply developed further in Lacanian analysis.

25 Fink (2015) noted, "There is no singular theory of love in Lacan's work as a whole" (p. 64). As with many aspects of Lacanian analysis, the form presented here is based on certain currents in clinical, Anglophonic Lacanian analytic literature.

26 Spero (1996) focused his reading of Genesis on Adam rather than on Eve or on Adam and Eve together, though Eve and Lilith play important roles in his interpretation. The focus may partly stem from the Talmudic and midrashic texts he closely incorporated.

27 Spero (1996) also concluded his essay by further utilizing his reading of the fall to inform Lacan's (1973/1978) comments on the original sin of psychoanalysis: that "something, in Freud, was never analysed" (p. 12). Spero argued that Freud "had to become the very symbol of negation . . . upon which all future analyses would be predicated," curiously—though not without cause—identifying Freud with both the Tree of Knowledge and the phallus.

28 One can recognize here the opening of the medical model onto the primal scene of Eden. This is arguably another consequence of imposing a developmental reading: the appearance of "orthopedics in its etymological sense" (Lacan, 1986/1992, p. 10; see Lacan, 1966/2006, pp. 78, 251).

29 For example, his account of the Oedipus complex does not explicitly account for the role of the phallus.

30 Admittedly, Adam is the focus of the narrative of creation (though not, perhaps, of the fall), but it is interesting that Parker (1999) and Spero (1996) spend considerably more time developing their ideas in relation to Adam rather than to Eve. As noted, Piskorowski's (1992) work has a more equitable focus, and Rashkow (1993) noted, as of her writing, "traditional exegesis has concentrated on 'Adam's Fall'" (p. 75).

84 Lacanian psychoanalysis and Christianity

References

Beattie, T. (2014). Nothing really matters – rhapsody for a dead queen: A Lacanian reading of Thomas Aquinas. In C. Davis, M. Pound, & C. Crockett (Eds.), *Theology after Lacan: The passion for the Real* (pp. 34–57). Eugene, OR: Wipf and Stock.

Cantin, L. (2002). From delusion to dream. In R. Hughes & K. R. Malone (Eds.), *After Lacan: Clinical practice and the subject of the unconscious* (pp. 87–102). Albany, NY: State University of New York Press.

Cazacu, P. (2013). *Orthodoxy and psychoanalysis: Dirge or polychronion to the centuries-old tradition?* New York, NY: PL Academic Research.

Chaudhari, P. (2013). Freedom for relationship: An initial exploration of the theology of Zizioulas and the psychoanalytic insights of Winnicott in dialogue. *Pastoral Psychology, 62,* 451–460.

Chaudhari, P. (2019). *Dynamis of healing: Patristic theology and the psyche.* New York, NY: Fordham University Press.

Chrysostomos, Abp. of Etna. (2004a). *Orthodoxy and psychology.* Etna, CA: Center for Traditionalist Orthodox Studies.

Chrysostomos, Abp. of Etna. (2004b). Scholarly imprudence: Comments on contemporary trends in Orthodox spiritual writing and Byzantine historiography. *Orthodox Tradition, 21*(1), 2–15.

Copjec, J., Jöttkandt, S., Kerr, L., & Gorelick, N. (2009). *Umbr(a): Islam, 1.* (n.p.): The Center for the Study of Psychoanalysis and Culture.

Crockett, C. (2007). *Interstices of the sublime: Theology and psychoanalytic theory.* New York, NY: Fordham University Press.

Damick, A. S. (2011). *Orthodoxy and heterodoxy: Exploring belief systems through the lens of the ancient Christian faith.* Chesterton, IN: Conciliar Press.

Davis, C., Pound, M., & Crockett, C. (2014a). Introduction: Traversing the theological fantasy. In C. Davis, M. Pound, & C. Crockett (Eds.), *Theology after Lacan: The passion for the Real* (pp. 1–18). Eugene, OR: Wipf and Stock.

Davis, C., Pound, M., & Crockett, C. (Eds.). (2014b). *Theology after Lacan: Passion for the Real.* Eugene, OR: Wipf and Stock.

DeLay, T. (2015). *God is unconscious: Psychoanalysis and theology.* Eugene, OR: Wipf and Stock.

Dunlap, A. (2014). *Lacan and religion.* New York, NY: Routledge.

Fink, B. (1995). *The Lacanian subject: Between language and jouissance.* Princeton, NJ: Princeton University Press.

Fink, B. (2015). Love and/in psychoanalysis: A commentary on Lacan's reading of Plato's Symposium in Seminar VIII: Transference. *Psychoanalytic Review, 102*(1), 59–91.

Freud, S. (1953a). The interpretation of dreams. In J. Strachey (Ed. & Trans.), *The standard edition of the complete psychological works of Sigmund Freud: Volume V (1900–1901)* (pp. 339–622). London, UK: Hogarth Press Limited. (Original work published 1900)

Freud, S. (1953b). Totem and taboo. In J. Strachey (Ed. & Trans.), *The standard edition of the complete psychological works of Sigmund Freud: Volume XIII (1913–1914)* (pp. 1–162). London, UK: Hogarth Press Limited. (Original work published 1913)

Freud, S. (1957). On the universal tendency to debasement in the sphere of love (contributions to the psychology of love II) (1912). In J. Strachey (Ed. & Trans.), *The standard edition of the complete psychological works of Sigmund Freud: Volume XI (1910)* (pp. 177–190). London, UK: Hogarth Press Limited. (Original work published 1912)

Freud, S. (1964). Moses and monotheism. In J. Strachey (Ed. & Trans.), *The standard edition of the complete psychological works of Sigmund Freud: Volume XXIII (1937–1939)* (pp. 3–140). London, UK: Hogarth Press Limited. (Original work published 1939)

Hallonsten, G. (2007). Theosis in recent research: A renewal of interest and a need for clarity. In M. J. Christensen & J. A. Wittung (Eds.), *Partakers of the divine nature: The history and development of deification in the Christians traditions* (pp. 281–293). Cranbury, NJ: Associated University Presses.

Hierotheos, Met. of Nafpaktos. (2005). *Orthodox psychotherapy: The science of the Fathers.* (E. Williams, Trans.). Livadeia, GR: Birth of the Theotokos Monastery.

Kalinich, L. J. (1988). The Logos in Lacan. *St. Vladimir's Theological Quarterly, 32,* 367–383.

Kalinich, L. J. (1990). Psychoanalysis and the quest for truth. *St. Vladimir's Theological Quarterly, 34,* 356–360.

Lacan, J. (1977). *Ecrits: A selection.* (A. Sheridan, Trans.) New York, NY: Tavistock/Routledge. (Original work published 1966)

Lacan, J. (1978). *The seminar of Jacques Lacan, book XI: The four fundamental concepts of psychoanalysis.* (A. Sheridan, Trans.). New York, NY: W. W. Norton. (Original work published 1973)

Lacan, J. (1992). *The seminar of Jacques Lacan: Book VII: The ethics of psychoanalysis 1959–1960.* (D. Porter, Trans.). New York, NY: W. W. Norton. (Original work published 1986)

Lacan, J. (1998). *The seminar of Jacques Lacan, book XX: On feminine sexuality, the limits of love and knowledge, 1972–1973.* (B. Fink, Trans.). New York, NY: W. W. Norton. (Original work published 1975)

Lacan, J. (2006). *Écrits.* (B. Fink, Trans.). New York, NY: W. W. Norton. (Original work published 1966)

Lacan, J. (2013). *The triumph of religion: Preceded by discourse to Catholics.* (B. Fink, Trans.). Malden, MA: Polity Press. (Original work published 2005)

Lacan, J. (2015). *Transference: The seminar of Jacques Lacan, book VIII.* (B. Fink, Trans.). Malden, MA: Polity Press. (Original work published 1991)

Lapin, A. (2007). What is "psychotherapy" in the context of Orthodox Christianity? *World Cultural Psychiatry Research Review, 2,* 80–86.

Leupin, A. (2004). *Lacan today: Psychoanalysis, science, religion.* New York, NY: Other Press.

Lossky, V. (1957). *The mystical theology of the Eastern Church.* (Fellowship of St. Alban & St. Sergius, Trans.). Crestwood, NY: St. Vladimir's Seminary Press. (Original work published 1944)

Mantzaridis, G. I. (1984). *The deification of man: Saint Gregory Palamas and the Orthodox tradition.* (L. Sherrard, Trans.). Crestwood, NY: St. Vladimir's Seminary Press.

Moncayo, R. (2012). *The signifier pointing at the moon: Psychoanalysis and Zen Buddhism.* London, UK: Karnac Books.

Morelli, G. (2006). *Healing: Orthodox Christianity and scientific psychology.* Fairfax, VA: Eastern Christian Publications.

Nietzsche, F. (2006). *The gay science.* (T. Common, Trans.). Mineola, NY: Dover. (Original work published 1887)

Nobus, D., & Quinn, M. (2005). *Knowing nothing, staying stupid: Elements for a psychoanalytic epistemology.* New York, NY: Routledge.

Parker, K. I. (1999). Mirror, mirror on the wall, must we leave Eden, once and for all? A Lacanian pleasure trip through the Garden. *Journal for the Study of the Old Testament, 83*, 19–29.

Piskorowski, A. (1992). In search of her father: A Lacanian approach to Genesis 2–3. In P. Morris & D. Sawyer (Eds.), *A walk in the Garden: Biblical, iconographical and literary images of Eden* (pp. 310–318). Sheffield, UK: JSOT Press.

Pound, M. (2007). *Theology, psychoanalysis, trauma.* London, UK: SCM Press.

Raschke, C. (2014). Subjectification, salvation, and the Real in Luther and Lacan. In C. Davis, M. Pound, & C. Crockett (Eds.), *Theology after Lacan: The passion for the Real* (pp. 58–70). Eugene, OR: Wipf and Stock.

Rashkow, I. (1993). *The phallacy of Genesis: A feminist-psychoanalytic approach.* Louisville, KY: Westminster/John Knox Press.

Rashkow, I. (2000). *Taboo or not taboo: Sexuality and family in the Hebrew Bible.* Minneapolis, MN: Fortress Press.

Rashkow, I. (2007). Psychology and the Bible: What hath Freud wrought? *Svensk exegetisk årsbok, 72*, 31–48.

Reich, W. (1980). *Genitality in the theory and therapy of neurosis.* (M. Higgins & C. M. Raphael, Eds., P. Schmitz, Trans.). New York, NY: Farrar, Straus, and Giroux. (Original work published 1927 under the title *Die Funktion des Orgasmus*)

Romanides, J. S. (1998). *The ancestral sin.* (G. S. Gabriel, Trans.). Ridgewood, NJ: Zephyr.

Schneider, C. (2009). The transformation of Eros: Reflections on desire in Jacques Lacan. In A. Pabst & C. Schnedier (Eds.), *Encounter between Eastern Orthodoxy and radical Orthodoxy: Transfiguring the world through the Word* (pp. 271–289). Burlington, VT: Ashgate.

Skomra, A. (Ed.). (2005). *Umbr(a): The Dark God.* (n.p.): The Center for the Study of Psychoanalysis and Culture.

Spero, M. H. (1996). Original sin, the symbolization of desire, and the development of the mind: A psychoanalytic gloss on the Garden of Eden. *Psychoanalysis and Contemporary Thought, 19*, 499–562.

Steffler, A. W. (2002). *Symbols of the Christian faith.* Grand Rapids, MI: Eerdmans.

Thermos, V. (2002). *In search of the person: True and false self according to Donald Winnicott and St. Gregory Palamas.* (C. Kokenes, Trans.). Montreal, Quebec, Canada: Alexander Press.

Thermos, V. (2010). *Thirst for love and truth: Encounters of Orthodox theology and psychological science.* Montreal, Quebec, Canada: Alexander Press.

Thermos, V. (2011). Towards a theological understanding of psychopathology and therapy. *International Journal of Orthodox Theology, 2*(3), 101–119.

Vergote, A. (1983). From Freud's "Other scene" to Lacan's "Other." In J. H. Smith & W. Kerrigan (Eds.), *Interpreting Lacan* (pp. 193–221). New Haven, CT: Yale University Press.

Ware, T. (1993). *The Orthodox Church.* New York, NY: Penguin.

Wyschogrod, E., Crownfield, D., & Raschke, C. A. (1989). *Lacan and theological discourse.* Albany, NY: State University of New York Press.

Yannaras, C. (1996). Psychoanalysis and Orthodox anthropology. In J. T. Chirban (Ed.), *Personhood: Orthodox Christianity and the connection between body, mind, and soul* (pp. 83–89). Westport, CT: Praeger.

Yannaras, C. (2005). *On the absence and unknowability of God: Heidegger and the Areopagite.* (H. Ventis, Trans.). New York, NY: T&T Clark International. (Original work published 1967)

Yannaras, C. (2011). *Relational ontology*. (N. Russell, Trans.). Brookline, MA: Holy Cross Orthodox Press. (Original work published 2004)

Yannaras, C. (2012). *The enigma of evil*. (N. Russell, Trans.). Brookline, MA: Holy Cross Orthodox Press. (Original work published 2008)

Yannaras, C. (2013). *Against religion*. (N. Russell, Trans.). Brookline, MA: Holy Cross Orthodox Press. (Original work published 2006)

Žižek, S. (2009a). *First as tragedy, then as farce*. New York, NY: Verso.

Žižek, S. (2009b). *"God is dead, but he doesn't know it": Lacan plays with Bobok*. Retrieved from www.lacan.com/essays/?p=184

Part II

Chapter 5

Oedipus at Eden

The stories of creation and the fall in Genesis have received much attention from expositors throughout history (Rashkow, 2000). Within this multitude of exposition, several psychoanalytic readings have been produced (e.g., Fodor, 1954; Rashkow, 1993, 2000), including some from Lacanian perspectives (Parker, 1999; Piskorowski, 1992; Schreiber et al., 2019; Spero, 1996). Interestingly, these Lacanian interpretations generally treat the Genesis narratives as developmental parables, conflating Adam and Eve with children undergoing the Oedipus complex. The basic gist of these readings (Parker, 1999; Piskorowski, 1992; Spero, 1996) is that the events of the fall are moments of the Oedipus complex and that the expulsion from the Garden is the entrance into the symbolic world. In this sense, Boer (2006) was correct in observing that for many expositors "the eating of the forbidden fruit by the woman and the man is necessary at a number of levels" (p. 325). For Boer, "the transgression and its punishment is absolutely necessary for the purposes of Genesis 1 [dominion, multiplication, filling the earth] to be fulfilled" (p. 326); or for Parker (1999), "the expulsion from Paradise is just as necessary, and just as painful, as a child's maturation and subsequent socialization through the Oedipal stage" (p. 20).

The problem with these readings of the Genesis narrative is twofold. First, from the perspective of Orthodox Christians, any reading in which sin is *necessary* is at odds with our understanding of God. For the Orthodox, death and sin are intimately linked, for death came into the world through sin (Rom. 5:12), and, reciprocally, it is "through the fear of death" that humanity has been "subject to lifelong bondage" in sin (Heb. 2:15). God could not be the source of death or sin, for "God did not make death" (Wis. 1:13, RSV) and God "tempts no one" (Jas. 1:13). Beyond the Scriptures, the Fathers and Mothers of the Church, as well as tradition, testify to this (Romanides, 1998). Lossky (1978) put it succinctly: "God has not produced evil" (p. 65). It is therefore problematic to consider the serpent a collaborator of God's (Parker, 1999; Spero, 1996). An Orthodox understanding of the Genesis narratives will not generally be inconsistent with an Orthodox view of God, much like a Lacanian perspective of a clinical case would not rest upon principles of ego psychology.

The second problem is from the psychoanalytic perspective. Boer (2006) was correct in suggesting that previous psychoanalytic readings of the Genesis

DOI: 10.4324/9781003214359-7

92 Oedipus at Eden

narratives are founded "in the context of the nuclear family—no matter how meta-phorical those terms might end up being" (p. 313). By reading these accounts as developmental narratives/parables in a more literal sense, previous expositors have perhaps missed the role of the narrative in its own context. For Boer, this context was the role of the narrative in the historical situation of Israel, though we will cen-ter the discussion on the spiritual context of the narrative in the Orthodox Church.

Orthodox Christians do not by necessity believe in the literal, historical accu-racy of the Genesis narratives. Although some Orthodox Christians do support such a reading (e.g., Rose, 2000), this is not a doctrine and certainly not a dogma. Rather, Met. Kallistos (Ware, 1993) wrote:

> The opening chapters of Genesis are of course concerned with certain *reli-gious* truths, and are not to be taken as literal history. Fifteen centuries before modern Biblical criticism, Greek Fathers were already interpreting the Cre-ation and Paradise stories symbolically rather than literally.
>
> (p. 218n2)

Fr. John Breck (2005) also noted the Church Fathers and historical figures were not inclined to literal interpretations of Genesis. Yannaras (2004/2011) called "attempts to fit it [the narrative of the fall] into a historical context" "doubtful" (p. 116). He also noted, "It is not the historicity of the story that is an element of *revelation*, but its symbolic character. If we deny its historicity, we do not find ourselves outside the boundaries of the Church's experience and witness" (Yannaras, 2008/2012, p. 51). The story is, in many ways, an "etiological parable" (Breck, 2006, para. 6), one that speaks about the origins of beliefs and—most importantly—reveals some-thing about God and humanity. In this sense, the Orthodox reading of the creation story may be parallel in nature to the Lacanian reading of texts such as *Totem and Taboo* (Freud, 1913/1953). These stories, or myths, are not valuable as historical or chronological accounts. Rather, they are valuable precisely because they aim to open up the reader rather than to close the reader off by accounting for all events in a historical recording. The religious context of the narratives pertains to the truths communicated within them. The theological interpretations of these stories are therefore important, as reading the text outside of a theology (in this case, outside the mind of the Church) leads only to literary criticism.

Thus, a reading that takes seriously both Orthodox and Lacanian perspectives will not read the story as a developmental parable per se. While the story includes obvious themes of humanity at its origins, these scriptures are important for their religious truths, which may involve some developmental interpretation but not in a way that draws a very concrete equivalence between Adam and the Oedipal child. Rather, considering the representative nature of these stories, the use of log-ical moments in reviewing them yields not a developmental sequence for Adam or Eve, but a retrospective view of how the story—as an etiological parable—yields a similar reading of the speaking being as the logical moments of subjectivity in Lacanian psychoanalysis.

Oedipus at Eden 93

As a final preliminary note, prediscursive reality is not something about which it means anything to hypothesize, yet faith in such a reality seems to animate interpretations of childhood development in the Garden of Eden. Lacan (1975/1988) noted, "at first, there is language, already formed" (p. 2). Similarly, he wrote that "It was certainly the Word that was in the beginning, and we live in its creation" Lacan (1966/2006, p. 225). Language permeates the creation story from the beginning, as it is through the Word that God creates (Jn. 1:3). Lossky (1978) put this concern into theological terms when he noted, "The narrative of creation, let us not forget, is expressed in the categories of the fallen world" (p. 67). Elsewhere, he wrote more extensively:

> There is an inevitable confusion in theological reasoning, so that clear expression becomes impossible: the plane of creation and that of the fall are superimposed upon one another, and we are only able to conceive of the first in images which belong to the second.
>
> (Lossky, 1944/1957, p. 109)

This is a strikingly similar description to Fink's (1995) discussion in analytic terms:

> We may try to think ourselves back to a time before words, to some sort of presymbolic or prelinguistic moment in the development of *homo sapiens* or in our own individual development, but as long as we are thinking, language remains essential.
>
> (p. 24)

Because of this inherent afterwardsness (*Nachträglichkeit*), readings of the Genesis narratives that rely on interpretations of a prediscursive reality (or, similarly, on a refinding of a lost meaning of the text) miss the mark both analytically and religiously. Thus, as with Freud's (1950/1966) patient Emma, the story of creation is a product of deferred action. Whatever the creation and the fall entailed, it is written down only after the fact and cannot be read as a chronological–historical series of events. To find something more in the narrative of the fall requires reading it as an account of a trauma realized only in retrospect. Boer (2006) also made this point, suggesting that narrative (the meaningful, chronological organization of events) is the method that fantasy takes to conceal trauma.

Yet another effort at analyzing the Genesis narrative of the fall is necessary in order to engage Lacanian and Orthodox perspectives in a fresh way. In rereading the fall narrative, the approach we adopt herein seeks to focus on the text as a spiritual and theological expression of the mind of the Church. We endeavor to position Lacanian psychoanalysis and the Orthodox faith as dialogical partners, both positioned to interact in a productive and mutually enriching way, eschewing the temptation to subjugate one to the other.

The reading of Genesis here progressively addresses moments of the story rather than following a verse-by-verse exposition of the text. Additionally, and consistent with the reviewed literature, the focus is primarily on the story of the fall.

94   Oedipus at Eden

First, this section addresses the prohibition God places in the garden and how to understand it in relation both to Orthodoxy and psychoanalysis. Second, it presents a rereading of the Oedipus complex and its relation to the fall. Third and finally, the consequences of the fall are discussed from an analytic perspective.

Prohibition

One of the pivotal aspects of the Genesis narratives is the prohibition enunciated by God in Genesis 2:16–17: "You may freely eat of every tree of the garden; but of the tree of the knowledge of good and evil you shall not eat, for in the day that you eat of it you shall die." The most apparent Lacanian reading of the prohibition is to consider it a manifestation of the Name-of-the-Father (e.g., Parker, 1999). The identification of the Edenic prohibition with the No of the Father leads to the equating of the fall with separation and positions God as the source thereof, and it is here any Orthodox discussion must start.

For previous Lacanian expositors (Parker, 1999; Spero, 1996), this prohibition is the action through which God collaborates with the serpent in order to facilitate the psychic fall of humanity so as to promote subjective development. This is perhaps an operable reading for a non-Orthodox Christian audience, yet for an Orthodox Christian, God's status as tempter is not credible. Furthermore, the understanding of the prohibition as the interdiction of the Name-of-the-Father is not warranted within Orthodoxy.

This is because the prohibition is interpreted within Orthodoxy not as a legal interdiction with a promise of a punishment but as a warning without threat (Yannaras, 2008/2012). "God does not forbid the first couple to eat of 'the tree of the knowledge of good and evil.' He simply warns them" (p. 24). For the Orthodox, God's words regarding the fruit are not spoken because he is hoarding some wealth or because he denies some benefit to humanity. Instead, he intended for Adam and Eve to eat of the fruit when they were morally ready to do so (Romanides, 1998), as they were created neither perfect nor imperfect, neither mortal nor immortal, but in a liminal state meant to move toward union with God (Lossky, 1978; Ware, 1993). This union, in Orthodoxy, is deification or *theosis*, which is union with God in his energies (rather than in his essence). As such, the problematic part of Adam and Eve's eating of the fruit is not the attempt to seize the godhead *per se* ("you will be like God," Gen. 3:5), but the attempt to become God in essence and to become God without God, who freely offers himself in his energies; it is the break in the relational connection between God and humanity that is at stake.

In Yannaras' (2008/2012) reading of the early chapters of Genesis, he viewed Adam and Eve (or humanity, as Yannaras read the narrative as an iconographical depiction of humanity) as facing two choices, or

> two existential possibilities: that life should be realized as *relation* (self-transcendence and self-offering [*kenosis*]), bringing with it knowledge of the potentialities of existence as *faith* (trust exercised in communion); or that

knowledge should be sought as an individually possessed certainty, and life as a finite but individually managed existential event.

(p. 25)

Thus, becoming god through union with God in his energies (life as relation) is juxtaposed with any attempt to seize the Godhead or to become God in essence. With this understanding, Yannaras (2008/2012) framed the temptation of Adam and Eve (and every person) as "the temptation of existential absolute completeness and self-containedness, the temptation of a nonexistent, imaginary equality with God" (p. 39). Visible here is the influence of Lacan on Yannaras, and it is important to understand the seizure of the essence of God, of nonexistent equality with God, as an imaginary object.

In sum, because God intended Adam and Eve to enter into union with him, his words regarding the fruit are a warning of the consequences of a break in the relationship between God and humanity rather than a prohibition of the fruit as an unacceptable object.

Whether the words of God are a warning or a prohibition may appear at first to be a negligible detail from an analytic perspective; after all, either a threat of castration or a warning of castration might equally impose the castration complex. For example, there is the warning of castration that causes castration anxiety in the case of a little boy, whom Freud (1938/1964) briefly referenced, who had been

acquainted with the female genitals through being seduced by an older girl. After these relations had been broken off, he carried on the sexual stimulation which had been set going in this way by zealously practising manual masturbation; but he was soon caught at it by his energetic nurse and was threatened with castration, the carrying out of which was, as usual, ascribed to his father.

(p. 276).

In this case, the threat is communicated not by the father, but by an intermediary, namely, the boy's nurse, and the threat is attributed to the father in the form of a warning (i.e., the nurse warns of an angry and prohibitive father). This is where the imaginary father appears, "the father who has fucked up the kid," or perhaps who will (Lacan, 1986/1992, p. 308). Worth noting here is that Freud (1938/1964) also states immediately after his discussion of this boy that two factors are important in considering the threat of castration: the enunciation of the threat and the knowledge of sexual difference. For those wishing to interpret God's words as an interdiction, regardless of whether it was necessary for humanity to fall, the question arises how such an interdiction would operate in the absence of sexual difference, the knowledge of which follows after the fall. Following in the tracks of previous authors, if we accept the parable of development, and if the analytic threat of castration rests upon the foundation of sexual difference, we reach a contradiction that God's words cannot possibly serve this function. Of course, taking into account the *Nachträglichkeit* of the story leads away from this conundrum

96 Oedipus at Eden

and to the question of what the narrative means to its community rather than to its protagonists.

A second example of the castration threat, important to this latter question, comes from Freud's (1909/1955) notes on Little Hans' phobia, in which his mother produces a threat to send Hans to the doctor for castration. In Little Hans's case, his phobia is representative of his desire for his father to express anger—to announce some form of castration threat himself—to separate Hans from his mother (Fink, 1997; see Lacan, 2004/2014). Even though the real father is the agent of castration, the child mistakes the real father for the imaginary father (Lacan, 1986/1992). In this case, some appearance of the angry father, the imaginary father, would relieve Hans of the anxiety of being absorbed by the mother. This misperception (of the imaginary father in the place of the real father), the desire for castration and separation from the mother, offers a new gloss on the narratives produced by previous analysis of the narrative of the fall, which saw in Adam an attempt to remain with the mother (through a foreclosure of the-Name-of-the-Father).

How does this relate to God's words in the Garden? The assumption of the words as a prohibition is allowed only through the assumption of an imaginary God whose anger, jealousy, and threat of castration underlie the narrative. Similarly, the tendency to impute to Adam an attempt at foreclosure may be more indicative of our own neurotic tendencies than anything else—what good obsessive does not see paradise as some land of unlimited, pre-castration *jouissance* from which one would refuse to leave? With respect to the role the text plays in its community, certain forms of theological community (including some secular theologies) seem to play the role of Little Hans, reading desirously in Genesis about an imaginary god good enough to threaten castration for those who seek to disobey his commands to differentiate from the mother. This is a way of sustaining both the fantasy of lost *jouissance* and the castration that protects the subject from it. Orthodoxy does not provide this reassuring way out.

In the narrative of the fall, the serpent presents God to humanity as a liar jealously protecting his power. The serpent thus initiates a shift of Adam and Eve's view of God toward seeing him as a rivalrous other. What is at issue in the fall is not God as the symbolic father whose word Adam and Eve transgress. Rather, it is that the serpent entices Adam and Eve to view God as a little other, a mirror image. The relationship between humanity and God shifts to the imaginary, a type of relationship pervasive in psychosis and which Bergeron (2002) characterized as one "of strength and power" (p. 77). It is the serpentine view of God as other in the imaginary that precipitates the fall (and for that matter, that underlies the willingness of expositors to read the story of the fall as one of arbitrary prohibition and punishment).

Thus, while other authors see the fall as God's symbolic castration of humanity to prevent psychosis, Orthodox theology would suggest it is the slide into psychotic rivalry with God that leads to the fall in the first place. The fall is in

Oedipus at Eden 97

some way recapitulated by those who read God in this narrative (or perhaps more generally) as arbitrary, vengeful, and wrathful. The parts of Orthodox theology that appear polemical (such as that of Kalomiros [1980] and Romanides [1998]) are polemical precisely in their insistence that this god is not the God of Orthodoxy. The gap between the imaginary, the symbolic, and the real appearances of God opens up as central to investigating the Genesis narratives from both Orthodox and Lacanian perspectives. Such an investigation supports the argument that Lacanian psychoanalysis and Eastern Orthodox theology can substantially inform one another's views of humanity. Having been introduced to the imaginary God here, we will next center around a reconsideration of lack in the Garden of Eden based on the three registers.

The garden of Oedipus

Previous authors (Parker, 1999; Piskorowski, 1992; Spero, 1996) focused on the action of the creation and fall narratives as an instance of the Oedipus complex. Castration, which is the culmination of the Oedipus complex, is but one form of object lack and the one these authors emphasized. Lacan outlined three forms of object lack: privation, frustration, and castration (Lacan, 1994/2021). Each corresponds to different agents and objects based on Lacan's formulations of the real, imaginary, and symbolic (see Table 5.1).

Taking this structural configuration and applying it to the fall narrative provides a wider impression than simply interpreting the story as a matter of the Oedipus complex as a developmental model. It is this wider formulation that creates new pathways of interpretation ripe for exploration. This model serves as a guide for the following discussion, which views the narrative from the perspective of real, symbolic, and imaginary, in turn.

Real

The agent of castration is the real father that manifests the paternal function and effects the symbolic castration by the deprivation of the imaginary phallus. That is, the real agent removes, at least in the subject's understanding, both the mother's imaginary phallus (the child as phallus) and the subject's capability to be the imaginary phallus. Spero (1996), Parker (1999), and, to a lesser extent, Piskorowski

Table 5.1 Three types of lack of object

Agent	Lack	Object
Real father	Symbolic castration	Imaginary phallus
Symbolic mother	Imaginary frustration	Real breast
Imaginary father	Real privation	Symbolic phallus

Source: Adapted from Lacan (1994/2021, p. 207).

98 Oedipus at Eden

(1992) emphasized this aspect of the narrative of the fall—God the real father (in their readings) bars the subject (Adam and Eve) from remaining undifferentiated and psychotic in the Garden of Eden. It is easy to see in what way God and the serpent are collapsed in these readings, the latter serving only as a representative of the former. The condensation of the two figures reflects the fantasy of the God as the real father, a sort of family romance of a God who endorses the ambitious sin of humanity.

However, by shifting the narrative into the Orthodox perspective, it becomes clear that the Tree of Knowledge of Good and Evil does not serve as the imaginary phallus here, nor is Eden the mother. The object of Adam and Eve's fall is neither the fruit (which was "good for food," Gen. 3:6 and intended for humanity to enjoy eventually) nor sexuality (which existed before the fall), but precisely the opposite of sexuality: the object is the *essence of God*, the attempted seizure of which is a denial of relational being, and an insistence on autonomous existence. This is *apotheosis* rather than *theosis*. However, no such assumption of the divine essence is possible; this is the imaginary phallus. The serpent entices Adam and Eve to seek something—perhaps the only thing—which is truly impossible: to become like God in essence.

For Yannaras (2008/2012), the Tree of the Knowledge of Good and Evil is precisely "the potentialities of *knowing* both *evil* (the mode of createdness [autonomy]) and *good* (the mode of Godhead [relation]" (p. 41). There is no way to "equality with God as ontic atomic self-sufficiency," which is "the rational fallacy or wishful delusion of possessing the nonfinitude of the Uncreated" (p. 42). This is the preoedipal *jouissance*, which never existed except as a fantasy of the already castrated.

One question remains here: Why is the serpent the real father? When the object is clear—apotheosis as the imaginary phallus—the agent becomes clear. The serpent is the real father as it is the serpent who brings Adam and Eve face-to-face with their "want-to-be," their *lack of being* (*manque-à-être*). The prohibition that Freud produced was the incest taboo, yet it is the way in which the incest taboo brings the subject face-to-face with its lack that effects its journey through the defiles of symbolic relations, not the relationship with the mother as such. The serpent provides the interdiction by suggesting that atomic self-sufficiency—the rejection of lack—is the meaning of deity rather than relation. Furthermore, this shift in interpretation resolves the fantasy of Eden as a lost paradise of *jouissance*. Although previous authors treated Eden as a true paradise which Adam and Eve refused to leave (in attempting foreclosure), this new framework shows the imaginary nature of the object.

Thus, Adam and Eve, at the intervention of the real father, defy the imaginary father who stands in for him through the seizure of the Godhead in the imaginary—this is truly the moment of *Oedipus Rex* (or perhaps of the primal horde). The confusion of God and the serpent is further developed when considering the imaginary in the following. Formulating this new approach in Lacanian terms, the first row of Table 5.1 could be reconfigured as shown in Table 5.2.

Oedipus at Eden 99

Table 5.2 First stage

Agent	Lack	Object
Real serpent	Symbolic castration	Imaginary: Godhood-in-essence

Source: Adapted with permission from Lacan (1994/2021, p. 207).

Symbolic

At the level of the symbolic, the mother appears as the one who effects imaginary frustration of the real breast (Evans, 1996). The mother's absence is the advent of her symbolic presence, and it is the mother as absent that frustrates the child who expects not only his or her needs to be met but also his or her demand for love. The absence of God appears at the time of temptation, as he is not there to intervene but is named in his absence ("Did God say", Gen. 3:1). Rather than reading God's absence as a fact of historical import (or reading him as present in the serpent), the retroaction of the narrative leaves interpretive freedom regarding the nature of God's absence. Understanding the narrative of the fall as a condensation of multiple narratives—real, imaginary, and symbolic—allows other possible perspectives. Considering both Orthodox and Lacanian formulations, the absence of God here is an expression of the human experience ex post facto. How it is that God makes his appearance here as symbolic mother (rather than symbolic father) will again be clarified by the object.

Life is central in the narratives of the creation and the fall, not only in the Tree of Life, but in the care God, as birthgiver of all creation, shows in breathing "into his [Adam's] nostrils the breath of life" (Gen. 2:7, RSV), in Adam's naming of Eve ("the mother of all living," Gen. 3:20), and in God's own warning against eating prematurely from the Tree of Knowledge of Good and Evil. God's presence, as life-giving, is the fullness of life, the object in the real. However, God's life-giving presence is condensed with immortality, incorruptibility, power, and plenitude—it may assume many faces.[1] Adam and Eve seek the imaginary face of the object when they attempt to seize godhood (self-sufficient power and plenitude in godhood-in-essence). They experience imaginary frustration of the real face of the object at the moment when God, in his withdrawal at the conclusion of the narrative, enunciates his internal Trinitarian[2] dialogue: "Behold, the man has become like one of Us, knowing good and evil; and now, he might stretch out his hand, and take also from the tree of life, and eat, and live forever" (Gen. 3:22, NASB).[3] Immortal life of the organism is the real face of the object in the narrative. Immortal life, or "indestructible life," is of course the lamella of Lacan's (1973/1978) seminar, of which "the *objets a* are merely . . . representatives" (p. 198). Taking life as the real object of imaginary frustration, God's role as symbolic mother in the narrative becomes clear.

Regarding the frustration itself, it must be clarified again that death in Orthodoxy is not from God—the decision of humanity introduced death in its truest

100 Oedipus at Eden

sense: spiritual death, which is separation from God, who is life (Romanides, 1998). Yannaras (2008/2012) explained:

> When Man chooses to realize existence as *nonrelation*, as self-sufficient autonomy, then access to the fruit of the tree of life, access to immortality, is ruled out. And the denial of access, the privation of immortality, does not constitute a punishment; once again it constitutes a blessing "that evil should not become immortal."
>
> (p. 25)[4]

Thus, humanity chooses what leads to spiritual death (separation from God), and God, in his symbolic presence (as absence in separation), effects the "privation of immortality" (the frustration of immortality, in Lacanian terms) as a blessing. The fact that humanity is corruptible reflects the loss of the lamella and the loss of the fullness of God's presence. Adding these insights to Table 5.2, then, Table 5.3 is produced.

Imaginary

The imaginary God appears as Adam and Eve perceive themselves in competition with God for the divine essence: as the serpent says, "God knows that when you eat of it your eyes will be opened, and you will be like God, knowing good and evil" (Gen. 3:5). Again, the collapse of the serpent and God into the same agent is understandable at this moment, as it is the misrecognition of the imaginary father for the real father Lacan (1986/1992) described at the end of the Oedipus complex. In this case, Adam and Eve misrecognize God for the serpent who deceives them, elevating God to the level of "the Great Fucker" (p. 307), the one hoarding the divine essence. It is the misrecognition of God as the imaginary father that motivates Adam and Eve's fear of God (as they hide from him) and which lays the foundation of that strain of Christianity which sees humanity as "sinners in the hands of an angry God" or as totally depraved and predestined to eternal torture. As Lacan (1986/1992) further noted, "It is this imaginary father and not the real one which is the basis of the providential image of God" (p. 308), the one good enough and strong enough to curse and to bless.

The imaginary God here is the one who causes real privation of the symbolic phallus. What might it mean to experience privation of that which symbolizes

Table 5.3 Second stage

Agent	Lack	Object
Real serpent	Symbolic castration	Imaginary: Godhood-in-essence
Symbolic God	Imaginary frustration	Real: Immortality

Source: Adapted with permission from Lacan (1994/2021, p. 207).

Oedipus at Eden 101

lack? The masculine subject has the symbolic phallus by undergoing the paternal function (i.e., being castrated in the imaginary) and the feminine subject lacks the symbolic phallus by virtue of being not-all under the paternal function (Moncayo, 2008). In other words, privation corresponds to the feminine subject, who undergoes privation of the symbolic phallus in the real. The object of privation is again important to investigate.

In the narrative of creation and the fall, the symbolic object is that which is present in the story only in relation to the fact that it never makes a true appearance: the Tree of Life. Just as life appeared at the level of the imaginary as the Tree of Knowledge (and the essence of God) and at the level of the real as immortality, so it appears at the symbolic as the Tree of Life itself, the symbol of what Adam and Eve lack. This is clarified by the Orthodox perspective that Adam and Eve were created "neither mortal nor immortal" (Theophilus of Antioch, *To Autolycus*, 2.27, M. Dods, Trans., 1885). Typically, Western Christian frameworks of the story presume a fall from perfection (incorruptibility and immortality), leaving only the Tree of Knowledge as a potential symbol of lack. With the understanding that Adam and Eve lacked immortality, the Tree of Life becomes the very symbol of this lack, as it is the only tree from which it is clear they have not eaten. In fact, God expels them from the Garden to prevent that very act.

The expulsion of Adam and Eve from the Garden to prevent access to the Tree of Life reflects a privation in the real of the symbol of lack. In other words, Adam and Eve (and all of humanity) are, with respect to the Tree of Life, in the feminine position. In this sense, the expulsion from Eden—while commonly attributed to the angry God as a form of punishment—can also be understood as the creation of the possibility of the Church, which as the Bride of Christ, exists not-all under the castration of Life. Indeed, the privation of the Tree of Life, the mercy of God in allowing physical death, is what both places a limit on evil and what makes possible union with God in his energies (the possibility that is definitively not-all under the castration of the imaginary phallus of apotheosis). Configuring this to the format of Table 5.3, the full table (Table 5.4) appears.

Consequences of the fall

With this new perspective of the narrative of the fall, new significance is produced in the consequences that follow from the fall. First, sexuation is considered in

Table 5.4 Full table

Agent	Lack	Object
Real serpent	Symbolic castration	Imaginary: Godhood-in-essence
Symbolic God	Imaginary frustration	Real: Immortality
Imaginary God	Real privation	Symbolic: Tree of Life

Source: Adapted with permission from Lacan (1994/2021, p. 207).

102 Oedipus at Eden

relation to Adam and Eve's reaction to their fall. Second, the significance of the lamella in the narrative and in Orthodox theology is examined. Third, God's pronouncements to Adam and Eve in Genesis 3:16–19 are reviewed for their analytic significance.

God as lamella

The lamella, for Lacan (1973/1978), is "the libido, *qua* pure life instinct, that is to say, immortal life, or irrepressible life . . . indestructible life" (p. 198). Understanding the presence of God as life itself (and separation from which is death), God's presence is comparable to the lamella. Furthermore, the lamella is characterized by its absence in all sexed beings. However, the lamella, in its absence, is represented by the *objets a* that stand in for it. "It is of this that all the forms of the *objet a* that can be enumerated are the representatives, the equivalents. The *objets a* are merely its representatives, its figures" (p. 198).

Considering the identification of the lamella with God's life-giving presence, it could be said that it is of God's presence that all the forms of the *objet a* that can be enumerated are the representatives. In other words, the *objet a* provides, in its own presence as an absence, the representative of that which is not representable.

The lamella is directly connected to sexuality, as "it is precisely what is subtracted from the living being by virtue of the fact that it is subject to the cycle of sexed reproduction" (Lacan, 1973/1978, p. 198). This is because "sexuality is established in the field of the subject by a way that is that of lack" (p. 204). In subjectification, the speaking being enters into relation to the Other based on the superimposition of the lack of the subject and the lack of the Other, and it is this lack that animates human sexuality. The lamella, as immortal life, is banished, and "the living being, by being subject to sex, has fallen under the blow of individual death" (p. 205). It is individual death, the fact that humanity cannot reproduce itself asexually and must experience the cessation of individuality, which corresponds to sexed reproduction.

For Lacan (1973/1978), the lamella flees due to the sexual reproduction of the speaking being under death. Sex and death are indelibly linked. Orthodoxy supports the goodness of sex (Ware, 1993), yet views death as an evil event—how is it that sex could come with death? Vladimir Lossky (1978) approached this challenging terrain with theologically sound insight:

> The Fall has changed the very meaning of the words. Sexuality, this 'multiplying' that God orders and blesses, appears in our universe as irremediably linked to separation and death. This is because the condition of man has known, at least in his biological reality, a catastrophic mutation.
>
> (p. 67)

For the Orthodox, the fall—that is, the introduction of death—did not create sex, nor did sex lead to death. Rather, death irrevocably altered sex such that it is now "irremediably linked to separation and death" (Lossky, 1978, p. 67), a fact Lacan continually pressed the analytic world to face. In this sense, it was death that first was introduced, not as individual death but in the fleeing of the lamella, the indestructible life of the presence of God, which Adam and Eve jettisoned when they chose existence as nonrelation. The lamella's absence and the *objets a* that irrupt as the jetsam of its catastrophic departure are the factors that structure human sexuality and psyche in the aftermath of the fall. The anthropology revealed in the Orthodox view of the fall is surprisingly consistent with analytic considerations of the speaking being.

Sexuation

Sexuality is commonly linked to the narrative of the fall, despite the absence of any explicit connection in the text of the narrative. This may be due in part to the immediate consequence of the fall for Adam and Eve: "Then the eyes of both were opened, and they knew that they were naked; and they sewed fig leaves together and made themselves aprons" (Gen. 3:7). Parker (1999) perceived the clothing of Adam and Eve as connected to sexual differentiation in his review of the fall from a Lacanian perspective:

> The result of the eating of the fruit is, interestingly enough, not plenitude, or a fulfilment of desire, or even a knowledge of good and evil, but a "knowledge of nakedness," that is, of sexual differentiation, or knowledge of a Lacanian "lack." Just how much Adam and Eve desire to return to each other, to the original unity, is possibly suggested by their attempt to cover their nakedness, and thereby obliterate their sexual differentiation.
>
> (p. 28)

This is an important observation, but why is it that the Knowledge of Good and Evil produces knowledge of sex? Regarding the Knowledge of Good and Evil, Yannaras (2008/2012) noted the Tree of Knowledge represents knowledge of Good as life in relationship to God and Evil as autonomous self-sufficiency. The knowledge that Adam and Eve attain at the fall is, then, the knowledge of evil in their new, autonomous experience. The sexual differentiation of which Adam and Eve become aware is due to, as Parker (1999) suggested, the fact that sexuality is coordinated to lack—and it is the relation to lack that is the only possible form of structure after the fall. Although Parker read an "original unity" into the text (p. 28), Yannaras (2008/2012) argued that sexuality and nakedness are part of relation when one pursues the mode of relational existence; Adam and Eve "hide the characteristics that differentiate the sex of the human being" only because they have chosen self-sufficiency and wish to defend against their objectification by one another (p. 43). For Yannaras, Adam and Eve are not trying to return to some previous state, but to prop up their new individual (rather than personal) existences.

104   Oedipus at Eden

From an Orthodox perspective, then, the hiding of the sexes pertains to the refusal of the object. Significantly, sexuality is not introduced in the fall, but what sexuality is before the fall is unknowable. What is introduced in the fall is not the penis but the phallus as symbol of lack. The human decision to exist as atomic self-sufficiency is the very grounds of revelation of what is lacking; this is why the fall precipitates sexuation as a relation to symbolic phallus or the object, depending on the subject's position in sex (and setting aside for the moment the signifier of lack in the Other).

Orthodoxy and psychoanalysis are both able to witness the significance of the loss of indestructible life in organizing the sexual principles of human personality. Furthermore, God's pronouncements to Adam and Eve in the wake of the fall may further shed light on the structure of the psyche.

God makes three pronouncements after the fall, one to the serpent, one to Eve, and one to Adam. This reading focuses on his words to Eve and Adam, as recounted in Genesis 3:16–19:

> To the woman he said, "I will greatly multiply your pain in childbearing; in pain you shall bring forth children, yet your desire shall be for your husband, and he shall rule over you." And to Adam he said, "Because you have listened to the voice of your wife, and have eaten of the tree of which I commanded you, 'You shall not eat of it,' cursed is the ground because of you; in toil you shall eat of it all the days of your life; thorns and thistles it shall bring forth to you; and you shall eat the plants of the field. In the sweat of your face you shall eat bread till you return to the ground, for out of it you were taken; you are dust, and to dust you shall return.

God's words to Eve observe two major consequences: pain in bringing forth children and desire for her husband, who "shall rule over" her. Understanding the fall as the moment of sexuation, and taking some liberty with the correlation of femininity and hysteria and masculinity and obsession,[5] God's words to Eve reflect the position, to some degree, of the feminine and the hysteric: the pangs of *Penisneid* and the demand for a child—or substitute phallus—from the father, and the desire of the master. God does not present this relationship as preferable nor worthy of enforcement, but simply makes the observation that, as a consequence of the fall, this relationship will ensue. In other words, God does not instantiate hysteria, but he observes hysteria as a consequence of the fall's introduction of the phallus and sexuality.

Similarly, God's words to Adam observe the obsessive position. Whereas the consequences of the fall for Eve are expressed in terms of her relation to the phallus (child) and to the master, Adam's are expressed in his relationship to work—there is no Other in Adam's new position. Adam's relationship will be to the ground, which he will dutifully toil, assuming the obedience of the obsessive. Further, he will engage in such until the day he dies—laboring under the master, waiting for his death, without ever accounting for his own life.

Summary of the fall

Thus, this reading of the fall narrative is conducted not as a matter of chronology, history, or development, but treats the story as a series of logical moments pertaining to various human experiences. Considering the story's etiological nature and expression in categories of the fallen world allows a fuller and more fruitful reading that highlights the actual correspondence between Orthodox theology and Lacanian theory.

Indeed, the significant consonance—and even overlap—of the Orthodox Christian and Lacanian analytic views of anthropology or human nature are illustrated by the narrative of the fall. Rather than remaining limited to some form of noncompetition (or nonoverlapping magisteria [Gould, 1997]), Orthodoxy and psychoanalysis share more in common in their views of human nature, sexuality, death, and sin than do Orthodoxy and many other forms of Christianity. Similarly, the Orthodox view of the speaking being is much closer to Lacanian psychoanalysis than are some forms of analysis today. Thus, these fields are more apt and able to cooperate and engage in substantial reciprocal contribution.

The Orthodox view of God—as essentially absent—offers psychoanalysis a new way of relating to religion and religious practice. Rather than simply analyzing religion from the outside, psychoanalysis has the opportunity to engage with Orthodoxy in a more intimate manner. Indeed, analysis may have knowledge from clinical experience to transmit, particularly regarding the ways such an absent God may have already made his appearance within analysis. The lamella, *das Ding*, and Lacan's (1975/1998) own more extensive excursion on mysticism are all predicated on the pregnant absence of some Thing and point toward possible connection with the God of the Orthodox Church precisely in his absence and unknowability. It is in this direction that the present analysis will continue.

Notes

1 "Face" is used here more in an analytic sense and not in a religious one—this is not to advocate any sort of modalism, but rather to note the effects of the energies of God (i.e., his presence) are multifaceted. Clarification of this point is in the discussion of the lamella in Chapter 6.

2 This is, obviously, a Christian gloss.

3 The more literal NASB is utilized here as it expresses God's words as a complete thought. The RSV reads "Behold, the man has become like one of us, knowing good and evil; and now, lest he put forth his hand and take also of the tree of life, and eat, and live for ever" (Gen. 3:22) which leads directly to the next thought: "therefore the Lord God sent him forth from the garden of Eden, to till the ground from which he was taken" (Gen. 3:23).

4 Yannaras' (2008/2012) use of "privation"—at least in Norman Russell's translation—is evocative of Lacan's own delineation of frustration, privation, and castration, but Yannaras does not pursue this distinction or comment on his choice of words (nor does Russell). As such, it might be more analytically accurate to read the above quote as "the frustration of immortality," particularly as immortality is, in the end, granted by God, just as the real object may well be provided by the mother—after a time (Evans, 1996).

106 Oedipus at Eden

5 Fink (1997), for his part, argued that "within limits, we can associate masculine structure with obsession, and feminine structure with hysteria" (p. 256n20). Obviously, not all cisgender women are hysteric nor all cisgender men obsessive, nor is it the case that Lacan's (1975/1998) discussions of masculinity and femininity in *Encore* are reducible to obsession and hysteria.

References

Bergeron, D. (2002). The work of the dream and jouissance in the treatment of the psychotic. In R. Hughes & K. R. Malone (Eds.), *After Lacan: Clinical practice and the subject of the unconscious* (pp. 71–85). Albany, NY: State University of New York Press.

Boer, R. (2006). The fantasy of Genesis 1–3. *Biblical Interpretation, 14*(4), 309–331.

Breck, J. (2005, May 2). Meaning of meanings of Scripture? *Life in Christ.* Retrieved from https://oca.org/reflections/fr.-john-breck/meaning-or-meanings-of-scripture

Breck, J. (2006, November 1). On reading the story of Adam and Eve. *Life in Christ.* Retrieved from https://oca.org/reflections/fr.-john-breck/on-reading-the-story-of-adam-and-eve

Evans, D. (1996). *An introductory dictionary of Lacanian psychoanalysis.* New York, NY: Routledge.

Fink, B. (1995). *The Lacanian subject: Between language and jouissance.* Princeton, NJ: Princeton University Press.

Fink, B. (1997). *A clinical introduction to Lacanian psychoanalysis: Theory and technique.* Cambridge, MA: Harvard University Press.

Fodor, A. (1954). The fall of man in the book of Genesis. *American Imago, 11*, 203–231.

Freud, S. (1953). Totem and taboo. In J. Strachey (Ed. & Trans.), *The standard edition of the complete psychological works of Sigmund Freud: Volume XIII (1913–1914)* (pp. 1–162). London, UK: Hogarth Press Limited. (Original work published 1913)

Freud, S. (1955). Analysis of a phobia in a five-year-old boy. In J. Strachey (Ed. & Trans.), *The standard edition of the complete psychological works of Sigmund Freud: Volume X (1909)* (pp. 3–152). London, UK: The Hogarth Press Limited. (Original work published 1909)

Freud, S. (1964). Splitting of the ego in the process of defence. In J. Strachey (Ed. & Trans.), *The standard edition of the complete psychological works of Sigmund Freud: Volume XXIII (1937–1939)* (pp. 271–278). London, UK: Hogarth Press Limited. (Original work published 1938)

Freud, S. (1966). Project for a scientific psychology. In J. Strachey (Ed. & Trans.), *The standard edition of the complete psychological works of Sigmund Freud: Volume 1 (1886–99)* (pp. 295–397). London, UK: Hogarth Press Limited. (Original work published 1950)

Gould, S. J. (1997). Nonoverlapping magisteria. *Natural History, 106*(2), 16–22.

Kalomiros, A. (1980). *The river of fire: A reply to the questions: Is God really good? Did God create hell?* Seattle, WA: St. Nectarios Press.

Lacan, J. (1978). *The seminar of Jacques Lacan, book XI: The four fundamental concepts of psychoanalysis.* (A. Sheridan, Trans.). New York, NY: W. W. Norton. (Original work published 1973)

Lacan, J. (1988). *The seminar of Jacques Lacan: Book 1: Freud's papers on technique, 1953–1954.* (J. Forrester, Trans.). New York, NY: Cambridge University Press. (Original work published 1975)

Lacan, J. (1992). *The seminar of Jacques Lacan: Book VII: The ethics of psychoanalysis 1959–1960.* (D. Porter, Trans.). New York, NY: W. W. Norton. (Original work published 1986)

Lacan, J. (1998). *The seminar of Jacques Lacan, book XX: On feminine sexuality, the limits of love and knowledge, 1972–1973.* (B. Fink, Trans.). New York, NY: W. W. Norton. (Original work published 1975)

Lacan, J. (2006). *Écrits.* (B. Fink, Trans.). New York, NY: W. W. Norton. (Original work published 1966)

Lacan, J. (2014). *The seminar of Jacques Lacan, book X: Anxiety.* (A. R. Price, Trans.). Malden, MA: Polity Press. (Original work published 2004)

Lacan, J. (2021). *The object relation.* (A. Price, Trans.). Malden, MA: Polity Press. (Original work published 1994)

Lossky, V. (1957). *The mystical theology of the Eastern Church.* (Fellowship of St. Alban & St. Sergius, Trans.). Crestwood, NY: St. Vladimir's Seminary Press. (Original work published 1944)

Lossky, V. (1978). *Orthodox theology: An introduction.* (I. [Ian] Kesarcodi-Watson & I. [Ihita] Kesarcodi-Watson, Trans.). Crestwood, NY: St. Vladimir's Seminary Press.

Moncayo, R. (2008). *Evolving Lacanian perspectives for clinical psychoanalysis: On narcissism, sexuation, and the phases of analysis in contemporary culture.* London, UK: Karnac Books.

Parker, K. I. (1999). Mirror, mirror on the wall, must we leave Eden, once and for all? A Lacanian pleasure trip through the Garden. *Journal for the Study of the Old Testament, 83,* 19–29.

Piskorowski, A. (1992). In search of her father: A Lacanian approach to Genesis 2–3. In P. Morris & D. Sawyer (Eds.), *A walk in the Garden: Biblical, iconographical and literary images of Eden* (pp. 310–318). Sheffield, UK: JSOT Press.

Rashkow, I. (1993). *The phallacy of Genesis: A feminist-psychoanalytic approach.* Louisville, KY: Westminster/John Knox Press.

Rashkow, I. (2000). *Taboo or not taboo: Sexuality and family in the Hebrew Bible.* Minneapolis, MN: Fortress Press.

Romanides, J. S. (1998). *The ancestral sin.* (G. S. Gabriel, Trans.). Ridgewood, NJ: Zephyr.

Rose, S. (2000). *Genesis, creation, and early man: The Orthodox Christian vision.* Platina, CA: Saint Herman Press.

Schreiber, E., Schreiber, G., Avissar, S., & Halperin, D. (2019). Genesis through Lacan: A shift in God's discourse toward therapeutic management. *International Journal of Applied Psychoanalytic Studies, 16*(3), 181–194.

Spero, M. H. (1996). Original sin, the symbolization of desire, and the development of the mind: A psychoanalytic gloss on the Garden of Eden. *Psychoanalysis and Contemporary Thought, 19,* 499–562.

Theophilus of Antioch. (1885). To Autolycus. In A. Roberts, J. Donaldson, & A. Cleveland Coxe (Eds.), *Ante-Nicene Fathers.* Buffalo, NY: Christian Literature Publishing Co. Retrieved from www.newadvent.org/fathers/02042.htm

Ware, T. (1993). *The Orthodox Church.* New York, NY: Penguin.

Yannaras, C. (2011). *Relational ontology.* (N. Russell, Trans.). Brookline, MA: Holy Cross Orthodox Press. (Original work published 2004)

Yannaras, C. (2012). *The enigma of evil.* (N. Russell, Trans.). Brookline, MA: Holy Cross Orthodox Press. (Original work published 2008)

Chapter 6

God in analysis

While cataphaticism (and apophaticism of essence) leads to the dead God of philosophy, the apophaticism (of the person) of the East maintains an avowal of the "absence and unknowability of God" (Yannaras, 1967/2005). This avowal rests firmly on the grounds of the essence/energies distinction in Orthodox theology, which insists on both God's absolute unknowability and unapproachability in essence and his revelation and relational engagement in his energies. This is no small doctrinal dispute as cataphaticism and apophaticism lead to such divergent approaches to God that Vladimir Lossky (1978) confidently referred to "two monotheisms" (p. 27).

The unique position of the Orthodox Church as a Christian Church that affirms both the Incarnation and the mystical unknowing more characteristic of Eastern religions makes its relationship to psychoanalysis unique. Although some of Lacan's comments about God hold steady (due to commonalities between Eastern and Western Christian traditions such as the Incarnation or biblical cannon), his general approach to God, particularly in his imaginary and symbolic appearances, does not resonate with the conception of God in the apophatic East.

In considering an alternate approach to understanding the God of the Orthodox Church from a Lacanian perspective, the Other *jouissance* of *Encore* (Lacan, 1975/1998) and the not-all of femininity represent one approach, which will be discussed in Chapter 7. However, a better starting point for approaching God as understood in Orthodoxy arrived in Lacan's teaching 13 years prior, in his seminar on *The Ethics of Psychoanalysis* (Lacan, 1986/1992). It is in this year of his seminar that Lacan developed his conception of *das Ding*, or the Thing.

The Thing, for Lacan (1986/1992), is "at the heart of a subjective world" (p. 71). It is that around which the universe of the subject's signifiers arranges itself in accordance with the pleasure principle. In presenting his conception of the Thing, Lacan differentiated the object and the Thing in the following way: "an object, insofar as it is a created object, may fill the function that enables it not to avoid the Thing as signifier, but to represent it" (p. 119).

The vase is Lacan's (1986/1992) example of the object in this sense, as the vase creates a nothing in its center by surrounding it. Thus, the vase is "an object made to represent the existence of the emptiness at the center of the real that is called

DOI: 10.4324/9781003214359-8

the Thing, this emptiness as represented in the representation presents itself as a *nihil*, as nothing" (p. 121). The vase presents its nothing as a representation of the emptiness that is the Thing; it is a representative (vase) of the representation (nothing) of the Thing.

The Thing itself, which "is not nothing but literally is not" (Lacan, 1986/1992, p. 63) bears striking resemblance to the Orthodox conception of God in his essence.[1] Although DeLay (2015) objected to conflating God and the Thing, his logic is primarily based on the concern that a God in the real is an Aristotelian unmoved mover, one who is lifeless. However, the unmoved mover—the God of philosophy, which Yannaras (1967/2005) and Lossky (1944/1957) rejected—fits much more aptly the description of the dead God of the symbolic. The God DeLay seeks to avoid is the cataphatic notion of God-in-essence, but all cataphaticism is inherently symbolic as it seeks to map the entire geography in its domain. Apophaticism is similar to the function of the *koan* in Zen Buddhism: "not to explain reality but to open the mind" (Moncayo, 2012b, p. 116).

Lacan (1986/1992), in his explication of the death of God, outlined what he viewed as a successive development of the concept of God, which follows movement from the murder of the primal father to "the animal totem, then a more-or-less powerful and jealous god, and, finally, the single God, God the Father. The myth of the murder of the father is the myth of a time for which God is dead" (p. 177). This observation is not without merit, and Lacan read in the death of the God-Man (θεάνθρωπος), who is subsequently resurrected and forever guarantees the consequence of his murder (the command to love God), a "certain atheistic message in Christianity itself" (p. 178).

Yannaras (1967/2005) vociferously agreed with the atheism of Christianity, and even went so far as to argue that "the God that is conceived reductively on the basis of ideals drawn from human moral experience is the same dead God as the God of classical metaphysics who was defined by the logic of determinism" (p. 45). The death of God is the only logical conclusion of the assumption of the cataphatic, Aristotelian conception of God. Indeed, Yannaras redoubled his objections to this conception of God, noting:

> The "death of God," the testimony to his absence, is a fact only for those who seek God persistently, but who, within the constraints of western rationalist theology—its individualistic fideism or mysticism, its utilitarian ethics, the authoritarianism of the churches—can ascertain nothing else than his absence.
>
> (pp. 50–51)

Because this form of unbelief decries God precisely in his Western garb, Yannaras quoted approvingly Heidegger's comment that "atheistic thought that denies the God of philosophy, the God as *causa sui*, is perhaps closer to the divine God" (as cited in Yannaras, 1967/2005, p. 51).[2] This divine God is not the god of the philosophers, thus, DeLay's (2015) concerns are well-founded, but still miss the God of Orthodoxy.

110   God in analysis

To clarify this, it may help to recall Lacan's (1986/1992) comparison of the Gods of Moses the Egyptian and Moses the Midianite. Moses the Egyptian is a "rationalist" (p. 174) who seeks to preserve the monotheism of Akhenaton, whose religion provides organization "in the substantive unification of the world centered on the sun" (p. 173). In contrast to this is "the inspired, obscurantist Moses" (p. 174), the one whose God of the burning bush is a jealous God placing laws and demands upon the people. These are essentially the two Gods DeLay (2015) contrasted, the former based on symbolic organization and the latter based on jealousy and—though Lacan does not say it—anger, who, after all, had to be talked out of massacring his recently rescued people. DeLay preferred the latter. Lacan (1986/1992), for his part, identified monotheism with the symbolic prohibition.

Lacan (1986/1992) then made an apparently tangential comment about the Temple of Solomon. He asked rhetorically about the architecture of the building "a question that cannot be answered by any document, by any material image," which is: "How was this temple to be constructed so as to avoid all the traps of art?" (p. 175). It is here Lacan begins to approach what it might mean for God to appear in the real.

The prohibition of images (Ex. 20:4) is meant to avoid the captation of the image, which is a kind of idolatry. This, and the Temple's symbolic significance as "the cover of what was at its center, the Ark of union" (Lacan, 1986/1992, p. 175), suggest Lacan may be accurate in imputing to (cataphatic) monotheism an inherent priority of the symbolic. In this sense, Islam is much closer to a manifestation of a pure priority of the symbolic, a pure monotheism, between its insistent aniconism[3] and its monistic deity. Although Islam upholds the life of Jesus (e.g., Surah 4:157), its denial of his deity (Surah 5:17), that is, of the Incarnation, is what renders Islam a religion with priority of the symbolic in its (Islam's) traditional forms; it is only the Incarnation that provides Christians the ability to create iconography.

Indeed, Lacan's observation about the Temple of Solomon and its avoidance of imagery is proper to the Hebrew Bible rather than the Old Testament as such. In other words, the Incarnation, which alters the reading of the books of the Hebrew Bible for the Christian (Behr, 2006), creates a new, Christian understanding of the Temple. This is most clear in the Iconoclastic controversies of the 8th and 9th centuries (Ware, 1993).

The Iconoclasm of Emperor Leo III, whose edicts forbade the veneration of icons, fell in line with the Jewish and Islamic bans on graven images (Ware, 1993). This iconoclasm, given further ratification by the secondary repression of Leo V, was ultimately condemned in the seventh ecumenical council, the Second Council of Nicaea. The condemnation of Iconoclasm rested on the grounds of the Incarnation. As St. John of Damascus (1898, M. H. Allies, Trans.), one of the stoutest defenders of the holy icons, wrote:

> You see that the divine beauty is not set forth in form or shape, and on this account it cannot be conveyed by an image (ουκ εικονιζεται) it is the human

God in analysis   111

form which is transferred to canvas by the artist's brush. If, therefore, the Son of God became man, taking the form of a servant, and appearing in man's nature, a perfect man, why should His image not be made? If, in common parlance, the king's image is called the king, and the honour shown to the image redounds to the original, as holy Basil says, why should the image not be honoured and worshipped, not as God, but as the image of God Incarnate?

(Apologia Against Those Who Decry
Holy Images, I.52)

The Incarnation of the Word of God makes possible the construction of images— since God became man, it is possible to represent his image as incarnated. Images are not (it is generally held) to be made of God the Father (Ware, 1993), but of Christ, who is "the image of the invisible God" (Col. 1:15). Furthermore, icons in the Orthodox Church are "windows to heaven" (Zelensky & Gilbert, 2005); they do not represent earthly reality but depict instead the deified saints (Ware, 1993). Icons are subject to criticism when they come too close to presenting the human form with realism, for which reason statues are generally avoided in the Orthodox Church (Curnow, 2007).

The significance of this is that the symbols of God—as Word, for example, or in the symbolism of the Old Covenant—and the imagery of God as revealed in the presence of Christ are the necessary appearances of God in the symbolic and imaginary for any conception of his absence to circle around the real. It is that which does not or cannot appear in the symbolic and imaginary that is real. It is through expression in the first two registers that the third can be conceived—only in outline.

Yannaras (1967/2005) followed Heidegger in discussing the necessity of both being and nothingness: *beings* are the phenomenological revelation of things in experience; *Being*, however, "remains outside, it escapes notice, the truth of Being is elusive" (p. 53). The truth of Being is aletheia ($\alpha\lambda\eta\theta\epsilon\iota\alpha$),[4] unhiding or revelation, "emergence from oblivion or self-concealment—that is, out of nothingness" (p. 53). Truth and oblivion are then two modes of being. Rather than affirming rationalist ontological trappings, this means "Being ceases to signify the cause or principle of beings" (p. 53); that is, it does not stand for some unmoved mover or Cartesian guarantor of truth (as affirmation), but refers only to "the *mode* by which that which *is* comes accessible to us either as truth (reducing oblivion to nothing) or as oblivion (reducing manifestation to nothing)," nothing being key to being in either sense (p. 53). It is this discussion that led Yannaras to suggest "Heidegger comes then to recognize, in his own manner, the apophaticism of—at least—New Testament theology" (p. 55).

God's essence is in oblivion, in "the darkness wherein He who is beyond all created things makes his dwelling" (Lossky, 1944/1957, p. 27). It is only in specific moments of theophany ($\theta\epsilon o\phi\alpha\nu\epsilon\iota\alpha$), in which God is manifested in his energies, that something can be said about who God shows himself "to be" in the mode of truth. Further, Christ's manifestation of God, as a revelation, is possible only because of God's essential absence (or presence in oblivion). It is the iconography

112   God in analysis

of the Church as well as the affirmations of the Word of God as revealed in truth (e.g., in Christ, in the creeds and definitions of the Ecumenical Councils, in Scripture, etc.) that undergird the Church's apophaticism.

Returning to Lacan's (1986/1992) gloss on *Moses and Monotheism* and the death of God, it is key here to understand Lacan is addressing God's representation in Western, onto-theological formulations. Lacan is, in a sense, smashing the conceptual Dagons of the Christian West. However, Lacan's skepticism of Christian ontology (mistakenly displaced onto the Septuagint's *he who is*) is an echo of the same critique that forms the foundation of Eastern Christianity, namely, that God's mode of being in oblivion precludes cataphaticism. It is "conceptual fabrications" (Yannaras, 1967/2005, p. 54) that are elevated to "the place of the absence of God" (p. 52) that one could say Lacan (1986/1992) opposed. In a polemical critique that would suit an apophatic theologian, Lacan cracked that while God made man in his image, "man no doubt paid God back in kind" (p. 196). In considering the image of God, Lacan noted, "one doesn't see in the image, beyond the capture of the image, the emptiness of God to be discovered. It is perhaps man's plenitude, but it is also there that God leaves him with emptiness" (p. 196). The image hides the emptiness.

This leads back to the discussion of the Thing. Lacan's (1986/1992) elaboration of the lures involved in sublimation in relation to *das Ding* describes the same idolatry:

> At the level of sublimation the object is inseparable from imaginary and especially cultural elaborations. It is not just that collectivity recognizes in them useful objects; it finds rather a space of relaxation where it may in a way delude itself on the subject of *das Ding*, colonize the field of *das Ding* with imaginary schemes. . . . In forms that are historically and socially specific, the *a* elements, the imaginary elements of the fantasm come to overlay the subject, to delude it, at the very point of *das Ding*.
>
> (p. 99)

Reversing the polarization of Lacan's (1986/1992) transposition of theological concepts into analytic terms, this formulation is easily transposed into theological terms: The affirmative theological propositions proffered by the conceptual systematism of the West raise, through imaginary and cultural elaborations, conceptual fabrications to the level of God-in-essence, occluding the absence of God at the center of the subjective structure. God himself undergoes *aphanisis* in such systems, appearing only at the level of meaning and fading at the level of being.

St. Paul revised the theology of the Temple in line with this new path in his first epistle to the Corinthians, writing to the Christians there: "Do you not know that you are God's temple and that God's Spirit dwells in you?" (1 Cor. 3:16) and "Do you not know that your body is a temple of the Holy Spirit within you, which you have from God?" (1 Cor. 6:19). In Solomon's Temple, the Holy of Holies was occupied by the Ark of the Covenant, as Lacan observed; in the Second Temple, the Holy of Holies was empty (Josephus, *The Wars of the Jews*, 5.219), occupied only by the Foundation Stone (*m. Yoma* 5:2) marking the absence of the Ark. The Holy of Holies, where only the high priest would enter, is emptied of the symbolic presence of God and left empty—until St. Paul described the position of the Holy of Holies itself inside the Christian, wherein "the Holy Spirit dwells" (1 Cor. 3:16) and wherein Christ is the High Priest (Heb.).[5]

Indeed, regarding the entry into the Holy of Holies only by the high priest, St. Paul commented that "by this the Holy Spirit indicates that the way into the sanctuary is not yet opened as long as the outer tent is still standing (which is symbolic for the present age)" (Heb. 9:8–9). However, Christ's entrance into the Holy of Holies through "the greater and more perfect tent (not made by hands, that is, not of this creation)" (Heb. 9:11) is the mark of the end of the ritual sacrifice precisely as he completes it. St. Paul noted:

> Where a will is involved, the death of the one who made it must be established. For a will takes effect only at death, since it is not in force as long as the one who made it is alive.
>
> (Heb. 9:16–17)

The faith which is called Christian culminates not in the priority of the symbolic, which emptied the human mind of imaginary captation in the Old Covenant, but in the accession of the real in Christ, "who has become a priest, not according to a legal requirement concerning bodily descent" that is, not by the Law, "but by the power of an indestructible life" (Heb. 7:16). Thus, just as the absence of God as indestructible Life, as lamella, occurs at the fall, so, too, does the theophany of Christ make manifest in truth the same indestructible Life which had been theretofore only in oblivion. In his death, which could not continue indefinitely, Christ instituted a New Covenant, a new will, in which the Temple of God is the body of the Christian.

The subjective structure of the Christian is organized around the Holy of Holies, the essential absence of God, which is made bearable by the ministrations of the High Priest who manifests the Life that the absence withdrew. This is what enables the connection between Lacan's *Ding* and the God of the Eastern Church. This adds a new perspective to Lacan's (1986/1992) statement that "the Thing only presents itself to the extent that it becomes word, hits the bull's eye, as they say" (p. 55).[6] *Das Ding*, God in his essence, presents itself (reveals itself in truth, αληθεια) only to the extent it becomes Word, the *Logos* of God, and hits the mark—or, it could be said, is ἀναμάρτητος (anamartétos), that is, not one who misses the mark or one who is sinless. It is God's appearance as Word in Christ that gives any notion of the invisible God. Christ's sinlessness, rather than fulfilling legal obligation, is a mark of his completion of the mission of man, to become deified and unified with God, the "first true human being" (Behr, 2006, p. 108).

It is only insofar as the Church maintains its imagery at the level of the iconography of the Incarnation and its theology at the level of apophatic negation that it maintains the emptiness of the Holy of Holies of the Christian subject. It is the empty altar that is the center of Orthodoxy, and to this extent, any religious system

114   God in analysis

that places conceptual and imaginary notions of God in the Holy of Holies succumbs to the captation of idolatry.

Subjectivity, essence, energies

The distinction Yannaras (1967/2005) made between oblivion and truth, between nothingness and manifestation, and between essence and energy pertains not only to God but also to human persons (Louth, 2005). Fr. Andrew Louth (2005) summarized Yannaras's (1967/2005) main argument:

> A person's mode of existence is freely revealed through his energies, and revealed in a communion, which is a synergy between the person who is revealed and the person who accepts the disclosure of the other in such a revelation. What is revealed is not the nature of the person, but the mode of existence, and this mode of existence is literally an ecstatic ek-sistence . . . a "standing outside" oneself towards the other, in a free act of ecstatic or erotic longing.
>
> (Louth, 2005, p. 9)

This is true of the human as well as the divine; the other can only be perceived in the appearance of energies. However, the environment, such as it is, offers countless ambiguous stimuli, let alone illusions, that blur the appearance of energies with the occurrence of happenstance—it is for this reason, and for the hope of a better answer, that Gideon tested God twice with the fleece (Judg. 6:36–40).

What is it that testifies to energies *qua* energies? Lacan (1973/1978) approached a similar problem with the following dictum: "a signifier is that which represents a subject for another signifier" (p. 207). For Lacan, the subject of the unconscious undergoes *aphanisis*, or a fading, in alienation in language. "The first signifier . . . emerges in the field of the Other and represents the subject for another signifier, which other signifier has as its effect the *aphanisis* of the subject" (p. 218). Insofar as the first signifier[7] emeries in the field of the Other, representing the subject for another signifier, the other signifier concretizes the subject. In somewhat more straightforward language, when the mother calls the child, two signifiers are in play—the signifier of the mother and the mother's signifier of the child. It is insofar as the mother's discourse, which assumes these signifiers, excludes parts of the subject that the second signifier undergoes primal repression.

This other, second signifier[8] is the *Vorstellungsrepräsentanz*, "the central point of the *Urverdrängung*" (Lacan, 1973/1978, p. 218). Thus, the *Vorstellungsrepräsentanz* is that which is repressed as the representative of the representation of the lack of the subject. This primal repression serves as "the point of attraction, through which all other repressions will be possible" (p. 218). This is the source of unconscious desire. Ultimately, the function of the signifier is

> to reduce the subject in question to being no more than a signifier, to petrify the subject in the same movement in which it calls the subject to function, to

God in analysis   115

speak, as subject. There, strictly speaking, is the temporal pulsation in which is established that which is the characteristic of the departure of the unconscious as such—the closing.

(p. 207)

It is the opening and closing—the appearance and disappearance of the subject—that corresponds to Yannaras's (1967/2005) balance between truth and oblivion. The subject is in oblivion until it appears in truth, in the disclosure or unhiding as it occurs in parapraxes, dreams, and acts. While Lacan (1973/1978) viewed this as "a matter of life and death" (p. 218), for Yannaras, it is a matter of relation. This may be in part due to Lacan's insistence the subject must choose between being and meaning; for Yannaras, the essence of the subject is *always obliviated*, and the energies are what open and close. Introducing the essence and energies distinction to Lacan's formulation suggests that while the energies of the subject must fall on the side of being or meaning, there is always some part of the subject that falls outside the truth, and it is this that renders any statements of God (or any human person) at best only ever half-said (Lacan, 1991/2007), and which separates Eastern from Western apophaticism.

The appearance of the subject in energetic expression, for Lacan (1973/1978), occurs at the level of the unconscious (in non-meaning). For Yannaras (2008/2012), there is no strict differentiation between the conscious and unconscious, but between relation and non-relation, which is the *vel* of Yannaras' subject. Furthermore, Yannaras took seriously Lacan's postulation that the subject appears in the place of the Other. Yannaras supported this idea by arguing the conception of the human hypostasis (manifestation of being) as an ontological being has practical uses at times, but the hypostasis is "directly accessible to common empirical verification only through the mediacy of *relation*" (p. 130).[9] This approaches something close to intersubjectivity.

Lacan (1975/1998) gave a second dictum regarding the representation of the subject: "a sign is not the sign of some thing, but of an effect that is what is presumed as such by a functioning of the signifier" (p. 49). The effect presumed by a functioning of the signifier is the subject. Lacan's example of a sign is that of smoke on a deserted island—"there is no smoke that is not a sign of a smoker" (p. 49). Of course, this example is an echo of the one Lacan (1973/1978) gave in the 11th year of his seminar, when he suggested the signifier's representation of the subject to another signifier is similar to finding hieroglyphics on a desert island. What marks the difference between the sign and the signifier in such similar examples? This is less than clear, as Lacan noted in regard to the hieroglyphics, "You do not doubt for a moment that, behind them, there was a subject who wrote them" (p. 199). In the third year of his seminar, Lacan (1981/1993) left a formulation that may prove helpful here:

The signifier may extend over many of the elements within the domain of the sign. But the signifier is a sign that doesn't refer to any object, not even

116 God in analysis

> to one in the form of a trace, even though the trace nevertheless heralds the signifier's essential feature. It, too, is the sign of an absence. But insofar as it forms part of language, the signifier is a sign which refers to another sign, which is as such structured to signify the absence of another sign, in other words, to be opposed to it in a couple.
>
> (p. 167)

The signifier is understandably similar to the sign, as it is essentially a form of a sign, one that signifies the absence of another sign. Signifiers always refer to one another in their differences (or oppositions). The subject is represented to another subject in the sign that refers to an object (which is the best view of one subject from the space of another). A fingerprint, for example, is a trace of the absence of a particular finger, but it is the function of signifying (which opposes fingerprints against one another as signifiers) that allows the realization of it as a sign.

For Yannaras (2008/2012), the hypostasis manifests in numerous ways, but most especially in its "human *personal* otherness," which discloses "an active subjective identity, that is, an actual call to *relation*, as a mark and readiness for the struggle for *relations*" (p. 131). This is inclusive of the unconscious, as "involuntary physical operations . . . are marks and active signifiers of personal otherness—signifiers that refer to a signified existential identity accessible to knowledge (which is always incomplete) by means of the empirical immediacy of *relation*" (p. 131). Here described is the appearance of signs, the markers of the absent (fading) subject. Yannaras was noting the implications of Lacan's (1975/1998) recognition that the subject's "sign is capable of arousing desire. Therein lies the mainspring of love" (p. 50).

Thus, the energies that reveal a hypostasis are differentiated (by the function of the signifier) from happenstance when they are received as signs of another subject. The psychotic, locked out of the signifying process, interprets everything as signs of the Other; when all else fails, relation returns in the real.

A point must be made here, which is that Yannaras's (2008/2012) perspective on Lacan's idea of the subject appearing in the place of the Other furnishes a relational interpretation of psychoanalytic principles. However, this form of relational thought is not predicated on the imaginary identifications that characterize many forms of intersubjectivity. Instead, it is predicated on the inclusion of humanity in the essence/energies distinction, allowing that the human hypostasis is in no way able to be fully known, fully seen, or fully heard. Just as the conflation of divine essence and energies leads to a cataphatic God of imaginary and symbolic formulations, so too the conflation of human essence and energies leads to the therapeutic formulations that rely on the patient being understood. The apophaticism that preserves simultaneously the presence and absence of the human hypostasis articulates a pathway to walk alongside psychoanalysis in avoiding the pitfalls of solipsism at one extreme and oceanic feeling at the other.

Vorstellungsrepräsentanz

If in some way God can be understood in connection to the Thing, it is not as a representative thereof, nor as an ontologically weighted concept. The two relate to the extent that neither can be said to be. The Thing is "something strange to me, although it is at the heart of me, something that on the level of the unconscious only a representation can represent" (Lacan, 1986/1992, p. 71). The Thing is essentially absent, only represented by the *Vorstellungsrepräsentanz*, which is the site of repression. The Thing's absence is known by what signifier of its absence is repressed. This is the sense in which the *Vorstellungsrepräsentanz* is the representative of the representation of the drive.

It is around the Thing that the *Vorstellungen* organize, around which they gravitate. The *Vorstellungen* are located between the point of perception and that of consciousness, and Lacan (1986/1992) clarified the *Wortvorstellungen* are at the level of the preconscious (*Vorbewusstsein*) where they "reflect in a discourse" what occurs at the level of the *Vorstellungsrepräsentanz* in the unconscious "according to an economy of words" (p. 63). Thus, the *Vorstellungsrepräsentanz* is what

> regulates by means of the pleasure principle the investment of the *Vorstellungen*, and the structure in which the unconscious is organized, the structure in which the underlying unconscious mechanisms are flocculated. And it is this which makes the small curds of representation, that is to say, something which has the same structure as the signifier—a point on which I insist.
>
> (p. 61)

The *Vorstellungsrepräsentanz*, therefore, forms the structure and investment of the universe of *Vorstellungen* as they link with the *Vorstellungsrepräsentanz* around the Thing. This is the function of the *Vorstellungsrepräsentanz* as the representative of the representation of the drive.

This structural review is important to demonstrate that the Thing is not, in experience, the same Thing for everyone. For example, Lacan (1986/1992) noted that "the burning bush was Moses's Thing" (p. 174). The possible "solutions" to the Thing are multiform (p. 215). Lacan suggested the identification of (the cataphatic) God with the Thing is one possible solution, "the most massive example" of Freud's (p. 214). There is also the sublimation of Freud's death drive, the teleology of evolution, the woman of courtly love, and the "Supreme-Being-in-Evil" of Sade, manifested also in the theology of the Manicheans and perhaps of the Cathars (p. 215). Most simply, Lacan (1986/1992) suggested that art, religion, and science devise methods of representing, avoiding, and denying the Thing (respectively).

Lacan (1986/1992) recognized the tendency to find God in "the field of the Thing . . . onto which is projected something beyond" (p. 214). Here again, however, it should be stressed that the God of the Orthodox is not one of ontological affirmation, which is the one Lacan clearly had in mind, but one found only in the

118   God in analysis

ascents of negation. God revealed himself in the Word, in Christ, and it is in relation to the revelation of Christ that the Church can make cataphatic statements—it should not escape notice that the creeds and definitions of every Ecumenical Council recognized by the Eastern Orthodox Church principally pertain to Christology (Ware, 1993). Thus, while Lacan[10] (1986/1992) can affirm that "this Thing doesn't exist to start with" (p. 134), this is not necessarily in opposition to the Unknown God of Orthodoxy, about whom it may be said that "within the limits set by the semantics of our language, the limits of our world, it makes better sense to say *God does not exist* than to say *God exists*" (Yannaras, 2004/2011, p. 57).

The Thing, unique to each person, is represented by a representation; if the burning bush was Moses' Thing, it is so in the sense that it is the *Vorstellungsrepräsentanz* representing the Thing, representing the absence of a deity upon whom no one can gaze without death (Ex. 33:20), whose name is only the most fundamental assertion language can make, that is, that someone speaks.[11] In other words, the burning bush represented not God's presence but precisely his absence. The *Vorstellungsrepräsentanz* is nothing more than the theological vase that reminds us that God does not exist within the network of words and images available to the human mind. In addition to the burning bush, this is even more clearly shown when Elijah sought to make an appeal to God:

> The Lord passed by, and a great and strong wind rent the mountains, and broke in pieces the rocks before the Lord, but the Lord was not in the wind; and after the wind an earthquake, but the Lord was not in the earthquake; and after the earthquake a fire, but the Lord was not in the fire.
>
> (1 Kg 19:11b–12a)

The work of systematic and cataphatic theologies—of any religion—is to cover over, or to repress, the absence and unknowability of God. Apophaticism is the Church's praxis for continually uncovering this repression.

Furthermore, it will come as no surprise to the Orthodox that sexuality undergirds everything in psychic life, as sexuality is the residue of God's absence. The human mind as we know it after the fall is constantly grappling with separation from the personal God who calls the subject into existence, for whom the soul longs, relationship with whom is true *eros*, of which even apparently debased forms of eroticism are echoes.

The absence of God poses a problem for positive theology as it seeks to capture God's being within the conceptual framework of the human mind. Conceptual fabrications elaborated in theological systems or secular thought are methods of attempting to solve this absence. Indeed, even outside of religion, the absence of indestructible life is clearly at work in the body of modern science and technology, which alternatively seeks methods of prolonging individual life and prolonging the life of humanity, either on this planet (through ecological intervention) or another.

The emptiness at the center of being, the site of the primally repressed absence of God and cause of erotic desire, is the center of the structuring of the investment

God in analysis 119

of the *Vorstellungen*. If "good and bad already belong to the order of the *Vorstellung*" (Lacan, 1986/1992, p. 63), what does it mean for Orthodox praxis that the psyche is organized around the Thing and not around the good and the bad? Here, the ethics of psychoanalysis may clarify the ethics of the Orthodox faith. However, in order to see that which orients us to the beyond of the *Vorstellungen* and draws us beyond the pleasure principle, the Church's approach to *jouissance* must be explored.

Notes

1 Moncayo's (2012a) essay on "Trace and trait" fleshes out some of the similarities here. For example, similar to Yannaras's (1967/2005) two forms of apophaticism, Moncayo wrote that negation in Western syllogism is essentially a positive tool, and "the logic of contradiction leads to the negation of the negation and to the experience of emptiness" (p. 38). Further discussion is included herein.
2 This appears to be Yannaras's own translation from *Identität und Differenz*.
3 Grabar (2003) offered an interesting overview of aniconism in Islam, including some instances in which Muslims have used religious imagery.
4 Of course, this Heideggerian consideration of truth was not lost on Lacan (Freeland, 2013).
5 The Book of Hebrews is, in the Orthodox Church, traditionally attributed to St. Paul (St. Athanasius Academy of Orthodox Theology, 2008, p. 1652).
6 This is originally a play on "*faire mouche*" and "*faire mot*" (Porter, 1992, p. 55n2).
7 This is the "unary signifier" in Lacan's (1973/1978, p. 218) parlance at the time.
8 The "binary signifier" (Lacan, 1973/1978, p. 218).
9 "Empirical" should be understood here not in its scientific definition (i.e., the quality of being repeatable and observable) but as a reference to phenomenological experience.
10 The words quoted here are from an interlocuter in Lacan's (1986/1992) seminar identified only as "Mr. X" (p. 134). Lacan's response to Mr. X is affirmative, and it is this affirmation noted here.
11 Moncayo (2012a) connects the name of God in Jewish and Christian faith to connection between the symbolic and the real in the unary trace (p. 27).

References

Behr, J. (2006). *The mystery of Christ: Life in death*. Crestwood, NY: St. Vladimir's Seminary Press.
Curnow, T. (2007). *Pantokrator: An introduction to Orthodoxy*. Angerton Gardens, UK: Cambridge Scholars Publishing.
DeLay, T. (2015). *God is unconscious: Psychoanalysis and theology*. Eugene, OR: Wipf and Stock.
Freeland, C. (2013). *Antigone, in her unbearable splendor: New essays on Jacques Lacan's The Ethics of Psychoanalysis*. Albany, NY: State University of New York Press.
Grabar, O. (2003). From the icon to aniconism: Islam and the image. *Museum International, 55*(2), 46–53.
St. John of Damascus. (1898). *Against those who decry holy images*. (M. H. Allies, Trans.). London: Thomas Baker. Retrieved from https://sourcebooks.fordham.edu/basis/johnda mascus-images.asp

120 God in analysis

Lacan, J. (1978). *The seminar of Jacques Lacan, book XI: The four fundamental concepts of psychoanalysis.* (A. Sheridan, Trans.). New York, NY: W. W. Norton. (Original work published 1973)

Lacan, J. (1992). *The seminar of Jacques Lacan: Book VII: The ethics of psychoanalysis 1959–1960.* (D. Porter, Trans.). New York, NY: W. W. Norton. (Original work published 1986)

Lacan, J. (1993). *The seminar of Jacques Lacan: Book III: The psychoses, 1955–1956.* (R. Grigg, Trans.). New York, NY: W. W. Norton. (Original work published 1981)

Lacan, J. (1998). *The seminar of Jacques Lacan, book XX: On feminine sexuality, the limits of love and knowledge, 1972–1973.* (B. Fink, Trans.). New York, NY: W. W. Norton. (Original work published 1975)

Lacan, J. (2007). *The seminar of Jacques Lacan: Book XVII: The other side of psychoanalysis.* (R. Grigg, Trans.). New York, NY: W. W. Norton. (Original work published 1991)

Lossky, V. (1957). *The mystical theology of the Eastern Church.* (Fellowship of St. Alban & St. Sergius, Trans.). Crestwood, NY: St. Vladimir's Seminary Press. (Original work published 1944)

Lossky, V. (1978). *Orthodox theology: An introduction.* (I. [Ian] Kesarcodi-Watson & I. [Ihita] Kesarcodi-Watson, Trans.). Crestwood, NY: St. Vladimir's Seminary Press.

Louth, A. (2005). Introduction. In C. Yannaras (Ed.), *On the absence and unknowability of God: Heidegger and the Areopagite* (pp. 1–14). New York, NY: T&T Clark International.

Moncayo, R. (2012a). *The emptiness of Oedipus: Identification and non-identification in Lacanian psychoanalysis.* New York, NY: Routledge.

Moncayo, R. (2012b). *The signifier pointing at the moon: Psychoanalysis and Zen Buddhism.* London, UK: Karnac Books.

Porter, D. (1992). Notes. In *The seminar of Jacques Lacan: Book VII: The ethics of psychoanalysis 1959–1960.* (D. Porter, Trans.). New York, NY: W. W. Norton.

St. Athanasius Academy of Orthodox Theology. (2008). Notes. In *The Orthodox Study Bible.* Nashville, TN: Thomas Nelson.

Ware, T. (1993). *The Orthodox Church.* New York, NY: Penguin.

Yannaras, C. (2005). *On the absence and unknowability of God: Heidegger and the Areopagite.* (H. Ventis, Trans.). New York, NY: T&T Clark International. (Original work published 1967)

Yannaras, C. (2011). *Relational ontology.* (N. Russell, Trans.). Brookline, MA: Holy Cross Orthodox Press. (Original work published 2004)

Yannaras, C. (2012). *The enigma of evil.* (N. Russell, Trans.). Brookline, MA: Holy Cross Orthodox Press. (Original work published 2008)

Zelensky, E., & Gilbert, L. (2005). *Windows to heaven: Introducing icons to Protestants and Catholics.* Grand Rapids, MI: Brazos Press.

Chapter 7

Jouissance and the body of the Church

The *jouissance* of the subject is, as Lacan (1975/1998) taught, related to the position the subject assumes in language and sexuation. To consider the relationship of the Orthodox Church to *jouissance* necessitates some speculation regarding the position of Orthodoxy within the regulation of the phallic function of language.

The Church considers itself the Bride of Christ. This is not a simple metaphor, but a position derived from Scripture, already in the Gospels (Mt. 25:1–13) and fully formed by the time of St. Paul's epistle to the Ephesians, wherein he explicitly states that the mystery of marriage "is a profound one, and I am saying that it refers to Christ and the Church" (5:32). This is seen also in the practice of the Church, such as in the Bridegroom Matins of Holy Week that anticipates Christ's arrival. The role of the Church as the Bride of Christ suggests a feminine position of the Church in relation to God. If we can avoid foreclosure—if we do not take for granted that the construction of the Church as feminine is an artifact of cultural assumptions—and take up the insights of psychoanalysis as an ally, we may be able to encounter another logic behind the language of the Church.

Sexuation

In contrast to the sociocultural distinctions of anatomical sex, gender identity, and gender expression, Lacanian analysis contributes a distinction between these and psychoanalytic sex. The assumption of sexual position in Lacanian psychoanalysis arises through *sexuation* (see Lacan, 1975/1998). In other words, a person might be a *masculine* subject or a *feminine* subject in the sense of their psychoanalytic position notwithstanding their genetic makeup, gender identity, gender expression, or sexual orientation.

Male and female are not "opposite sexes" for Lacanian analysis. This is because "there is no such thing as a sexual relationship" (Lacan, 1975/1998, p. 12). There is some ambiguity in Lacan's statement (Fink, 1991) as with many of Lacan's teachings, but the statement is a negation of any sense of complementarity in the relationship between the sexes or in sexual relationships. This is because *"each sex is defined separately with respect to a third term"* (Fink, 1991, p. 65). For this reason, the determining factor of masculinity and femininity is not the relation of

DOI: 10.4324/9781003214359-9

122 Jouissance and the body of the Church

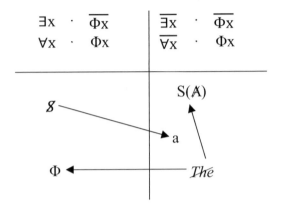

Figure 7.1 Diagram of sexuation
Source: Moncayo (2008, p. 80).[1]

the one to the other (and thus they are not opposites) but the relation of each to this third term, which is the phallic function (Φx). The phallic function is polyvalent and could be understood as the function of the Law, language, or symbolic castration (see Fink, 1991). Lacan (1975/1998) connected it to the operation of alienation. Man and woman—in the analytic sense—assume different positions in relation to the phallic function (Fink, 1991). Lacan (1975/1998) provided a diagram to illustrate each sexual position in relation to their partners and to the third term. (For theoretical clarity, we refer to Moncayo's [2008] version of the diagram in Figure 7.1.)

The left side of the diagram represents the masculine position and the right represents the feminine position, and "every speaking being situates him or herself on one side or the other" (Lacan, 1975/1998, p. 79). The formulae in the upper portion describe the conditions of masculinity and femininity, while the lower portion describes the partners that masculine and feminine subjects take.

Masculine subjectivity

The formulae on the masculine side are $\exists x\ \overline{\Phi x}$ and $\forall x\ \Phi x$. The first formula, $\forall x\ \Phi x$, signifies "it is through the phallic function that man as whole acquires his inscription" (Lacan, 1975/1998, p. 79). Fink (1991) provided a gloss for this, that, "the whole of a man falls under the phallic function" (p. 68). Alienation within language is total for the masculine subject. However, Lacan (1975/1998) noted the phallic function "is limited due to the existence of an x by which the function Φx is negated: $\exists x\ \overline{\Phi x}$" (p. 79).

That is, $\exists x\ \overline{\Phi x}$ signifies "there exists a subject that is not subject to the law of castration" (Moncayo, 2008, p. 81). This points to the primal father, whom

Jouissance and the body of the Church   123

no law subjected. Lacan described this formula as "the father function" (Lacan, 1975/1998, p. 79) and suggested it is the exception here that establishes the rule of the phallic function. Moncayo (2008) described the way the imaginary (primal) father establishes the phallic function:

> It is only by appeal to the primal and imaginary father that men can appear to have the phallus within the imaginary. But by virtue of this very appeal, the son falls to the position of a castrated signified for the master signifier of the Other (imaginary father).
>
> (p. 81)

Another way of saying this is that it is in the attempt to overcome lack, which is impossible, that man acknowledges and assumes his lack. Moncayo (2008) argued the father function is "a moment in the construction of masculine subjectivity wherein the father functions as the imaginary father, as the holder of an imaginary phallus that appears uncastrated" (p. 81). Fink (1991) noted the father function continues, as "incestuous wishes live on indefinitely in the unconscious" (p. 72).

Fink (1991) also related Lacan's account of masculinity to set theory, in which Lacan was "very interested": "set theory is directly concerned with problems related to the part and the whole. Man can be taken as a whole because there is a definable boundary to his set," that is, the father produces a limit (p. 70). Knowing where the limit of the function makes it possible to determine what is within the limits of the set of those who have undergone the function (every man except the father).

Regarding the diagram, the masculine side contains $ and Φ. $ is the masculine subject, and the Φ is the master signifier (S_1) (Lacan, 1975/1998). The vector $\$\rightarrow a$ demonstrates that the masculine subject relates to the Other *as object*—"$ never deals with anything by way of a partner but object a inscribed on the other side of the bar" (Lacan, 1975/1998, p. 80). The masculine subject enjoys only the object, not the Other or a woman as such.

Feminine subjectivity

Feminine subjectivity is defined by two formulae as well: $\overline{\exists x}\ \overline{\Phi x}$ and $\overline{\forall x}\ \Phi x$. $\overline{\exists x}\ \overline{\Phi x}$ notes "there is not one x which is not submitted to the phallic function" while $\overline{\forall x}\ \Phi x$ notes "for not-all women, the phallic function is valid" (Moncayo, 2008, p. 82). Moncayo resolved the tension between these two by reading the former as representative of women as a set (again, in the sense of set theory) and the latter as a reference to "the singular or the part as determining of symbolic feminine structure as such" (p. 82). He suggested that while there is (in the imaginary) a singular man, the primal father, there is no equivalent singular woman; "the man and the woman are inventions on the side of masculinity" (Moncayo, 2008, p. 82). In this sense, "there is no such thing as Woman" (Lacan, 1975/1998, pp. 72); that is, Woman with a capital W or *the* woman. Regarding the second formula, that of the not-all, "the whole of a singular woman is not in the phallic function" (Moncayo, 2008, p. 83).

To understand the not-all, Fink's (1991) discussion of set theory is again important. Just as the exception of the father establishes the limit that makes possible the whole (of a man) to be situated within the phallic function on the masculine side, the feminine side states there is no exception ($\overline{\exists x\ \Phi x}$) and therefore no specified limit on the whole of a woman in relation to the phallic function.

Fink (1991) as well as Moncayo (2008) was careful to acknowledge the sensitivity of Lacan's (1975/1998) statements about women, such as "there is no such thing as Woman" (p. 72). Fink clarified that a woman is only not-all (or not whole) in relation to the phallic function and is "not somehow less 'complete' than man" (p. 74). Moncayo provided a more extensive engagement with the issue, but essentially hews closely to Lacan's understanding of the phallus as a signifier of lack rather than the actual penile organ (Lacan, 1966/2006). In this logic, a man is only complete on the imaginary level (with the imaginary phallus) and is precisely lacking insofar as he has the phallus at the symbolic level. Woman, for Moncayo (2008), lacks the imaginary phallus, yet, because of not being fully under the phallic function, "not having is having" for a woman (p. 53). The issue is not phallocentrism, then, but the operation of language in the phallic function.

Thus, Lacan (1975/1998) wrote "La,"[2] the feminine definite article, under erasure (with a line through it) notating the not-all of a woman (p. 80). A woman's partners, then, are the symbolic phallus Φ and the signifier of the lack in the Other $S(\text{\AA})$. The relation to Φ suggests a woman's ability to access phallic *jouissance*, while the relation to $S(\text{\AA})$ is something more than a relation to lack and notates access to an Other *jouissance* (Fink, 1991).

Feminine *jouissance*

Sexuation requires a return to the discussion of *jouissance*, as feminine *jouissance* is critical to understanding sexuation. As not-all of a woman falls under the phallic function, a woman is not entirely within phallic *jouissance* (Lacan, 1975/1998). Moncayo (2008) presented with perspicacity his understanding of this Other *jouissance*. Moncayo noted there are "three *jouissances*,"[3] the first of which has been discussed already, which is phallic *jouissance* (p. 96). Phallic *jouissance* is the result of the imposition of the phallic function and is in the symbolic. There is also a *jouissance* of the Other, which is "the Imaginary face of the Real" (p. 96)—this would be akin to the real *jouissance* as imagined by the obsessive. Moncayo noted this *jouissance* of the Other can be found in psychosis and perversion. In contrast to these two forms of *jouissance*—that of the All of the absence of castration (the *jouissance* of the Other) and of the All of the presence of castration and the not-all of desire (phallic *jouissance*)—there is another form of *jouissance* in relation to the not-all of the Law: Other *jouissance*. This Other *jouissance* is "beyond, not before, the paternal function" (Moncayo, 2008, p. 96). That is, it is not the *jouissance* of the Other but an Other *jouissance* experienced by a feminine subject not-all under the phallic function.

Jouissance and the body of the Church 125

This form of *jouissance* is important presently, as it is closely linked by Lacan (1975/1998) to mysticism and the religious ecstasy of, for example, Teresa of Ávila's *transverberation* (at least as portrayed by Bernini). Lacan asked in discussing this Other *jouissance* "doesn't this jouissance . . . put us on the path of ex-sistence? And why not interpret one face of the Other, the God face, as based on feminine jouissance?" (p. 77).

The *Jouissance* of the Church

Considering that the feminine position within sexuation is that of the not-all and the subject is not-all under the law of the phallic function ($\overline{\forall x}\ \Phi x$), the Church's position with respect to the law may offer context for the consideration of the Church taking the feminine position with respect to God. Perhaps the best starting point for this consideration is the Orthodox application of *oikonomia* (οἰκονομία). *Economy* is descended in English from the Greek *oikonomia*, which referred originally to the ordering of the household (Meyendorff, 1974). It is used in Orthodoxy to refer to the ordering of the household of God, and, more specifically, to the practice of the clergy flexibly applying the law on a case-by-case basis. Thus, while the Orthodox Church has the law in its cannons and traditions, the Church generally practices economy in the application of the law and rules of practice (Ware, 2000).

For example, Orthodox Christians are expected to maintain fasts at various times throughout the year. The Nativity fast, which occurs during the 40 days before the feast of the Nativity of Christ (or Christmas), involves abstention from the consumption of meat, dairy, and frequently of fish, alcohol, and oils as well (e.g., Antiochian Orthodox Christian Archdiocese of North America, n.d.).[4] However, the American holiday of Thanksgiving arrives during this fast. As such, the Church affirms that American Orthodox are welcome to break the fast for the day to celebrate the holiday appropriate to their culture (e.g., Kostoff, 2015). This flexibility is consistent throughout the life of the Church, which is indicative of its position that rules of living are not legal standards[5] but guidelines received as from a doctor for the spiritual health of the believer (Ware, 2000). Rather than a set of rules pleasing to God, the law in this sense is oriented *beyond the law*, to the place of the absence of God and to the erotic relationship that grounds the psyche. The relationship of the Christian to the rule of living in Orthodoxy is that of the not-all; the Christian falls not-all under the rule of the law, nor does the law take on the ontological weight of morality.

The Orthodox view of God is in contrast to those from various religions and traditions over millennia who have identified God with the primal father ($\exists x\ \overline{\Phi x}$), whether as an invisible and whimsical fury or through some representation of his authority on earth. This is essentially in line with Lacan's readings of God as built upon imaginary and symbolic elaborations of the father. This view of God as the primal father—the one who really enjoys, perhaps even enjoying the punishment and torment of the unbelievers—is essentially pagan, whether found within the Orthodox Church or in other traditions.

126   Jouissance and the body of the Church

Similarly accompanying the idea of the primal father's rule is the expectation that all will have undergone the paternal function ($\forall x\ \Phi x$), leading to the legalism found in many religious traditions. Such legalism ranges from explicit rulemaking to implicit communal regulation of adherent behavior, such as in socially shaming those who do not practice their faith in specific ways. This engagement with the phallic function in some cases coincides with the internalization of the moral law, even if the tradition suggests such laws do not apply. This leads to the institution of an expectation within these traditions to have not only correct behaviors but correct thoughts and feelings as well.[6]

With respect to Christianity, the masculine formulae of sexuation are particularly pertinent in considering the theology of substitutionary atonement, especially penal substitutionary atonement. In penal substitutionary atonement, there is a law so overwhelming in its force that even God cannot abrogate it except by the execution of the only person not subject to its force. In an unexpected inversion, it is the father in this narrative who is castrated in his inability to overcome the primal law, while it is the perfect son who is the exception that is murdered *specifically because the law does not apply to him* (because he is innocent), just as the primal father was. Moreover, the human person in this view was originally a perfect creature who willingly violated the primal law that required the consequence of death in the first place. In other words, the fundamental identity of the human person is *guilty*, an identity that itself requires a legal framework such as the idea of God's Justice. It is the circular twist of this story that God satisfies the demands of transcendent Justice, or the primal law, by murdering the innocent so the guilty may go free.

Because the foundational understanding of creation, sin, the fall, and salvation in substitutionary atonement are all oriented toward the violation of God's law and the restitution of his honor, they are inherently bound to the morality of behaviors. Indeed, the systems of morality often applied at the level of daily praxis are oriented to the level of the *Vorstellung*, leaving the Christian to determine whether an action is right or wrong in relation to the law. This approach to morality leads to certain foreseeable outcomes, such as a deontological focus that characterizes certain behaviors as intrinsically or naturally wrong, or the ambitious social agendas that some segments of Christianity seek to impose on everyone in society. This language leaves little to the imagination about the way in which such Christians structure morality—specifically within the network of *Vorstellungen* and not with respect to the Thing.

Substitutionary atonement and the adherence to a moral order that often accompanies it are products of a masculine position dedicated to the phallic function in one way or another. The regulation of *jouissance* within such an order is oriented toward the retention or withholding of *jouissance* from the Other (such as in the refusal to enjoy sexual conjugation, which is devoted solely to procreation) or the fantasy of the *jouissance* of the Other that will finally arrive after marriage vows.

In considering the Orthodox Church's relation to sexuation, it must first be noted that the Church is characterized by *conciliarity*, meaning that while there is a spiritual head of the Church in the Ecumenical Patriarch, there is not one bishop who holds jurisdiction over all others ($\overline{\exists x \; \Phi x}$). This is not a rejection of the primal father as the primal father never became established, neither theologically nor in episcopal polity. Furthermore, the Church's praxis orients the Christian to something beyond the law and beyond the *Vorstellungen* ($\overline{\forall x} \; \Phi x$). The orientation of the Christian to the beyond of the law is drawn from the "Mystical Theology of the Eastern Church" (Lossky, 1944/1957), whose bishops have been exclusively monastic since the 14th century and whose mystical spirituality guides the way of the Church (K. Ware, 1986; T. Ware, 1993). The absence of God—the exclusion of God from all positivistic methods of thought and apprehension—forms the crux of the Orthodox Church's not-all approach to the law, which is further structured by the soteriology of true eroticism rather than penal substitution. In relation to the phallic function, the Church is structured as feminine.

The question arises, then, in what way the Church approaches *jouissance*. Kalinich (1988) offers a beginning here by locating *jouissance* "within the mystical theological tradition" of the Orthodox Church:

> Vital to the union or deification, the *theosis* in this system, is a notion of self-abandonment or self-emptying, applicable not just to the path of spiritual ascent, but to sexuality as well. The person or subject expresses himself most truly in a renunciation of the self. Self-assertion leads only to disintegration. In contrast, in the death of the self is life. In the little death of sexuality is *jouissance*. In the *jouissance* of sexuality is an icon of the *jouissance* of deification.
>
> (pp. 377–378)

The overwhelming nature of *jouissance* is found in the deification of the human person, who undergoes self-emptying in *kenosis* that reveals the meaning of Christ's advisement that "he who finds his life will lose it, and he who loses his life for my sake will find it" (Mt. 10:39). This directive goes beyond the pleasure principle and beyond the good of the individual.

The Church offers two pathways to deification: marriage and monasticism (Ware, 1986). Following Kalinich's insight, these pathways also structure the Church's approach to *jouissance*. In the case of marriage, an apparently minor difference in the mystery of marriage between the Orthodox Church and Western Christian traditions will illuminate the structure of this approach.

The Church has never considered marriage a concern only of civil authorities; however, the Church also did not have a specific rite of marriage for almost a millennium (Meyendorff, 2000). Rather, the couple would marry civilly and have their marriage recognized in the Church by the reception of the Eucharist (and, later, by the crowning that would take place in the context of the Eucharist). The eventual development of the marriage ceremony as a sacrament took different courses in the East and West. Notably, there are two inheritances from the Roman legal system that continue in Western traditions generally: the administration of

128 Jouissance and the body of the Church

the sacrament by the couple and the exchanging of vows. Both of these reflect the original civil character marriage had even within the Church, though their meaning is understood differently within Christian ceremonies. The civil view of marriage as a contractual engagement fits well with the increasing understanding, at least in U.S. society, of marriage as a way of reaching Oneness—being One with one's soulmate, for example, through complementary administration of the marriage, and the pleasurable regulation of the *jouissance* approached therein through the vows made to one another. When the focus of marriage is upon the partner, it is possible even with the best of intentions to hold the marriage, or the phallic *jouissance* contained within it, as the overarching goal of the marriage, as a sort of sublation or *Aufhebung*. When this occurs, it can lead some Christians, as Wehr (2011) observed, to view "sex within marriage . . . as the key to fulfilment where, at last, self-discipline is no longer needed" (p. 93). This is an essentially masculine perspective, as each partner reaches for the exception to the phallic function, where union with and enjoyment of the other is expected to lead away from castration.

In its own approach to marriage, the Orthodox Church recognizes the mystery of marriage as performed by the priest (Meyendorff, 2000), the third person standing in for Christ, who is God's presence-in-absence. This signifies the Orthodox marriage as discontinuous with the civil laws that might bind the couple contractually; similarly, no vows are exchanged in the Orthodox wedding ceremony. Rather, the priest makes appeals to God for the marriage to be preserved. For the Orthodox Church, it is the presentation of God's presence-in-absence as a third term that precludes the mystery from collapse into the dyad regulated by the Law.

In this way, rather than orient toward the imaginary phallus, the Orthodox Church presents the signifier of the lack in the Other, $S(A)$, marking it as already present in the marriage by orienting the couple to Christ through the priest, making God, to borrow Lacan's (1975/1998) playful description, "the third party in this business of human love," "the *ménage à trois*" (p. 70). The signifier of the lack in the Other is, in this case, what signifies the lack in the marriage which is incomplete to the extent that it leads to deification.

Marriage is not the opening of the couple onto the paradise of unlimited sexual *jouissance*. The Orthodox communion fast, which always precedes the acceptance of the Eucharist, is an absolute fast—from food, from liquid other than water—and from sex with one's spouse (Oikonomou, 2002). The restriction of the marriage bed, which is found in St. Paul's rather amusing admonishment to "not refuse one another [sexually] except perhaps by agreement for a season, that you may devote yourselves to prayer" (1 Cor. 7:5), is a form of castration only in the sense that symbolic castration limits what is already never possible. The couple, never able to achieve plenary genitality, is castrated only with respect to the imaginary phallus. The form of castration practiced here by the Church is not by threat but by the assumption of the lack, in which the subject of marriage shifts from seeking the object in the other to acknowledging the absence, which the object represents only in its inability to satisfy, at the center of being.

Thus, marriage is not a way to regulate *jouissance* in the sense of the pleasure principle—that is, by minimizing it. By maintaining the presence of God
as an absence in the marriage, the couple seeks something beyond imaginary,
genital unification; the couple seeks deification through the marriage. Sexual
jouissance is regulated in marital abstinence to avoid the perpetually masturba-
tory nature of sexual (phallic) *jouissance*, the "jouissance of the idiot" (Lacan,
1975/1998, p. 81). Where this operation is effective, the couple is opened to the
Thing, through the signifier of the lack in the Other, and to the possibility of
the Other *jouissance* this opens. The regulation of the phallic *jouissance* is conducted not by introducing pleasure (or a limit) but by "a higher order *jouissance*
beyond the phallus" (Moncayo, 2008, p. xiv). Yannaras (1979/1984) came close
to this when he noted the Church does not reserve *eros* for sexual reproduction (or
genitality). "True *eros*," he wrote, "lies neither in the psychological and physical
aspects of the reproductive process, nor in the institution of marriage, but only in
the Church's *asceticism*" (p. 165). This asceticism, which is a spiritual praxis and
devotion, is found in marriage as well as in monasticism. It is the relation to the
Thing that opens the pathway to *eros*.

Monastic life, then, is the other method of regulating phallic *jouissance* in the
Orthodox tradition. As with the standards of living recognized generally by the
Orthodox (no sex outside of marriage; no sex within marriage while fasting),
the abstention from sex in monasticism is not a matter of avoiding the dirty or
profane. Regulating the *jouissance* of the idiot is an opening to the pursuit of
the Thing and the Other *jouissance* that accompanies it. The abstention from sex
in Eastern monasticism is not a matter of the elevation of the object in sublimation (which is arguably the case in Western mysticism),[7] nor is it the obsequious
avoidance of the Thing in religious obsession. Eastern monastic celibacy is much
closer to an aesthetic effort on the part of the monastic to maintain an "organization around this emptiness" of the Thing (Lacan, 1986/1992, p. 130), to clear the
obstacles to recognizing the Thing. As Met. Kallistos (Ware, 1986) described, the
prayer of the monastic aims "to advance beyond all language and images into
the mystery of God" (p. 165)

In both marriage and monasticism, the relation is not primarily to the other,
nor to the Other, but to the signifier of the lack in the Other. This is what marks
the feminine structure of the Orthodox Church's approach to *jouissance*. Apophaticism is the ground of relations with this signifier, which itself opens the way
beyond all signification to the Thing. Apophaticism extends beyond the sense of
negative statements about God. Apophaticism is the renunciation of epistemology. This is because "nothingness" is "placed as a non-restrictive (an unrestricted)
limit to thought that continues to raise questions" (Yannaras, 1967/2005, p. 54).
Yannaras observed in this context that the nihilism of Western philosophy serves
a function relative to apophaticism:

> As the refutation of exclusively conceptual affirmation of God and of the prac-
> tical necessity of God, nihilism stands for a radical denial of the "conceptual

idols" of God, and as the unrestricted limit to questioning it offers further possibilities of rescuing the divinity of God.

(p. 54)

For this reason, the experience of relation with God is infinite, because apophaticism, predicated on nothingness, is "the denial that we can exhaust the truth in its formulation" (p. 60). Rather than restricting God only to "types, myths and symbols" (p. 73), apophaticism is the "acceptance of unknowing as the sole category of 'knowledge'" (p. 74). Apophaticism falls not-all under the law because it does not end in negative statements but in the absence of statements altogether:

> The goal of this progressive denial (or "demythologization") is not a mental concept, but *beauty*, a presence of personal otherness, that cannot be objectified in affirmative or negative definitions. The unknowing of abstractive "demythologization" indicates a way out from the limits of natural ontology, disbelief in the God of analogical ascents—unknowing defines the annihilation of God as being.
>
> (p. 74)

The Other *jouissance* of Orthodoxy is found in its profound apophaticism that opens pathways beyond the Law of the symbolic and beyond the deception of the imaginary in the process of deification, which is the approach of "the Unknown in the darkness of absolute ignorance" (Lossky, 1944/1957, p. 25). The darkness of ignorance is where God appears as uncreated light, the brightness of which is as blinding now as it was on Mount Tabor when it appeared before the disciples of Christ (Mat. 17:1–8). It is not a simple experience of perception, but engulfs one's senses and one's intellect, and yet "surpasses at the same time both sense and intellect" (Lossky, 1944/1957, p. 221). This Other *jouissance*, the effulgence in excess of all human faculties—the direct apprehension of the divine—is the result of the opening up to the outside of all symbolic and imaginary bounds.

The body of the Church

The use of psychoanalysis in considering the Church's position in relation to sexual practice can be extended even further into the life of the Church in considering the tradition of male-only priesthood.

Fr. Thomas Hopko was a prominent and popular Orthodox priest and theologian, and he was Dean of St. Vladimir's Theological Seminary, teaching dogmatic theology for over 30 years. Fr. Hopko also had a popular podcast from 2008 to 2015 with Ancient Faith Radio, the premier Orthodox radio system in the United States. Fr. Hopko's theological construction of gender and sexuality in the Church has largely driven the modern discussion around the question of the "Male Character" of the Priesthood (1975, p. 141; see Dunn, 2010 regarding his prominence in this discussion). Fr. Hopko (1975) himself noted that the question of sexual difference has historically found very little attention in the life of the Church, such that all attempts at reasoning about the nature and possible reasons for sexual difference are modern phenomena—not that this discredits the discussion, but simply notes it is a very new one with little precedence in the Church.

For his part, Fr. Hopko (1975) attempts to link sexual difference not simply to culture or biology but to the theological significance of the differentiation of persons in the Godhead. Because God in himself is multiform and containing several hypostases, so humanity must have two forms in order to truly engage in pursuing God's likeness. For Fr. Hopko, there is a consonance between the Son and the male and the Holy Spirit and the female. This is to reproduce at the level of creation the Trinitarian *monarchia* of the Father at the level of the Uncreated (the Father being present at both levels). Just as the Logos is begotten and the Holy Spirit proceeds, so the male mans and the female womans. (It should be noted that Orthodox theology seldom makes the distinction between sex and gender that is common today [Purpura, 2017].) In this view, what is important is the "di-sexual spiritual existence" (Hopko, 1975, p. 152), which pairs somewhat arbitrarily men and the Logos and women and the Spirit. There is no clear connection between the anatomical organism—having as it does the penis, the vagina—and these categories of Logos and Spirit. In other words, Fr. Hopko—and he is not unique—collapses sex, gender, and gender expression into a single binary, in this case taking for granted that a male body accompanies the identity of a man (Dunn, 2010, made a similar observation about Fr. Hopko's anthropology).

Fr. Hopko (1975, 1993) also connects the maleness of the priest to the imaging of God: "The presbyter/bishop is always the living icon of the Father, whose divine icon is his only Son incarnate in human form" (Hopko, 1993, p. 173). This is in contrast to the feminine role of the Church as the Bride of Christ.

One gets the impression in reading Fr. Hopko and other prominent voices in the Orthodox Church that there is a struggle in this new question for the Church, namely, the struggle to justify the ancient answer to a question that until recently had never been asked in such a fulsome manner. This is not lost on Fr. Hopko or to his audience; in responding to criticism regarding his position, Fr. Hopko (1977) commented that:

> Some said that I had obviously decided, before any theological analysis and reflection, that only certain male members of the Christian Church may be ordained to the episcopate and the priesthood according to Orthodox doctrine, and that my writing was merely the attempt to "prove" what I had already prejudicially predetermined. . . .
>
> What I had hoped to do in the essay was to take as my starting point the absolutely indisputable fact that the Church—which has had women saints of all sorts, including women secular rulers, some of whom have been given the title "equal to the apostles"—nevertheless has never had women bishops and

132 Jouissance and the body of the Church

priests. I took this as a "given," as a matter of factual data. I then proceeded to ask the question: Are there sound theological reasons for this fact or not?

(pp. 161–162)

This latter question is pro forma; Fr. Hopko clearly has an answer in mind when titling the article in question "On the Male Character of Christian Priesthood," which may have otherwise born a title such as "Women and the Priesthood: Are there sound theological reasons for male priesthood?"

Dunn (2010) called to account this question-begging approach that assumes the theological significance of historical fact, noting that it is the mirror image of those who Fr. Hopko critiqued, who take for granted the necessity of women in the priesthood (privileging the historical present) and also beg the question. Dunn argued quite convincingly for the reopening of this discussion without any answer already in mind. Specifically, Dunn problematized the conflation of gender and sex in Fr. Hopko's writing, observing that Fr. Hopko's reliance upon the connection of the maleness of the priest to the maleness of Christ neglects the division Fr. Hopko himself introduces between sex and gender in allowing that males in the congregation play the role of the Bride along with females.

In fairness, Fr. Hopko (1993) countered this very argument 17 years prior, stating that "the ecclesial community *as community* requires no sacramental expression because, unlike its head and husband, the man Jesus Christ, the bride and body is itself always actually historically present in a way that Jesus is not" (p. 174). This argument sounds plausible but is not as decisive as it first seems. To say that the ecclesial community *as community* does not require sacramental expression does not make much sense, given that the Orthodox Church does not practice private mass and in fact the community is itself a sacramental presence (see Zizioulas, 1985; see also Papanikolaou, 2011). Thus, where in some Christian traditions mass may be celebrated with only the priest, the Orthodox Church does not practice this specifically because of the sacramental expression of the community. Fr. Hopko seems to be willing to disavow the crucial role of the community in the sacraments because they are historically present, as if this were the measure of the mystery. Indeed, "the eucharistic community constitutes a sign of the fact that the *eschaton* can only *break through* history but never be identified with it" (Zizioulas, 1985, p. 161). The community—specifically in the sacrament—is at that moment connected with the entirety of the Church, visible and invisible, and connected to the afterwardsness of all historicity. In view of this, Dunn's (2010) critique still stands.

Dunn (2010), focusing on the *Acts of Paul and Thecla*, argues that theologically, in addition to the gender of a person not pertaining to sacramental role, the anatomical sex of a person does not bear upon such roles either, comparing such an idea to the Donatist heresy that asserted the purity of the clergy was necessary for the efficacy of the sacraments. Dunn's implication is that anatomy no more than character should serve as a barrier to the validity of the sacraments.

The critique of the traditionalist perspective championed by Fr. Hopko can be taken farther, however. To the extent that Fr. Hopko wished the Logos and Spirit to correspond to men and women, his vision of women as subject both to Christ and to men is comparable to the insult suffered by the Holy Spirit in the doctrine of double procession that underlies the *filioque*. In this way, Fr. Hopko's argument is successful—he gives women the status of the Holy Spirit after all, albeit in a different way than intended.

The Nicene-Constantinopolitan Creed (also called the Nicene Creed) promulgated by the First Council of Constantinople codified the belief that the Holy Spirit "proceeds from the Father" as a dogma of the Church. However, the Western Church made an addition to this, that the Holy Spirit "proceeds from the Father and the Son" (see Ware, 1993, pp. 50–51). This addition was made first in Spain, then adopted in Charlemagne's Carolingian Empire, and eventually adopted by Pope Benedict VIII at the urging of the Holy Roman Emperor Henry II (Dix, 1945/2007, p. 487). Eastern Christians, including the Eastern Orthodox, do not include this addition in the Creed and to this day consider it a point of contention between Orthodox and Catholic Christians (Ware, 1993). While the distinction between "from the Father" and "from the Father and the Son" may seem negligible, the consequences are significant from both historical and theological perspectives. Discussing the divergence, Lossky (1967/1974) noted:

> It is understandable that a divergence in this culminating point, insignificant as it may seem at first sight, should have a decisive importance. The difference between the two conceptions of the Trinity determines, on both sides, the whole character of theological thought. This is so to such an extent that it becomes difficult to apply, without equivocation, the same name of theology to these two different ways of dealing with divine realities.
>
> (p. 80)

For Lossky, as for many Orthodox, the approach of the Trinity in the West (specifically in the Thomistic tradition) that seeks to understand God first as a simple essence and then to logically deduce through "relations of opposition" the distinct persons results in a depersonalization of the Divine (Papanikolaou, 2006, p. 66). The Father and the Son are distinct in the opposition of the paternal and filial, whereas the Holy Spirit must look for its logical distinction in a double opposition so as to properly institute itself as a person of the Trinity—thus, the Holy Spirit proceeds from the Father and the Son. However, this subordinates the Holy Spirit and obfuscates the hypostases of the Trinity as personal in favor of logically deducing the persons of the Trinity by reasoning beginning with the one essence.[8] Ware (1993) pointed out regarding the development of this Scholastic view of God that,

> emphasizing as it does the essence at the expense of the persons, it comes near turning God into an abstract idea. He becomes a remote and impersonal

134 Jouissance and the body of the Church

being, whose existence has to be proved by metaphysical arguments—a God of the philosophers, not the God of Abraham, Isaac, and Jacob.

(p. 215)

Conversely, the Orthodox approaches the Trinity not first through essence but through persons. This is clear in Zizioulas' (1985) discussion of the Trinity:

> The Father out of love—that is, freely—begets the Son and brings forth the Spirit. If God exists, He exists because the Father exists, that is, He who out of love freely begets the Son and brings forth the Spirit. Thus God as person— as the hypostasis of the Father—makes the one divine substance to be that which it is: the one God.
>
> (p. 41)

This describes well the conception of the *monarchia* of the Father—the Father as the source of divinity. Rather than looking for the identity of persons in the relation of opposition, Orthodox theology looks to "relations of origin": "the Son is begotten, the Holy Spirit *proceeds* from the Father. This is sufficient to distinguish them" (Lossky, 1944/1957, p. 55).

Returning to Fr. Hopko's construction that men and women correspond to the Logos and the Spirit, this alignment is based on the relation of opposition. Fr. Hopko (1993) argued that the relation between men and women "is a communion of being and life whose content is love among equals who share an identical nature uniquely 'enhypostasized' in personally distinct 'modes of existence' in imitation of Divinity" (pp. 166–167), that is, that men and women relate to God in distinct modes of existence similar to the begetting and proceeding of the Son and the Spirit. However, his simultaneous insistence that "men are to be the 'heads' of women" (p. 167) is a conception of humanity predicated on persons distinct from one another through opposition—the opposition of man to God, and of woman to man and God. This is a recapitulation of the double procession imposed upon the Holy Spirit in the *filioque*, and there is no less a substantial cost to this. If double procession depersonalizes the Trinity, the double relation of women serves no different function.

Even so, the Church has not ordained women to the role of priest or bishop, whether for reasons historical, cultural, or theological. The Lacanian conception of sexuation may provide another perspective for considering this matter.

Lacan's teaching that there is no such thing as a sexual relationship is precisely what is negated in the *filioque*. The approach of *essence* through the relation of opposition and the approach of *hypostases* in the relation of origin are two methods of dealing with the "unity-in-distinction" that is the Trinity (Papanikolaou, 2006, p. 52). The relation of opposition is predicated on the opposition of two terms—first of Father versus Son, then of Father/Son versus Spirit in the double procession. This complementarianism is a masculine attempt to achieve the unity of the One, which is already clear in its emphasis on essence. Taken to its

Jouissance and the body of the Church 135

conclusion, if God is most essentially the One, deification or union with God will result in *henosis* rather than *theosis*. The only other option is that God is entirely incommunicable and transcendent.

This negation also animates the appeal to complementarity in the sexes or in men and women, not just at the level of the real organism in anatomy, but at the level of theological anthropology. The subordination of women in the double relation to man and God is actually a necessity for the preservation of the fantasy of the One who has not been subjected to the paternal function. Lacan (1975/1998) was correct in identifying the superposition of the *objet a* over the S(Å) with *eudaemonism* and the pursuit of the pleasure principle. In short, the *filioque* brings to Christianity the obsessional and masculine approach to religion.

The *monarchia* of the Father, if truly transposed onto the sexual relationship, cannot possibly support the subordination of women under a double relation with God and man. Just as the Holy Spirit is not defined by dual opposition but by procession from the Father, so too women are not defined by an opposition to men but by a relation to the Father, in this transposition, irrespective of men. In other words, there is no such thing as a sexual relationship.

Why, then, a male priesthood? In addition to the cultural accident of patriarchy (in the sense of social psychology), sexuation may enlighten theological reflection. The traditionalist argument exemplified in Fr. Hopko's work relies upon the real penile organ, leaving aside broader questions relating to the significance given to this organ. The real phallus (Π) is distinguished in Lacanian psychoanalysis from the imaginary phallus (φ) and the symbolic phallus (Φ). The question of the Orthodox priesthood is whether the *maleness* of the priest pertains to Π, φ, or Φ. If it pertains to Π, then the priesthood is predicated on the penile organ and nothing more. If it pertains to φ, then the priesthood is predicated on power as the only one who has not undergone the phallic function of castration ($-\varphi$) is the primal father ($\exists x\ \overline{\Phi x}$); this form of priesthood is either that headed by a single Patriarch (the Pope) or that which devolves the authority of the Master to those who speak in his name (such as expositors of the infallible Word of God, the Bible). If it pertains to Φ, then the priesthood is primarily to be understood not based upon what it has but what it does not have. Moncayo (2008) noted that "within the Symbolic, masculinity only has a missing phallus or the signifier of a lack" (p. 53). This is precisely the role identified for the priest in the mystery of marriage, but it is also the role of the priest in the Church as a whole.

The priesthood is predicated on the symbolic phallus because it marks the not-having of the Church and serves as one of the two poles of the feminine Church. First, the feminine Church relates to the symbolic phallus as the mark of the desire of God and reference point in marriage and monasticism. Second, the feminine Church relates to the S(Å) in its mysticism, the pathway to which is open because of the symbolic (rather than imaginary) nature of the phallus in the priesthood pointing the way to this signifier of the lack in the Other. The lack in the Other the signifier signifies is the lack of the Church, which celebrates the energic presence of God in his essential absence; the experiential or phenomenological (rather than

136   Jouissance and the body of the Church

ontological) lack in God insofar as he desires relations with every human hypostasis; and to the lack in the believer that is presented to him or her in each fast and every icon.

In this view, the priesthood is not a male priesthood in that it retains the real or imaginary phallus but a masculine priesthood that retains the symbolic phallus. The restriction of this office to anatomical males is arguably due to two causes. First, the cultural accident of the male priesthood may be due in part to psychoanalytically masculine subjectivities having been understood by those in the Church as necessarily related to the penile organ in a tautological manner despite being contingent. Second, masculinely structured subjects relate to the *objet a* and to this extent benefit from the notion that women are a complement to men. In other words, rather than the *priesthood* being structured as masculine in the sense of having the symbolic phallus, the subset of *priests* that are masculinely structured have sought to superpose the object over the signifier of the lack in the Other.

In this way, the Church can credibly advocate for the masculine role of the priesthood in the sense of having the symbolic phallus without precluding anatomical females from the office. This consideration requires further discussion within the mind of the Church, but is noteworthy for extending Dunn's (2010) argument that "even if we concede the point that the priesthood is a 'masculine' ministry, this does not preclude women from being priests" (pp. 40–41). Indeed, it adds another layer to this argument by discussing the psychoanalytic importance of such masculinity.

Just as sexuation illuminates the role of masculinity in the priesthood, sexuation may similarly provide some foundation for the Orthodox understanding of God as masculine, if not male (Hopko, 1993). Although Lacan (1986/1992) apparently attributed the masculinity of God to the father whose image he bears, it may be worth considering as well that the masculinity of God is significant in that it fosters symbolic identification (in the Old Covenant, through actual castration) with the ego ideal rather than imaginary identification with the ideal ego and maternal desire. The benefit of this distinction is that it creates a space for lack by supporting separation from the imaginary universe.

Furthermore, finding a feminine person of God[9] would reduce the space of lack (both in God and in the Christian who bears his image), reducing the Christian God to the One of Gnosticism,[10] who in deepest reality is the *pleroma* (Roukema, 2010), the fullness of being, whose aeons emanate as hermaphrodites or as syzygies, male–female pairings that are complete unto themselves (Saarinen, 2011). Indeed, it is only when Sophia emanates without her male counterpart (i.e., when she acts from lack) that she creates the demiurge Yaldaboath, who creates the evil material universe (*Apocryphon of John*).[11] From this follows "a series of broken symmetries" (Pagels, 2005, p. 264). The only conceivable role of lack in such a system is evil. The material universe, *kenoma* (Martin, 2010), is always separated from the *pleroma* by the *Horos*, the limit (Edinger, 1999, p. 71), separating the really real from the effervescent, essentially opposing being with matter. The symbolism of God as masculine, then, is not necessarily without purpose and may

Jouissance and the body of the Church 137

serve an important function in safeguarding a truly Christian understanding of spiritual (and psychic) life.

These discussions of *jouissance* and sexuation in the Church provide a starting point for deepening the interaction of Lacanian psychoanalysis and Orthodox anthropology and are perhaps one of the areas richest with opportunity for mutual benefit. Particularly at the level of social issues pertaining to sex, the Church, finding itself without language in the modern age to understand its own behavior, is precisely in the same gap that psychoanalysis occupies as symptom and stands to gain from this commonality should it choose to do so.

Notes

1 From Evolving Lacanian Perspectives for Clinical Psychoanalysis, Raul Moncayo, Copyright (2008) and Imprint. Reproduced by permission of Taylor & Francis Group.
2 The English edition of Seminar XX (Lacan, 1975/1998) produces "Woman" with a line through it rather than "La" (p. 78). Moncayo (2008) reproduced the diagram with "The" under erasure (p. 80), which seems a more apt adaptation to English and is therefore used here.
3 This formulation is specific to Monacyo. Nobus (2015) identified "at least eight different types of jouissance" in Seminar XX alone (p. 30). It is true Lacan used a variety of terms to refer to qualify *jouissance* in Seminar XX and throughout his work, and there are certainly clear delineations in Lacan's use of the language of *jouissance*. Moncayo's (2008) formulation is used here because it accounts for these delineations in Lacan's use of *jouissance* in a way directly tied to a body of theory, clarifying the difference between and significance of each.
4 The citations of diocesan websites or informal posts by clergy are for illustrative purposes. The fasts are practices rather than promulgated rules. Fasting is always done in economical consideration (by the priest) of particular persons, and it is encouraged to be done in secret (Webber, 2007).
5 The Church takes pains to make sure this is general knowledge. For example, continuing with the theme of the Nativity, the Antiochian Orthodox Christian Archdiocese of North America (n.d.) provides on its public website *Guidelines for the Nativity Fast*:

> Fasting in itself is not a means of pleasing God. Fasting is not a punishment for our sins. Nor is fasting a means of suffering and pain to be undertaken as some kind of atonement. Christ already redeemed us on His Cross. Salvation is a gift from God that is not bought by our hunger or thirst.
>
> (Para. 3)

This is accompanied by the note that fasting is for spiritual deliverance from passions and to turn our eyes toward God. The Archdiocese notes that Christians who are pregnant or nursing, experiencing serious illness, fasting without prayer or almsgiving (i.e., fasting as a legal obligation instead of a spiritual practice), or fasting without spiritual guidance should not fast.
6 See McNulty (2005) for a fruitful discussion of this issue; however, McNulty's view that the Old Covenant was one of pure behavioral expectation is an oversimplification. For example, God's vehement response to the Israelites, who "trample upon the poor" (Amos 5:11) and "turn justice to wormwood" (Amos 5:7), is to defy their religious law:

> I hate, I despise your feasts, and I take no delight in your solemn assemblies. Even though you offer me your burnt offerings and cereal offerings, I will not

138 Jouissance and the body of the Church

> accept them, and the peace offerings of your fatted beasts I will not look upon. Take away from me the noise of your songs; to the melody of your harps I will not listen. But let justice roll down like waters, and righteousness like an everflowing stream.
>
> (Amos 5:21–24)

This insistence on righteousness beyond the law is present, too, in the Church's most universal prayer of penitence, which is also from the period of the Old Covenant, Psalm 50:16–17, 19:

> For thou hast no delight in sacrifice; were I to give a burnt offering, thou wouldst not be pleased. The sacrifice acceptable to God is a broken spirit; a broken and contrite heart, O God, thou wilt not despise . . . . Then wilt thou delight in right sacrifices.
>
> (Note that in the Septuagint, this Psalm is numbered 50; in the Masoretic Text that forms the basis of many translations, including the RSV, this is Psalm 51.)

7 Yannaras's (1967/2005) discussion of Western mysticism noted that due to the theological underpinnings of Western mysticism, what is involved is "not even a matter of an actual relationship, but rather a one-sided, psychological appeal on the subject's behalf to a *substantially* inaccessible object of desire—it is a matter of erotic self-hedonism" (p. 119). Yannaras's hard stance here presents the Western conception of Christ as an inaccessible object in much the same way the Lady is the inaccessible object that stands in for the Thing in sublimation. It should be stressed that Yannaras is merely reducing to its logical conclusion the view that direct communion with God is not possible (as in Pound, 2007).
8 For an important consideration of Lossky's views, including criticisms, see Papanikolaou (2006).
9 As in the case of those who view the Holy Spirit as feminine or the Father as Mother. See Hopko (1993) for a discussion of Orthodox theology and views of God as masculine or feminine.
10 There are, of course, numerous systems of Gnosticism. They are more or less conflated here as they are peripheral to the discussion and generally unified in their cosmology as far as the argument here is concerned.
11 Edinger (1999) perceptively noted that Sophia "appears in Jung's conception of the archetypal anima" (p. 41). Edinger's work addresses the Jungian nature of Gnosticism, and he intriguingly made connections not irrelevant to Lacanian analysis when discussing the *Horos*, or the limit, as a matter of splitting the psyche into subject and object.

References

Antiochian Orthodox Christian Archdiocese of North America. (n.d.). *Guidelines for the Nativity fast*. Retrieved from www.antiochian.org/node/18518

Dix, G. (2007). *The shape of the liturgy*. New York, NY: Continuum. (Original work published 1945)

Dunn, D. (2010). "Her that is no bride": St. Thecla and the relationship between sex, gender, and office. *St. Vladimir's Theological Quarterly, 54*(1), 37–68.

Edinger, E. F. (1999). *The psyche in antiquity, book two: Gnosticism and early Christianity, from Paul of Tarsus to Augustine*. Toronto, CA: Inner City Books.

Fink, B. (1991). "There's no such thing as a sexual relationship": Existence and the formulas of sexuation. *Newsletter of the Freudian Field, 5*(1–2), 59–85.

Hopko, T. (1975). On the male character of Christian priesthood. *St Vladimir's Theological Quarterly, 19*(3), 147–173.

Hopko, T. (1977). On the male character of the Christian priesthood: A reply to criticism. *St Vladimir's Theological Quarterly, 21*(3), 161–167.

Hopko, T. (1993). God and gender: Articulating the Orthodox view. *St. Vladimir's Theological Quarterly, 37*(2–3), 141–183.

Kalinich, L. J. (1988). The Logos in Lacan. *St. Vladimir's Theological Quarterly, 32*, 367–383.

Kostoff, S. (2015, November 24). Indulging not in food, but in giving thanks to the Lord! *Reflections in Christ.* Retrieved from https://oca.org/reflections/fr.-steven-kostoff/indulging-not-in-food-but-in-giving-thanks-to-the-lord

Lacan, J. (1992). *The seminar of Jacques Lacan: Book VII: The ethics of psychoanalysis 1959–1960.* (D. Porter, Trans.). New York, NY: W. W. Norton. (Original work published 1986)

Lacan, J. (1998). *The seminar of Jacques Lacan, book XX: On feminine sexuality, the limits of love and knowledge, 1972–1973.* (B. Fink, Trans.). New York, NY: W. W. Norton. (Original work published 1975)

Lacan, J. (2006). *Écrits.* (B. Fink, Trans.). New York, NY: W. W. Norton. (Original work published 1966)

Lossky, V. (1957). *The mystical theology of the Eastern Church.* (Fellowship of St. Alban & St. Sergius, Trans.). Crestwood, NY: St. Vladimir's Seminary Press. (Original work published 1944)

Lossky, V. (1974). *In the image and likeness of God.* (J. H. Erickson & T. E. Bird, Eds.). Crestwood, NY: St. Vladimir's Seminary Press. (Original work published 1967)

Martin, S. (2010). *The Gnostics: The first Christian heretics.* Harpenden, UK: Pocket Essentials.

McNulty, T. (2005). Wrestling with the angel. *Umbr(a): The Dark God, 1*, 73–84.

Meyendorff, J. (1974). *Byzantine theology: Historical trends and doctrinal themes.* New York, NY: Fordham University Press.

Meyendorff, J. (2000). *Marriage: An Orthodox perspective* (3rd ed.). Crestwood, NY: St. Vladimir's Seminary Press.

Moncayo, R. (2008). *Evolving Lacanian perspectives for clinical psychoanalysis: On narcissism, sexuation, and the phases of analysis in contemporary culture.* London, UK: Karnac Books.

Nobus, D. (2015). The sculptural iconography of feminine jouissance: Lacan's reading of Bernini's Saint Teresa in Ecstasy. *The Comparist, 39*(1), 22–46.

Oikonomou, D. (2002). Christian fasting. *Mozaik, 10*(2), 16–18.

Pagels, E. (2005). Exegesis and exposition of the Genesis creation accounts in selected texts from Nag Hammadi. In C. W. Hedrick & R. Hodgson, Jr. (Eds.), *Nag Hammadi, Gnosticism, and early Christianity* (pp. 257–286). Eugene, OR: Wipf and Stock.

Papanikolaou, A. (2006). *Being with God: Trinity, apophaticism, and divine-human communion.* Notre Dame, IN: University of Notre Dame Press.

Papanikolaou, A. (2011). Integrating the ascetical and the eucharistic: Current challenges in Orthodox ecclesiology. *International Journal for the Study of the Christian Church, 11*(2–3), 173–187.

Pound, M. (2007). *Theology, psychoanalysis, trauma.* London, UK: SCM Press.

Purpura, A. M. (2017). Beyond the binary: Hymnographic constructions of Eastern Orthodox gender identities. *The Journal of Religion, 97*(4), 524–546.

Roukema, R. (2010). *Jesus, gnosis, and dogma.* (S. Deventer-Metz, Trans.). New York, NY: T&T Clark International.

Saarinen, R. (2011). Syzygy: Love made strange. *Dialog, 50*(1), 71–80.

Ware, K. (1986). *The Orthodox way.* Crestwood, NY: St. Vladimir's Seminary Press.

Ware, K. (2000). *The inner kingdom: Volume I of the collected works.* Crestwood, NY: St. Vladimir's Seminary Press.

Ware, T. (1993). *The Orthodox Church.* New York, NY: Penguin.

Webber, M. (2007). *Bread & water, wine & oil: An Orthodox Christian experience of God.* Chesterton, IN: Conciliar Press.

Wehr, K. (2011). Virginity, singleness and celibacy: Late fourth-century and recent evangelical visions of unmarried Christians. *Theology & Sexuality, 17*(1), 75–99.

Yannaras, C. (1984). *The freedom of morality.* (E. Briere, Trans.). Crestwood, NY: St. Vladimir's Seminary Press. (Original work published 1979)

Yannaras, C. (2005). *On the absence and unknowability of God: Heidegger and the Areopagite.* (H. Ventis, Trans.). New York, NY: T&T Clark International. (Original work published 1967)

Zizioulas, J. D. (1985). *Being as communion.* Crestwood, NY: St. Vladimir's Seminary Press.

Chapter 8

The ethics of Orthodoxy

Given the central absence of the Thing, the revelation of the Thing's Word in the Incarnation, and the relation of the Orthodox to the Other *jouissance*, where are things left for the ethics of the Church? Yannaras (1979/1984), in his work on morality in the Orthodox Church, sharply distinguished between the Orthodox vision of morality and the stereotypical view of Western conceptions of morality. Among the most important elements of Yannaras' thought, the concepts of *good* and *evil* are not invested as they often are in the West—as proper or improper actions or as utile outcomes. Rather, "in the language of the text of Genesis, the distinction between *good* and *evil* refers to life and death—not to categories of behavior, not to regulative/moral rules, not to faithfully keeping or breaking some law" (Yannaras, 2008/2012, p. 24). Good and evil are nothing more than "life without limit" and "existential finitude and death," respectively (p. 25). As such, good and evil have no ontological contents[1]; they are experiential, and the knowledge of them (the Knowledge of Good and Evil) is an existential experience.

Yannaras (1979/1984) most clearly summarized this when arguing, "the morality of the Gospel relates to a real, existential transfiguration of man's nature, and not simply to a more complete deontology or Law which leaves human nature existentially unchanged" (p. 51). In other words, the mode of existence of the person, as person, must be relational and it is transfiguration in this relation that comprises morality—there is no Law in morality. Morality for the Orthodox could never be a set of rules, nor the ordering of goods. For Yannaras, the mode of relational engagement "requires the ascetic self-transcendence of individuality and the reality of personal relationship and self-offering" (p. 218). It is through *ascetic kenosis* that the Orthodox pursue *synergia*, first with God, then also with one another.

Yannaras (1979/1984) contrasted this form of asceticism with "holistic systems of individualistic utilitarianism and their totalitarian mechanisms," which are never truly threatened by supposed revolutions[2] that operate within the same system (p. 218). This includes, for Yannaras, the "capitalist-marxist polarization," as Orthodoxy rejects any system that restricts the good of humanity to commodities and consumer goods (p. 219). Yannaras centered the "existential action" of the Christian in "achieving the *personal* truth of man," that is, the human *hypostasis* in relationship rather than any impoverished concepts of individuality, education,

DOI: 10.4324/9781003214359-10

142   The ethics of Orthodoxy

or society (p. 218). The Christian, then, is to "renounce the service of goods" (Lacan, 1986/1992, p. 305). These might be "private goods, family goods, domestic goods, other goods that solicit us, the goods of our trade or our profession, the goods of the city, etc." (p. 303). In abandoning utilitarianism, the Christian abandons also utility as the good altogether; the ethics of Orthodoxy is the ethics of the martyrs, who "embody the truth of the Church, the truth of the true life which is communion and relationship with God" by realizing "a mode of existence which is the complete antithesis of individual survival, and has its historical prototype in the cross of Christ" (Yannaras, 1979/1984, p. 178).

The meaning of the fruit of the Tree of Knowledge of Good and Evil is that the individualistic mode of being, which is chosen by Adam and Eve, is precisely what introduces the experiential category of evil as finitude and death. It is not that a *connaissance* is delivered to the *nous* through the consumption of the fruit; the knowledge in question is the savoir faire of death. This is the Christian inversion of the will to live: Those who would perpetuate their individual existence accede to death while those who seek something beyond individual existence (i.e., who assume the place of death with respect to individuality) accede to life. Thus, while the first Adam sought from the first tree the divine essence that resulted in death, it is the second Adam who, taking up the second tree, assumed the place of death and instituted in himself the true union of the divine and human natures through the energies of God. It is the Christian commitment to the beyond of individual existence that orients all aspects of Christian life. In analytic terms, deontology (the following of the Law) and utilitarianism are moralities that see only the level of the *Vorstellungen*, that operate according to the logic of what is good for the human as an individual or a collection of individuals. This is the pleasure principle written into theology.

Lacan (1986/1992) reads in Kant the distinction between wellbeing (*Wohl*) and the Good (*Gut*) differentiated by the subject's orientation to *das Ding* on the horizon, *Wohl* regulating the distance from *das Ding* (through the pleasure principle) and "the *Gut, das Ding*" as resting beyond this. Setting aside the question of Kant,[3] Lacan's proposed ethical orientation is toward the *Gut*, the beyond of the pleasure principle, that is, toward the act of the subject according to the subject's desire. Lacan (1986/1992) contrasts this with "the service of goods" (p. 313) at the level of the *Wohl*, the submission to which is a sacrifice. Lacan connects this sacrifice to that which underlies *Civilization and Its Discontents*, and Lacan suggests that it is the sacrificed *jouissance* that "religion undertakes to recuperate," leading Lacan to make the sort of sweeping statement he at other times condemns, stating that the effort to recuperate the lost *jouissance* is "the single trait which is common to all religions; it is coextensive with all religion, with the whole meaning of religion" (p. 322). This evaluation is open to reconsideration in light of Lacan's later writings and is taken up in the discussion of *jouissance* in Chapter 7 of this volume, particularly related to a phallic *jouissance* and an Other *jouissance*.

Cataphatic religion that seeks to encapsulate God within the bounds of the symbolic and imaginary limitations of the human mind is the religion that is known for

The ethics of Orthodoxy   143

keeping its distance from *das Ding*. It is no coincidence that the most cataphatic of religions are typically those with the clearest Laws regulating the distance of the subject and the Thing, the greatest regulation of the *Wohl*. The restriction of valid religious teaching to the *Sola Scriptura* in certain Protestant groups or to the Salaf of Islam, in the path referred to by its exonym of Wahhabism, constrain the understanding of God to certain delimited defiles; they also promulgate strict regulations in observance of this. This is especially true of their regulation of the feminine, no doubt due in large part to the preventing sexism of earlier ages. However, it also seems such regulations are an embodiment of the pleasure principle, precluding exposure of the signifier of the lack in the Other that exposes the subject to the Other *jouissance* beyond the Law.

Returning to Lacan's ethics, "desire disappears under pleasure's sway" (Lacan, 2006, p. 652), indicating that the subjectivization of desire requires an orientation toward the *Gut* and not the *Wohl*. It is the pursuit of "the Good" (the *Gut*) beyond all pleasurable service to goods elsewhere. For this reason, the subject "cannot stand the extreme good that *das Ding* may bring" it (Lacan, 1986/1992, p. 73). The *jouissance* experienced in this case is not the phallic *jouissance* of the relation to the phallic object, but that related to the hole in the Other, to the signifier of the lack in the Other that the singularity of *das Ding* entails.

The ethics of Orthodoxy are centered on modes of being rather than on the Law or on particular goods. The orientation of the subject in Orthodox Christianity is toward God, understood in the context of his absence, with desire acting as a gravitation toward him beyond all goods of the world. This transcends the question of the good of the individual. Indeed, to the extent that a person seeks heaven because of its pleasurable qualities, that person moves away from the mode of being of relatedness and back toward atomism, in other words, moves back to an ethics of pleasure.

Instead, in Orthodoxy the subject seeks in kenotic self-transcendence to push beyond the pleasure principle altogether, embodying death, "being-for-death" (Lacan, 1986/1992, p. 320), to the extent the subject seeks something beyond life. It is not for nothing Christ warned "if any one comes to me and does not hate his own father and mother and wife and children and brothers and sisters, yes, and even his own life, he cannot be my disciple" (Lk. 14:26). This willingness to take one's place among the dead, to be "between life and death" like Antigone (Lacan, 1986/1992, p. 272), is clear in the lives of the saints.

St. Symeon the Fool in Christ—the prototype of the holy fool—is one such example.

Symeon had made the pilgrimage to Jerusalem with his mother, "a very old woman, about eighty" (Leontius of Neapolis, n.d., p. 134), for the Feast of the Exaltation of the Cross. While there, he met a young man about 22 years old named John. John was on pilgrimage with his parents and had married a girl that same year. Symeon and John became good friends and traveled away from Jerusalem together with their parents. On their way back, John pointed out to Symeon "the monasteries all around the holy Jordan," (p. 134), and "on a sudden impulse"

144 The ethics of Orthodoxy

(Ware, 2000, p. 160), the two conspired to abscond from their parents and become monks, "Symeon abandoning his old mother, John his parents and the young wife waiting for him at home" (p. 160). The sight of the monastery was a sign of something about which St. Symeon could not help but want to know more. John told Symeon that "Angels of God" lived in the monasteries, and Symeon inquired whether they might see them (Leontius of Neapolis, n.d., p. 134). John's response was "if we become like them, yes" (p. 134). Despite being "endowed with much intellect," Symeon was confronted with a knowledge that could only be acquired as a matter of a *going through*, an *ascesis* and purification at the cost of pleasure.

This rather striking act—the abandonment of kith and kin—was not sanitized by St. Symeon's hagiographer, who made "no attempt to gloss over the harshness and cruelty of what Symeon and John were doing to others—and, indeed, to themselves" (Ware, 2000, p. 160). This is clear in the text, which notes that when they had arrived at the monastery, the superior did not stop encouraging them in their decision due to "seeing the streams of tears pouring forth from their eyes" (Leontius of Neapolis, n.d., p. 137).

Lacan (1986/1992) described religion as, at bottom, an attempt at recuperating the *jouissance* sacrificed in sublimation. He identified this operation as the distinguishing feature between "religious work" and "an ethical form of catharsis" (p. 323). Lacan, following Aristotle, stated that catharsis pertained to the purification of desire, this purification being impossible "unless one has at least established the crossing of its limits that we call fear and pity" (p. 323). If religious work is the operation of recuperating the *jouissance* lost in sublimation, then the question is ultimately one of sublimation contra catharsis. Sublimation, in Lacan's formulation here, can be found at the level of the object, the raising of the object to the dignity of the Thing. Furthermore, "at the level of sublimation the object is inseparable from imaginary and especially cultural elaborations" (p. 99), meaning that sublimation is connected not to the Thing but to that which takes its place. Thus, while religion in Lacan's view occupies itself with recuperation of *jouissance* sacrificed in sublimation, the "religious work" of St. Symeon is oriented toward not the elaborative systems that colonize the space of *das Ding* but toward revealing precisely the ruptures of the real that *das Ding* brings with it.

Indeed, St. Symeon pushed past the bounds of pity and fear in pursuit of the Thing beyond all pleasurable limits. It is this movement beyond the pleasure principle that characterizes the Orthodox path. If this movement beyond pity and fear remains uncertain in the beginning of St. Symeon's story, the remainder of his hagiography illuminates the matter all the more. Commenting on St. Symeon, Yannaras (1979/1984) described how

> Christ does not destroy the Law, but shows that the Law is transcended in the Kingdom. And St. Symeon is a citizen of the Kingdom: in his person, he embodies transcendence of the Law, the "transgression," which is a scandal only to those of us who still live in need of the Law, in need of obedience,

The ethics of Orthodoxy 145

because we have not yet attained or know nothing about the 'end' of the Law which is the freedom of the saints.

(p. 72)

The end of the Law, the recognition that, finally, there is no Law and no Other, appears as a scandal to those unprepared for this experiential knowledge. Yannaras (1979/1984) then described how St. Symeon would intentionally cause moral scandal, such as when he entered "the women's public baths—'as it were to the glory of God'" (p. 72). That the morality of the Orthodox knows no ontological or deontological bounds is quite clearly visible in such acts by St. Symeon; the knowledge of good and evil is an experiential act and is predicated only on the relational or non-relational mode of existence of the hypostasis.

Even so, the "as it were to the glory of God" (Yannaras, 1979/1984, p. 72) raises the valid question, from a Lacanian perspective, as to whether the Orthodox saint is not a sadist. The *jouissance* of the saint seems to be placed, after all, in the body of the Other, which Lacan (1991/2007) noted is "ineliminable from the substance of the one who has said 'I am what I am'" (p. 66). Yet the God of de Sade—and Lacan insists he had one—is of course the materialist nature to whom the libertine appeals. It is because the materialist insists on pure immanence, on the whole world being the body of God, that "materialists are the only authentic believers" (p. 66). However, the sadist both relies on this collapse (i.e., relies on the natural order for *jouissance*), and yet also attempts to deny and countermand the Other while all the while obeying a Law (de Kesel, 2001/2009). Despite the fact that the sadist cannot be carelessly conflated with the pervert (Nobus, 2015), there seems to be a denial in the sadist of castration such that the sadist continues to view himself as the object of *jouissance* of the Other (nature). In other words, whereas in sublimation the object is raised to the dignity of the Thing, in the perverse solution, the subject takes the place of the Thing (de Kesel, 2001/2009).

In discussing sublimation, Lacan (1986/1992) suggested that art is related to hysteria and *Verdrängung* (repression), religion to obsession and *Verschiebung* (displacement), and science to paranoia and *Verwerfung* (foreclosure). Art organizes around the emptiness of the Thing, religion avoids it, and science forecloses its very possibility (p. 130). Perversion, and the *Verneinung* (denial) associated with it, are not included in this discussion. In this way, the sadist is one who, outside of sublimation, takes upon oneself the place of the Thing, who refuses to acknowledge (denies) the lack in the Other in the form of the symbolic phallus.[4]

The Orthodox saint is no sadist, then, precisely because the saint does not assume the place of the Thing, even when provoking scandal. Furthermore, Lacan's (1986/1992) equivocation of *Verschiebung* and the function of religion do little to square accounts with the profound apophaticism of the East. It is not a matter of avoiding the Thing through the ritualized do-gooding of Lacan's description of religion, nor is it related to the recuperation of what is lost in sublimation, namely, the fantasized real *jouissance* of the obsessive. Instead of an attempt to provoke the Law—"Christ does not destroy the Law" (Yannaras, 1979/1984, p. 72)—or

146 The ethics of Orthodoxy

to obey the Law, the Orthodox saint opens up to something beyond the Law, to that Other *jouissance* that is beyond, not before, the Law (Moncayo, 2008). This, again, testifies to the essentially feminine position of the Eastern Church.

In de Kesel's (2001/2009) exposition, art and ethics share in common the fact that an individual traverses the Law to produce something in which "society can subsequently recognize itself" (p. 191). This allows one to see why the saints are the models of the Church. They are the exceptions, not in the sense of categorical difference, but in the sense, they are made of the same stuff, so to speak, as everyone else, and yet find it within themselves to step outside every manner of Law, both secular (exemplified in the Martyr) and sacred (exemplified in the Fool). The saints, as pinnacles of Orthodox practice, serve as the center of ethics and aesthetics in the community (or "society") of the Orthodox Church.

Lacan (1986/1992) posited one question with "the force of a Last Judgment: Have you acted in conformity with the desire that is in you?" (p. 314). The desire within, the desire embodied in the absence of the Thing, represented in repressed form in the representative of the representation, is always, despite the vestments it dons in any given subject, the absence of the Life each subject seeks in relationship. It is in relation to this desire that the Christian pursues, through asceticism and the two paths of the Church (marriage and monasticism), the transcendence of the self that occurs in the abandonment of idols of God. The Christian embraces the death drive in pushing past the pleasure principle, abandoning the service of goods, and assumes instead "an ethos of hopelessness and *despair* as far as concerns the life offered by personal survival" (Yannaras, 1979/1984, p. 268). It is in relation to this desire that Orthodoxy can announce a similar measure of the Last Judgment to Lacan's: "it is not God's sentence but His existence that judges humanity" (p. 36).

Notes

1 Yannaras (1979/1984) used a somewhat different consideration of ontology when he remarked that the Church's ethics "relate to ontological realities and not to evaluative categories" (p. 37). First, it should be clarified that Yannaras is, in this instance, differentiating the ethics of the Church from the moral categories of Good and Evil: "the Church's ethics are 'beyond good and evil'" (p. 37). Second, Yannaras' consideration of ontology is not tied directly to the Western, atomic consideration of ontology; it relates to an existential relationship. His work *Relational Ontology* (Yannaras, 2004/2011) explored this concept specifically, though most of his other works cited here do as well, to greater or lesser degrees.
2 Lacan (1991/2007) also noted the ambiguity of "'revolution,' which, in the use made of it in the mechanics of heavenly bodies, can mean return to the start" (p. 55).
3 De Kesel (2001/2009) remarks "it is striking how little it seems to hinder Lacan that his reference to Kant illustrates precisely the opposite of what he wants to show" (pp. 110–111). Lacan's interpretation of Kant is not a recapitulation of Kant's own deontology.
4 Hence, Sade's libertine Saint-Fond noted, "We are so many gods" (Sade, 1797/1968, p. 243).

References

De Kesel, M. (2009). *Eros and ethics: Reading Jacques Lacan's Seminar VII.* (S. Jöttkandt, Trans.). New York, NY: SUNY Press. (Original work published 2001)

Lacan, J. (1992). *The seminar of Jacques Lacan: Book VII: The ethics of psychoanalysis 1959–1960.* (D. Porter, Trans.). New York, NY: W. W. Norton. (Original work published 1986)

Lacan, J. (2006). *Écrits.* (B. Fink, Trans.). New York, NY: W. W. Norton. (Original work published 1966)

Lacan, J. (2007). *The seminar of Jacques Lacan: Book XVII: The other side of psychoanalysis.* (R. Grigg, Trans.). New York, NY: W. W. Norton. (Original work published 1991)

Leontius of Neapolis. (n.d.). The life and conduct of Abba Symeon called the fool for the sake of Christ. In D. Krueger (Eds.), *Symeon the Holy Fool: Leontius's life and the late antique city* (D. Krueger, Trans.) (pp. 131–172). Berkeley, CA: University of California Press.

Moncayo, R. (2008). *Evolving Lacanian perspectives for clinical psychoanalysis: On narcissism, sexuation, and the phases of analysis in contemporary culture.* London, UK: Karnac Books.

Nobus, D. (2015, November 13). *Jouissance, desire, and the law: A close reading of Lacan's Kant with Sade.* Presentation at the SF Bay Area School of Lacanian Psychoanalysis, San Francisco, CA. (Lecture notes)

Sade, M. de. (1968). *Juliette.* (A. Wainhouse, Trans.). New York, NY: Grove Press. (Original work published 1797 under the title *La Nouvelle Justine, ou les Malheurs de la Vertu*)

Ware, K. (2000). *The inner kingdom: Volume I of the collected works.* Crestwood, NY: St. Vladimir's Seminary Press.

Yannaras, C. (1984). *The freedom of morality.* (E. Briere, Trans.). Crestwood, NY: St. Vladimir's Seminary Press. (Original work published 1979)

Yannaras, C. (2011). *Relational ontology.* (N. Russell, Trans.). Brookline, MA: Holy Cross Orthodox Press. (Original work published 2004)

Yannaras, C. (2012). *The enigma of evil.* (N. Russell, Trans.). Brookline, MA: Holy Cross Orthodox Press. (Original work published 2008)

Chapter 9

Ego and ego fate

One of the critical and most central questions of anthropology, as a field of philosophy and theology, is the question of the *self*. Orthodox anthropology has developed over the course of the Church's history, but many significant developments occurred in the centuries centered on the Christological controversies (Ware, 1993). These controversies largely revolved around disagreements about the person of Christ and his relationship to and between his humanity and divinity were resolved in a series of Ecumenical Councils, of which the Orthodox Church recognizes seven. These councils provide some of the fundamental dogma and doctrine regarding the person of Christ and anthropology. Of interest here are the First Council of Nicaea (the first Ecumenical Council), the Council of Ephesus (the third Ecumenical Council), and the Council of Chalcedon (the fourth Ecumenical Council).

The participants of the First Council of Nicaea (325 CE) debated the relationship of Christ and God in response to the Arian controversy (Ware, 1993). Arius and his disciples insisted Christ was a created being, a separate essence from the Father. St. Athanasius and others argued against the Arians that Christ was also truly God; the Council chose the term *homoousios* (όμοούσιος) to describe the relationship of Christ to the Father, that they are "one in essence" (Ware, 1993, p. 22). The Council decided in favor of those arguing for one essence, preserving the divinity of Christ.

The issue of Christ's divinity was largely resolved by the second Ecumenical Council in 381 CE (Ware, 1993); thereafter, the relationship of Christ's humanity and divinity was called into question when Nestorius' arguments rose to prominence. Nestorius grappled with the question of how God (in Christ, being of one essence with the Father) might also be born of a woman. He emphasized a sharp distinction between the two natures of Christ (the human and the divine) to the point of essentially arguing for two persons (Word and Christ), having conflated person and nature (Lossky, 1978). St. Cyril of Alexandria pressed the opposing argument that the two natures were more closely related and that Christ was indeed one person despite two natures. This controversy led to the Council of Ephesus (431 CE), which condemned Nestorius's teachings.

DOI: 10.4324/9781003214359-11

Ego and ego fate 149

The fourth Ecumenical Council, the Council of Chalcedon (451 BCE), was convened to respond to an extreme form of St. Cyril's argument:[1] that Christ was one in person and one in nature (Ware, 1993). The Council of Chalcedon declared that Christ was in fact one person in two natures—one person, of one essence with the Father and of one essence with humanity (Lossky, 1978).

The distinctions between nature and person upheld in these Councils rely upon certain terminology the Church Fathers appropriated for explicatory use. At the time of the first Council, *ousia* (οὐσία; whence ὁμοούσιος) was a philosophical term that had implications of ultimate being in the sense of the One, in which all identity would be reabsorbed (Lossky, 1978). In defending the same essence of the Father and the Son, the Fathers utilized this term but found it necessary to affirm the differentiation of Persons as well so that it was clear Father and Son will not ultimately collapse in one identity.

However, the vocabulary of ancient philosophy lacked a term for *person* in an ontologically meaningful sense; *persona* for the Latins and *prosopon* (πρόσωπον) for the Greeks signified a "delimiting, deceptive, and finally illusory aspect of the individual . . . the masked face of impersonal being" (Lossky, 1978, p. 40). This is because *prosopon* was the term for the masks utilized by ancient Greek actors (Hierotheos, 1998); *persona* served much the same function for the Latins, essentially having "nothing to do with the *ontology* of the person" (Zizioulas, 1985, p. 34). This created difficulties in referring to the Persons of the Trinity as *prosopa* or *personae* as these did not communicate the reality of the Person.

In seeking to resolve this, the Fathers repurposed another word that was essentially synonymous with ousia: *hypostasis* (ὑπόστασις); (Lossky, 1978). Hypostasis also referred to ontological being, but with reference to singularity or particularity and instance of the being, while ousia pertained more broadly to essence. The Fathers essentially redefined the term hypostasis to identify it with *prosopon*, thereby introducing the concept of *person* with the ontological signification intact—the person as a particular instance of the essence. This change of definition led to much confusion; the formulation of the Trinity in the West was based on the language of *persona*, so the Eastern Church read into the Western formulation of three *personae* in one essence a sort of modalism or Sabellian tendency. However, the Eastern Church's formulation of three hypostases, without understanding the term's redefinition, sounded to the Western Church like "tritheism" (Lossky, 1944/1957, p. 52)!

The ontological component of *hypostasis* provides space in the Orthodox Church for a formulation of the Trinity that approaches the concept first through persons rather than substance (Zizioulas, 1985). For Zizioulas, God is free from all necessity, including the necessity of being: He exists through his own free will.

It is precisely His trinitarian existence that constitutes this confirmation: the Father out of love—that is, freely—begets the Son and brings forth the Spirit.

150   Ego and ego fate

> If God exists, He exists because the Father exists. . . . God as a person—as the hypostasis of the Father—makes the one divine substance to be that which it is: the one God
>
> (Zizioulas, 1985, p. 41).[2]

Thus, God's mode of existence is love—the act of love free from necessity. It is this that "hypostasizes God, *constitutes* His being" (Zizioulas, 1985, p. 46). This means God himself "is not subject to the necessity of the substance," that is, God does not exist by necessity (p. 46).

However, the human is subject to the necessity of existence, and is thus not fully *person*, that is, has not been *hypostasized*. Becoming an "authentic person,"[3] for Zizioulas (1985), is a matter of theosis: "the authentic person . . . must be 'uncreated,' that is, unbounded by any 'necessity,' including its own existence" (p. 43). In this sense, theosis is "the eternal survival of the person as a unique, unrepeatable, and free 'hypostasis,' as loving and being loved" (p. 49). Although the person exists outside of salvation as a "hypostasis of biological existence" (p. 50), Zizioulas argued this existence is not an experience of the fullness of personhood because it is (a) determined by necessity; (b) separated into individuals (splitting nature)[4]; and (c) concludes "with the last and greatest passion of man, with the disintegration of the hypostasis, which is death" (p. 51). This biological hypostasis is "the 'mask' of hypocrisy, the fortress of individualism, the vehicle of the final separation, death" (p. 52).

In theosis, Zizioulas (1985) emphasized equally that neither the body nor eros, the two components of the hypostasis, should be destroyed in salvation. Rather:

> They nevertheless change their activity, adapt themselves to the new 'mode of existence' of the hypostasis, reject from this activity of theirs which is constitutive of the human hypostasis whatever creates the tragic [death-carrying] element in man, and retain whatever makes the person to be love, freedom and life.
>
> (p. 53)

Therefore, the fate of the human hypostasis in salvation is not reabsorption into some unitary One, but transformation through identification with the hypostatic union of Christ and in relationship to God (Zizioulas, 1985). Authentic personhood, for Zizioulas, is a matter of communion with God and freedom from necessity in energetic union.

Yannaras' (1967/2005) presented a similar account of the person, both in relationship to God and in the absence of this relationship. Yannaras contrasted the mode of existence of fallen nature—"natural autonomy"—with the mode of existence of Christ, in communion with God (pp. 91–92). The one who denies self-transcendent communion with God in his energies partakes in what is

> equally a *personal* existential event, an active reference of the freedom of the person, that yet refers its existence, not to a relationship to the Person of God,

Ego and ego fate   151

but to a non-relationship, to the reality of the void or of the natural distance between God and human kind—*outside* the mode of life.

(p. 107)

This is the existential reality that Zizioulas (1985) called the biological hypostasis.[5] The personal and relational are the ground of ontology in Zizioulas and Yannaras, not the generalized concept of *being*. To be is to be a person in relationship. Yannaras (1967/2005) is especially explicit in stating,

No personal hypostasis (whether divine or human) is a fragment or part of divine or human *being*; on the contrary, each person recapitulates and expresses the whole *mode of being*, complete divinity or humanity. Neither divinity nor humanity exist outside the existent *hypostases*, that is to say, outside the persons. The person hypostasizes being, it constitutes being as existent reality.

(p. 87)

There is no such thing as the abstract being (or essence) of God or humanity outside the specific hypostases that instantiate being. This safeguards persons from becoming enveloped in the conceptual definitions Yannaras saw plaguing Western theologians' approach to God (or the idea of God). It also protects the understanding of human nature as something personal and unique rather than abstract.

One final word remains to be said regarding *prosopon* as person: Yannaras (1987/2007) recounted the etymological significance of *prosopon* and its implication for understanding personhood. The derivation of *prosopon* from *pros*, "towards," and *ops*, "eye," "face," or "countenance," (p. 5) identifies the person as that which turns toward another. This illustrates and undergirds the Orthodox understanding of personhood as inherently relational rather than individualistic.

Lossky (1978) noted that theosis is "supreme synthesis, through man, of God and the created cosmos, wherein rests the meaning of all Christian anthropology" (p. 75). The Orthodox conception of deification is deeply connected to essentially every facet of the faith—Christology, beliefs about creation, and, most especially, anthropology.

Fate of the hypostasis

Regarding theosis, Meyendorff (1974) noted "Byzantine theologians seldom devote much explicit attention to speculation about the exact fate of souls after death" (p. 163). The Orthodox do not expend extensive energy hypothesizing about things so distant from experience. Even so, there is a benefit to considering some of the Orthodox discussion of the nature of hell and the scope of salvation.

On the topic of hell, Kalomiros (1980) delivered a polemic address about the relationship between the goodness of God and hell, and Kalomiros identified the same problem with Western theology as Romanides (1998), namely, that it attributes death to the work of God, either because God instituted it as punishment or

152 Ego and ego fate

because death is natural ("but is not God the creator of all natural things?", Kalomiros, 1980, p. 3). Kalomiros also distinguished between the angry and punitive God of the West and the God of the Eastern Church, whom he noted is "not just, with the human meaning of this word" (p. 9), "for he is kind to the ungrateful and the selfish" (Lk. 6:35). God's mercy transcends human justice. Kalomiros continued:

> God is good, loving, and kind toward those who disregard, disobey, and ignore Him. He never returns evil for evil, He never takes vengeance. His punishments are loving means of correction, as long as anything can be corrected and healed in this life. They never extend into eternity. He created everything good.
>
> (pp. 9–10)

This good and loving God, who offers mercy freely, does not impose punishment in eternal damnation. Rather, Kalomiros was bold to say, "Our salvation or our eternal death is not a question of God's decision," because his will is always for salvation, "but it is a question of *our* decision, it is a question of the decision of our free will which God respects absolutely" (p. 25).[6] God is judge in the very specific sense that he is the truth and the light; judgment before God is the exposure of our hearts before the truth and the light of God. Because of this, heaven and hell are in fact the same thing experienced in two ways: for those who love God, "those hearts will rejoice in seeing God's light;" for those who hate God, "these men will suffer by receiving on their opened hearts this penetrating light of truth" (p. 30). Heaven and hell are not places but direct experience of the light of God—the same God in two experiences.

As for the scope of salvation, Metropolitan Kallistos of Diokleia (Ware, 2000) wrote of the *apocatastasis* (ἀποκατάστασις), which is the final restoration of all things. This idea, a form of *universalism*, is controversial in the Orthodox Church, as the Church condemned Origen as a heretic for advocating *apocatastasis* at the fifth Ecumenical Council. However, as Met. Kallistos (Ware, 2000) noted, Origen was condemned for his entire theological system, which involved the pre-existence of souls and a pre-cosmic fall, ideas untenable in the broader context of Orthodox theology.

Met. Kallistos (Ware, 2000) advocated for separating the belief in the reconciliation of all with God from the rest of Origen's system, given numerous Scriptures that seem to strongly suggest the reconciliation of all. However, because of the freedom of the human will, Met. Kallistos noted the salvation of all is not "a logical certainty" but "a heartfelt aspiration, a visionary hope" (Ware, 2000, p. 200). The hope for the salvation of all, through free choice, is a hope not condemned by the Church. Indeed, St. Gregory of Nyssa expounded a final restoration inclusive even of the devil. Met. Kallistos illustrated the tension regarding beliefs about the afterlife with a story about St. Silouan the Athonite recounted by St. Sophrony:

It was particularly characteristic of Staretz [Elder] Silouan to pray for the dead suffering in the hell of separation from God . . . He could not bear to think that anyone would languish in "outer darkness." I remember a conversation between him and a certain hermit, who declared with evident satisfaction, "God will punish all atheists. They will burn in everlasting fire."

Obviously upset, the Staretz said, "Tell me, supposing you went to paradise, and there looked down and saw somebody burning in hell-fire—would you feel happy?"

"It can't be helped. It would be their own fault," said the hermit.

The Staretz answered him with a sorrowful countenance. "Love could not bear that," he said. "We must pray for all."

(Sakharov, 1999, as cited in Ware, 2000, p. 194)

Thus, in Orthodoxy, two primary issues in considering the fate of humanity are, first, that God does not utilize punitive measures, especially not for all eternity; rather, heaven and hell are the same experience of the light, truth, and love of God from differing perspectives. Similarly, as God always wills salvation and allows for human freedom, an Orthodox Christian is able to hope for the salvation of all.

The ego and narcissism

Narcissism is a subject often interrogated by psychoanalysis, and Moncayo (2008) offered a crucial investigation of narcissism and its "forms and transformations" (p. 3). He posited that Narcissism is a structural (not simply developmental) configuration, and is not psychopathological unless the different structures are insufficiently differentiated within the subject. Moncayo outlined primary, secondary, tertiary, and fourth-degree or end-state narcissism.

Prior to the assumption of the specular image in the Mirror Stage, there is not a unified ego for the child (Moncayo, 2008). This state of undifferentiation between the subject and Other is constitutive of primary narcissism. The experience of primary narcissism in this state is therefore not a narcissism of ego cathexis, but has as its prototype intra-uterine experience, which is "a profound connection and interpenetration of life processes" (p. 7). This primary narcissism is pre-subjective, in which there is a no-ego, though "no-ego does not mean no-identity but a different form of identity" (p. 8). Moncayo (2008) made much of the pre-subjective narcissism, noting the psychoanalytic understanding of selfhood can approach

the question of self before and beyond the ego. In the pre-subject and in the self as object there is self-experience, even identity in the sense of sameness without difference, and in the sense of identity with the object, as well as energy and libido, but there is no ego.

(p. 8)

154   Ego and ego fate

Moncayo (2008) does not perceive the psychoanalytic self as restricted to the imaginary structure of the ego. In exploring this concept, Moncayo associated secondary narcissism with the ideal ego in the identification with the *objet a*. In this identification, Moncayo characterized the ego, as specular image, as a mirror that absorbs rather than reflects light, and when sending light out of itself, the light that "the mirror projects onto the objects of the environment includes the shadow of the specular image as the visual and imaginary representations of the ego" (p. 23). Thus, the environment of the ego in secondary narcissism is inflected always with projections and misrecognitions from the ego. Secondary narcissism is the narcissism of the imaginary *objet a*.

Tertiary narcissism, for Moncayo (2008), pertains to the ego ideal and to the father rather than to the mother. The identification with the father here involves internalization of the father's will through an inscription[7] "that symbolically represents both the name and gaze of the father" (p. 31). This move is partially into the symbolic, but it may still serve an imaginary function as the Name-of-the-Father takes the place of the desire of the mother, masking the lack in the subject, at least for a time.

In contrast to these, Moncayo (2008) posited fourth-degree or end-state narcissism. End-state narcissism is the movement beyond the imaginary father and the ideal ego and ego ideal. The symbolic father and phallus, as absent and as lack, are able to facilitate the subject of the real, where "the metaphoric flower of the subject will emerge from the place where the ego died" (p. 40). For Moncayo,

> It is only with the fourth degree of differentiation within narcissism that the subject can rebirth itself in the absence of imaginary ego-identifications. The subject is reborn as a new signifier that appears thanks to the autonomy and dynamic self-creating capacity of the Symbolic. Paradoxically, the agency of the subject is limited to the act of leaving empty the place of ego-agency within the structure.
>
> (p. 39)

For Moncayo, this emptiness of the subject is the goal of analysis; for the self to be beyond ego, beyond identifications, in "the wondrous emptiness of unbeing" (Moncayo, 2012a, p. 76). Moncayo considered unbeing linked to *sinthome* and the *unary trace*, two other Lacanian concepts regarding something beyond the ego. The *sinthome* is related to the drive: "Since the drive cannot be extinguished, the symptom continues after analysis in the form of the *sinthome*" (Moncayo, 2012a, p. 78) which allows yet contains *jouissance* as a fourth ring in the Borromean knot (Thurston, 1996). The goal of the analysis is, in one sense, to identify with the *sinthome* (Moncayo, 2008). Moncayo (2012a) seems to prefer the unary trace, however, which "may be better described as a form of non-self or non-ego (rather than ego or self) that nonetheless undergirds and re-knots the symbolic functioning of the subject" (p. 76). This nonself "is a form of identification based on non-identification," and whatever is left of the ego after analysis "can only be articulated in the form of the negative" (p. 76).

This "subjective destitution or benevolent depersonalization" does not involve the dissolution of the symbolic nor does it result in a particular personality structure (Moncayo, 2012b, p. 208). Rather, the awareness that remains after this process may retain positive aspects of different poles of personality (Moncayo noted obsessive and hysteric traits) but is beyond such formulations.

The ego, then, is not a limit of psychoanalysis despite its defensive and often destructive function. Through analysis, an emptying of the ego leads to a new subjective awareness beyond the ego and beyond imaginary identifications. The fullness and wholeness of the specular image open into the emptiness of the subject of unbeing.

The fate of the ego

How does the Orthodox conception of the person, of hypostasis, fit with the construction of the ego in analysis? The hypostasis in Orthodoxy is predicated on relationship, as Yannaras (1979/1984, 1996, 1967/2005, 1987/2007, 2004/2011, 2008/2012) and Zizioulas (1985), among others, made clear. This articulation allows some framework to be established relating the psychic structure outlined by psychoanalysis and that understood in Orthodox theology.

In discussing the relational nature of the hypostasis, Yannaras (1996) even incorporated psychoanalytic principles in his formulation of the human person: "The subject is born once the signifier appears in the space of the Other" (p. 85). There is some connection in Yannaras' (1996, 2004/2011, 2008/2012) work between the subject and the hypostasis and between the ego and the self. Lacan viewed the subject of the unconscious as the seat of desire, which is the ultimate measure of the ethical act: "Have you acted in conformity with the desire that is in you?" (Lacan, 1986/1992, p. 314). Yannaras (2004/2011) established the desire of the hypostasis as "erotic desire for life-as-relation," which he noted "is easily confused with the unconscious disguises assumed by the sex drive" (p. 72). Reformulating Yannaras's comments based on the insights derived from the re-reading of the fall narrative, it could be said that rather than the desire for life-as-relation being confused with (or misrecognized in) the unconscious drive, it is the unconscious drive that makes present the desire for life-as-relation in the fallen world. Yannaras (2004/2011) seems elsewhere to have acknowledged this when he noted that "for human beings, the object of the sex drive is that individual . . . who attracts them precisely as a possibility of functioning in terms of life-as-relation" (p. 25).

Taking the drive as the residue of the absent Thing allows the connection between hypostasis and subject to become apparent. The subject and the hypostasis are both subject to the unconscious desire for the Thing. Yannaras distinguished hypostatic modes of existing, however; for him, each hypostasis chooses to be in life-as-relation or to be an "ontic atomicity" (see Yannaras, 2006/2013,

156 Ego and ego fate

p. 27). This echoes Zizioulas's (1985) distinction between authentic personhood and biological hypostasis, the former engaged in unbounded, relational deification, while the latter is "the fortress of individualism" (p. 52).

How might the distinction between personhood, in its fullest sense, and individuality be understood in psychoanalytic terms? Clearly, there is involved some principle of identity in this choice, but perhaps not precisely one of identification. Moncayo's (2008, 2012a) discussions of narcissism and the unary trace provide a strong foundation from which to garner understanding regarding the modes of existence that Yannaras and Zizioulas construct.

Yannaras (2008/2012) saw in the hypostasis of individual existence an insistence on power, self-fulfillment, and self-completeness. This mode of being is intimately linked with the imaginary identification of/with the ego, and perhaps even primordially linked in some way to the imaginary God, whose Being Adam and Eve attempted to seize. This mode of being corresponds most closely to secondary and tertiary narcissism in Moncayo's (2008) formulation, in the elision, the lack in the subject. It is only in end-state narcissism that the lack in the subject is fully assumed, just as in the Orthodox Church the Christian must assume his or her own lack through the apophatic and ascetic struggle against conceptual idolatry and legalism—the struggle against the imaginary and symbolic as forms of blotting out the real. Indeed, Moncayo (2008) referred to "empty subject of the real" as the subject in end-state narcissism (p. 38).

Although analysis and Orthodox asceticism do not necessarily share the same end, it is not without reason that Moncayo (2008) noted that "ultimately the practice of analysis is a spiritual satisfaction" (p. 159). He even went further, when speaking of the cost of being in analysis, that "mystical experience and Lacanian psychoanalysis share a practice of what Lacan calls subjective or mental/psychical destitution and benevolent depersonalization" (p. 166). Though Moncayo connected this most closely with Buddhism, it is similarly true of the kenotic asceticism of the Orthodox.

Revelation

The Orthodox Church announces it is the "fullness of Truth" (Ware, 1993, p. 308), but not that it is the arbiter of truth. In other words, it cannot be said that Orthodoxy is true, and all other religious or spiritual systems are false; rather, all religious and spiritual systems contain some form of truth, and Orthodoxy contains the fullness of the same truth.

The fullness of truth in the Orthodox Church is not bound up with complete revelation or an infallible text, but is rather summed up, non-comprehensively, in the Incarnation of the Word (see Bouteneff, 2006, p. 208). It is the revelation of an absent and unknowable God, whose absence one finds in the Thing, which in some way transcends the darkness of the Thing. The revelation of the word is the way "immortal life" (Lacan, 1973/1978, p. 198) "can run around" (p. 197)—that is, the absence of God is sensible not only in the gravitation of the Thing, but in

Ego and ego fate   157

the appearance at the level of Christ of what is missing, as he took imaginary and symbolic constraints upon himself only insofar as necessary to point to something Else—as an image of that something Else (Col. 1:15), as the only mediator of it (1 Tim. 2:5), as the High Priest of it (Heb. 3:1), as the one who points beyond himself by emptying himself (Phil. 2:6–7).

This revelation is important in Orthodoxy, as it is that which structures the Church's practice and its understanding of deification. What leads to salvation is the love of God experienced in *theoria*; this is qualitatively different from a sort of Thalassal, oceanic feeling in that it obtains a *personal relation*, one that is never complete in the genital sense.

The fate of the identification-based ego of the non-relational mode of being is clearly described by Kalomiros (1980): "These men will suffer by receiving on their opened hearts this penetrating light of truth," which is the love of God (p. 30). Those who have abided only in their defensive imaginary and symbolic identifications will by necessity experience the love of God for the relational hypostasis as painful, as a death drive pushing for the death of the ego. God himself announced that "man shall not see me and live" (Ex. 33:20). Yannaras (1979/1984) described the experience of hell as the realization of one's self-imposed "incarceration" in individualism while confronted with the existential reality of the call of Love (p. 33). This excessive desire for the hypostatic relationship causes in the ego a certain pain, a *jouissance* that appears at the level of enjoyment for those who have been prepared through ego death in life.

Yannaras (1979/1984) described the process of preparation, through Orthodox asceticism, as "surrender of self and *self-emptying*, through a love which is not of the order of social 'altruism' but an existential change, a process whereby individuality is 'emptied' of self-determination in its conduct and relinquishes its autonomous resistances" (p. 164). The emptying of the ego, indeed, its murder, is the center of the Gospel; this is why conformity with the Law is entirely insufficient for true life: "it is possible for someone to keep the whole of the Law without managing to free himself from his biological and psychological ego, from corruption and death" (p. 75). The drive for death of the ego in pursuit of indestructible life is summarized aphoristically by Christ: "Whoever would save his life will lose it, and whoever loses his life for my sake will find it" (Mt. 16:25).

The fate of the subject of the hypostasis of relation is one of openness to the supplementary *jouissance* that is the real experience of God's love (though this is the same fate to which the ego-based hypostasis is subjected). However, if the person is "*concrete, unique,* and *unrepeatable*" (Zizioulas, 1985, p. 47), does the emptying of the self, the traversal or transfiguration into the empty subject of the real, mean the erasure of all uniqueness?

Zizioulas (1985) concerned his work with the concreteness of the person as hypostasis (an instance of the substance) rather than simply an "'ecstasy' of the substance" (p. 46). This is wherein the distinction from oceanic feeling is important for Orthodoxy; the person must not be lost in a return to divinity in *henosis* rather than *theosis*, a spiritual devoration.[8] For the Orthodox, the process of

158 Ego and ego fate

deification is "not uniform, for there is no measure common to all where persons are concerned" (Lossky, 1967/1974, p. 192). The Thing is not the same Thing for every person; thus, reordering one's relation to the Thing, to the absence of God, and ultimately to God, does not occur the same way twice. The uniqueness of the person is a result of the mode of relatedness, the pursuit of God's presence in absence in one's own life. There is no nature outside of hypostasis, and no hypostasis that repeats another.

Ultimately, Lacan (1973/1978) himself offered an account of something like this process: the *Ich*, in which is inscribed the *Lust-Ich* or pleasure-ego, also has pressing in its space *Unlust*, the *jouissance* from the outside that takes its place as "non-ego, negation," a "foreign body" (p. 245; see also p. 240). This nonego of *jouissance* is related to Moncayo's (2012a) observation that "emptiness is a form of *jouissance* or a level of experience that Lacan (1972–3) said we know nothing of" (p. 37).

This nonego, or identification with something beyond the ego, appears in Kalinich's (1988) account of theosis, which empties the "narcissistic structure" of the ego (p. 378). This self-emptying is what is presented in a small way in sexual orgasm—the pursuit of the *petite mort* is an icon in the fallen realm of the erotic union the subject seeks with the Thing, in which the ego fades.

Moncayo (2012a) related the nonego to the unary trace. For Moncayo, the unary trace is "a signifier without a signified, is an S1 without an S2, a pure signifier without a story: the unary signifier is a signifier of the void" (p. 26). In being outside of syllogistic logic, *das Ding* and the unary trace appear in the same non-circumscribed area (or open set). Just as the Thing reflects the uniqueness of the hypostasis, "*das Ding*, or the unary trace as it refers to identity, represents the absolute difference of the things-in-themselves, or their lack of inherent nature" (p. 39). The unary trace is a connection between the symbolic and the real, allowing something to be

> perceived from the perspective of infinity or of the unconscious, both as the unknown in the sense of the unknowable or indefinable, and the unknown in the sense of the totality of causes that remain invisible or that have now disappeared.
>
> (p. 39)

It is the emptiness of the place of the absence of God that Orthodoxy maintains, and yet also affirms an appearance of the Thing in the Word. The image of God, the likeness of which the Christian always strives to achieve through the emptiness of ascesis, is the unary trace of the Orthodox Church: "The image of God in man, in so far as it is perfect, is necessarily unknowable" (Lossky, 1944/1957, p. 118). In other words, the image of God is the empty trace. The pursuit of God's likeness in ascesis is predicated on the self-emptying of Christ, which comports with the unknowable emptiness.

One final question is worth consideration at this late stage. If the pursuit of the likeness of God is the goal of Christianity, is there a point at which the Christian achieves completion, achieves some sort of genital and plenary fullness outside which nothing is? Mantzaridis (1984) considered a similar question at the end of his work on *The Deification of Man*: "This vision of God in deification, then, begins in the present and awaits its fulfilment and perfection in the Kingdom of God. But even in the age to come, the saints' vision of God will not be static" (p. 124). This is because "the saints, communing in the grace of God and rendered through this communion more and more able to contain the divine radiance, will receive grace upon grace from God Himself, its infinite and unfailing source" (p. 125). Theosis is a never-ending salvation, the subject always opened up further in its emptiness to the experience of the Other *jouissance* that appears as the subject falls ever faster toward its center of gravity, *das Ding*.

Notes

1 Of course, there is growing understanding that the so-called monophysites in the Oriental Orthodox Church, which separated from the rest of the Church after the Council of Chalcedon, are in fact largely consistent in belief with the Eastern Orthodox Church, identifying as miaphysites, and that the ongoing schism between Churches is an unfortunate product of miscommunication more than truly different belief.

2 Two notes belong here: first, Zizioulas (1985) is presenting here the *monarchia* of the Father, that is, the Father as the origin of God (Ware, 1993). The monarchy of the Father is based in part on the Nicene-Constantinopolitan Creed as it stood prior to the Western addition of the *filioque* (Ware, 1993, p. 211). The Creed originally addressed the procession of the Holy Spirit with the phrase "Who proceeds from the Father," based on Christ's words in John 15:26: "But when the Counselor comes, whom I shall send to you from the Father, even the Spirit of truth, who proceeds from the Father, he will bear witness to me." The *filioque* altered this so the Creed read "Who proceeds from the Father and the Son" (Ware, 1993, p. 211). This changed the relationships within in the Trinity rather significantly, and the monarchy of the Father is not consistently held in Western Christianity (see Lossky, 1967/1974, for more detailed theological consequences of the *filioque*).

Second, the presentation that follows of Zizioulas's conception of theosis (as hypostatic union) is not uniformly held within Orthodoxy; it should be noted that the Orthodox Church does not have a catechism in the same way as does, for example, the Catholic Church. The creeds and definitions of the Ecumenical Councils are held as unequivocal boundaries due to their synodal and lay acceptance, but many topics are left open to theological opinion, or *theologoumena* (see Bouteneff, 2006). Lossky (1978) noted that "a theology that constitutes itself into a system is always dangerous" (p. 15). Thus, while Zizioulas's (1985) beliefs regarding theosis center on hypostatic union, Lossky's (1944/1957) are centered on participation in the energies of God. For a fuller discussion of this difference and the strengths of Zizioulas's position, see Papanikolaou (2003).

3 There is a certain affinity here between Winnicott's insights and Zizioulas's. Thermos (2002) came close to this in considering Winnicott in dialogue with St. Gregory Palamas.

160   Ego and ego fate

4 Lossky (1944/1957) here agrees with Zizioulas: "It was only as a consequence of sin that these two first human persons became two separate natures; two individuals, with exterior relationships between them" (p. 123).
5 This existential reality is not unlike Lacan's account of the speaking being; indeed, Yannaras (1967/2005) seems to have had something similar to Lacan's explication of the subject in mind when he describes this reality, as he noted that "if personal *ecstasy* remains without any reference to an answering Person (apart from any 'sign' emerging in the 'place' of the Other, so that ecstasy may constitute desire and desire relationship), it ends up being an experience of the existential void, an experience of the absurdity of existence" (pp. 107–108). It should be noted that *On the Absence and Unknowability of God* was first published in 1967 and therefore contemporary with Lacan's seminar. Yannaras later addressed Lacan's teachings by name (in, e.g., Yannaras, 1996). Of course, Lacan's (1975/1998) Seminar XX was not delivered until later (1972–1973).
6 This emphasis on human will is not to the exclusion of the will of God, as might be misread if taken alone. Lossky (1978) noted:

> Man was created by the will of God alone; but he cannot be deified by it alone. A single will for creation, but two for deification . . . . The love of God for man is so great that it cannot constrain; for there is no love without respect.
>
> (p. 73)

Lossky (1944/1957) elsewhere noted the will of God is "perfect and saving" (p. 129). Kalomiros (1980) wrote that our salvation depends on our will because the will of God is always for salvation:

> Do not invite death by the error of your life, nor bring on destruction by the works of your hands; because God did not make death, and he does not delight in the death of the living. For he created all things that they might exist.
>
> (Wis. 1:12–14)

Again, "as I live, says the Lord God, I have no pleasure in the death of the wicked, but that the wicked turn from his way and live" (Ez. 33:11).
7 Moncayo (2008) used the term "unary trace" here (p. 31) but left the term without gloss. It seems he used it here in a way very similar to the ego-ideal. However, in a later work, he differentiated the unary trait and the unary trace: "the insignia of the ego-ideal, and the medals of honor of the Other are traits, while the unary trace represents subjective destitution, the headless subject, and the void itself" (Moncayo, 2012a, p. 27).
8 Lossky (1967/1974) noted that salvation considered as some sort of absorption into an undifferentiated Body of Christ "recalls the image of Uranus devouring his children" (p. 188).

References

Bouteneff, P. (2006). *Sweeter than honey: Orthodox thinking on dogma and truth*. Crestwood, NY: St. Vladimir's Seminary Press.

Hierotheos, Met. of Nafpaktos. (1998). *The person in the Orthodox tradition*. (E. Williams, Trans.). Livadeia, GR: Birth of the Theotokos Monastery.

Kalinich, L. J. (1988). The Logos in Lacan. *St. Vladimir's Theological Quarterly, 32*, 367–383.

Kalomiros, A. (1980). *The river of fire: A reply to the questions: Is God really good? Did God create hell?* Seattle, WA: St. Nectarios Press.

Lacan, J. (1978). *The seminar of Jacques Lacan, book XI: The four fundamental concepts of psychoanalysis.* (A. Sheridan, Trans.). New York, NY: W. W. Norton. (Original work published 1973)

Lacan, J. (1992). *The seminar of Jacques Lacan: Book VII: The ethics of psychoanalysis 1959–1960.* (D. Porter, Trans.). New York, NY: W. W. Norton. (Original work published 1986)

Lacan, J. (1998). *The seminar of Jacques Lacan, book XX: On feminine sexuality, the limits of love and knowledge, 1972–1973.* (B. Fink, Trans.). New York, NY: W. W. Norton. (Original work published 1975)

Lossky, V. (1957). *The mystical theology of the Eastern Church.* (Fellowship of St. Alban & St. Sergius, Trans.). Crestwood, NY: St. Vladimir's Seminary Press. (Original work published 1944)

Lossky, V. (1974). *In the image and likeness of God.* (J. H. Erickson & T. E. Bird, Eds.). Crestwood, NY: St. Vladimir's Seminary Press. (Original work published 1967)

Lossky, V. (1978). *Orthodox theology: An introduction.* (I. [Ian] Kesarcodi-Watson & I. [Ihita] Kesarcodi-Watson, Trans.). Crestwood, NY: St. Vladimir's Seminary Press.

Mantzaridis, G. I. (1984). *The deification of man: Saint Gregory Palamas and the Orthodox tradition.* (L. Sherrard, Trans.). Crestwood, NY: St. Vladimir's Seminary Press.

Meyendorff, J. (1974). *Byzantine theology: Historical trends and doctrinal themes.* New York, NY: Fordham University Press.

Moncayo, R. (2008). *Evolving Lacanian perspectives for clinical psychoanalysis: On narcissism, sexuation, and the phases of analysis in contemporary culture.* London, UK: Karnac Books.

Moncayo, R. (2012a). *The emptiness of Oedipus: Identification and non-identification in Lacanian psychoanalysis.* New York, NY: Routledge.

Moncayo, R. (2012b). *The signifier pointing at the moon: Psychoanalysis and Zen Buddhism.* London, UK: Karnac Books.

Romanides, J. S. (1998). *The ancestral sin.* (G. S. Gabriel, Trans.). Ridgewood, NJ: Zephyr.

Thermos, V. (2002). *In search of the person: True and false self according to Donald Winnicott and St. Gregory Palamas.* (C. Kokenes, Trans.). Montreal, Quebec, Canada: Alexander Press.

Thurston, L. (1996). Sinthome. In D. Evans (Ed.), *An introductory dictionary of Lacanian psychoanalysis* (pp. 191–192). New York, NY: Routledge.

Ware, K. (2000). *The inner kingdom: Volume I of the collected works.* Crestwood, NY: St. Vladimir's Seminary Press.

Ware, T. (1993). *The Orthodox Church.* New York, NY: Penguin.

Yannaras, C. (1984). *The freedom of morality.* (E. Briere, Trans.). Crestwood, NY: St. Vladimir's Seminary Press. (Original work published 1979)

Yannaras, C. (1996). Psychoanalysis and Orthodox anthropology. In J. T. Chirban (Ed.), *Personhood: Orthodox Christianity and the connection between body, mind, and soul* (pp. 83–89). Westport, CT: Praeger.

Yannaras, C. (2005). *On the absence and unknowability of God: Heidegger and the Areopagite.* (H. Ventis, Trans.). New York, NY: T&T Clark International. (Original work published 1967)

Yannaras, C. (2007). *Person and Eros.* (N. Russell, Trans.). Brookline, MA: Holy Cross Orthodox Press. (Original work published 1987)

Yannaras, C. (2011). *Relational ontology*. (N. Russell, Trans.). Brookline, MA: Holy Cross Orthodox Press. (Original work published 2004)

Yannaras, C. (2012). *The enigma of evil*. (N. Russell, Trans.). Brookline, MA: Holy Cross Orthodox Press. (Original work published 2008)

Yannaras, C. (2013). *Against religion*. (N. Russell, Trans.). Brookline, MA: Holy Cross Orthodox Press. (Original work published 2006)

Zizioulas, J. D. (1985). *Being as communion*. Crestwood, NY: St. Vladimir's Seminar Press.

Chapter 10

Concluding reflections

Orthodox Christianity and Lacanian psychoanalysis are both adamant in their principles and hesitant to engage in *ecumenism*. In part because of this similarity, both of these fields are able to approach one another with a combination of firmness and intellectual humility that is often not found in dialogues that are overincorporative, one field seeking to subsume the other, or in dialogues that are illustrations of the narcissism of small differences. We hope that this dialogue on anthropology demonstrates that Lacanian psychoanalysis and Orthodox Christianity each can enrich the other's concept of anthropology without compromising either's *Weltanschauung*.

Lacan seems to have had this sort of dialogue in mind—one that enriches without dilution—in some of his comments on religion. For example, Lacan (2005/2013) noted:

> There is a certain flippancy in the way science disposes of a field [religion] regarding which it is not clear how it can so easily lighten its load. Similarly, faith has, a bit too often for my taste, been letting science resolve problems when questions translate into suffering that is a bit too hard to handle.
>
> (p. 19)

If psychoanalysis can avoid this flippancy and faith can avoid shrinking from questions, the two can engage in dialogue that opens up new horizons of experience.

The rapprochement of psychoanalysis and Orthodoxy offers a unique opportunity. As Met. Kallistos (Ware, 1999) noted,

> Our Orthodox theology of human personhood needs to be much more fully elaborated. . . . Such elaboration is possibly the special task that will confront Orthodox (and non-Orthodox) theology in the coming century. Just as the doctrine of the Church has been the central issue in the twentieth century, so in the twenty-first century the central issue, the question of all questions, will perhaps be the meaning of the human person. Certainly what Fr. Georges Florovsky used to say about our Orthodox ecclesiology—that it is "still *im*

DOI: 10.4324/9781003214359-12

164   Concluding reflections

Werden, in the process of formation"—is even more true of our Orthodox anthropology.

(p. 39)

In exploring the meaning of the human person, the consonance between Lacanian psychoanalysis and Orthodox theology offers one possible avenue for further developing Orthodox anthropology. While Yannaras (1996) has taken significant steps in incorporating psychoanalytic insight into Orthodox understandings of the human person, there is much yet to be done in furthering Orthodoxy's expression of the person.

The reluctance that some Orthodox have toward psychoanalysis, and especially Freud (Chrysostomos, 2004), overlooks not only the perspicacity that psychoanalysis offers with respect to the fallen person (i.e., one subject to the passions) but the ways that psychoanalytic understandings of *das Ding, jouissance,* and desire may help orient the Christian in ascesis as well. Cazacu (2013) argued that psychoanalysis is fit for inclusion, in a modified (or "transfigured" way) in pastoral theology (p. 132). Cazacu's focus was not on the Lacanian tradition, and it seems likely that this form of psychoanalysis may offer an even higher yield.

We hope to have demonstrated the ways in which psychoanalysis can inform Orthodox practice. For example, the role of *jouissance* in the subject's relationship to the Other (and the signifier of the lack in the Other) offers the Orthodox Christian a new perspective in the position they take with respect to God not only in his presence but his absence. Similarly, the morality of Orthodoxy, which Yannaras (1979/1984) has made clear, relates not to the ordering of goods, finds in psychoanalysis another method of refocusing away from the lure of the *Vorstellungen* and toward *das Ding,* proximity to which relates to the Good. Furthermore, the skepticism that psychoanalytic epistemology reserves for understanding is also found in the Orthodox obstinance to cataphatic theological systemization.

Beyond the work we present here, there are several areas that could produce further dialogue between these fields. The discussion of sexuation and the Church that we began here has much more fruit to bear in considering the role especially of the feminine in the Church. The ethics of Orthodoxy have also received relatively little rigorous attention at the level of social issues. Psychoanalysis' engagement with such concerns—through discourse analysis or other means—offers a pathway for Orthodox considerations to go beyond the typical affirmations of deontological assumptions.

This book represents a step taken to reduce the disengagement Lacan observed between science and religion. While we have not sought (at least intentionally) to emulate Lacan's laborious writing style, we hold the same hope that the reading of this text will involve a certain work on the part of the reader. Indeed, the significance of this work can be measured best not in the intellectual constructions involved but in the working it does or does not produce in the reader.

At the end of his seminar, Lacan's lessons were filled with silence (Roudinesco, 1993/1997). In the first session of the 26th year, on November 21, 1978, Lacan silently wrote some knots on the board, made a mistake, and stopped. He apologized and left without any further comment. Although age and illness undoubtedly played a significant role in his silence,[1] it is hard to imagine another way to resolve the lessons of psychoanalysis.

Such silence is all that can be produced in the face of something real. St. Gregory of Nyssa wrote, "Anyone who tries to describe the ineffable Light in language is truly a liar—not because he hates the truth, but because of the inadequacy of his description" (as cited in Ware, 1986, p. 30). This is just as St. Porphyrios the Kapsokalivite taught:

> Gradually the words are lost. The heart is so replete that it suffices to say two words, "My Jesus!", and ultimately no words at all. Love is better expressed without words. But when a soul truly falls in love with the Lord, it prefers silence and spiritual prayer. The flood of divine love fills the soul with joy and exultation.
>
> (Holy Convent of the Life-giving Spring—Chrysopigi, 2005, p. 128)

Note

1 Roudinesco (1993/1997) recounted Lacan's diagnosis of cancer as well as "slight vascular disturbances of the brain" noticed by a neurologist friend of Lacan's, which explained his tendency to "'blanks,' fits of rage, automatic gestures, and a kind of aphasia" (p. 400).

References

Cazacu, P. (2013). *Orthodoxy and psychoanalysis: Dirge or polychronion to the centuries-old tradition?* New York, NY: PL Academic Research.

Chrysostomos, Abp. of Etna. (2004). *Orthodoxy and psychology.* Etna, CA: Center for Traditionalist Orthodox Studies.

Holy Convent of the Life-giving Spring – Chrysopigi. (2005). *Wounded by love: The life and wisdom of Elder Porphyrios.* (J. Raffan, Trans.). Limni, GR: Denise Harvey.

Lacan, J. (2013). *The triumph of religion: Preceded by discourse to Catholics.* (B. Fink, Trans.). Malden, MA: Polity Press. (Original work published 2005)

Roudinesco, E. (1997). *Jacques Lacan: Outline of a life, history of a system of thought.* (B. Bray, Trans.). New York, NY: Columbia University Press. (Original work published 1993)

Ware, K. (1986). *The Orthodox way.* Crestwood, NY: St. Vladimir's Seminary Press.

Ware, K. (1999). Man, woman and the priesthood of Christ. In T. Hopko (Ed.), *Women and the priesthood* (pp. 5–53). Crestwood, NY: St. Vladimir's Seminary Press.

Yannaras, C. (1984). *The freedom of morality.* (E. Briere, Trans.). Crestwood, NY: St. Vladimir's Seminary Press. (Original work published 1979)

Yannaras, C. (1996). Psychoanalysis and Orthodox anthropology. In J. T. Chirban (Ed.), *Personhood: Orthodox Christianity and the connection between body, mind, and soul* (pp. 83–89). Westport, CT: Praeger.

Index

Note: Page locators in **bold** represent a table.

Adam and Eve: expulsion (fall), lesson
of 78–80, 91, 94–96, 98–100, 142;
imaginary father, misrecognition of
100; knowledge, sexual differentiation
103–104, 122; lack, symbolic object of
101, 103; perfection of, perceived 41
alienation: desire, as objet a 22–23;
from immortality 25; the real, before
alienation 66, 74; of subject from self
15, 17, 21, 29–31
ambiguity 11, 121
anthropology: connection to the real 5–6,
9, 39; orthodox 71–72; self, concept of
12–13, 148, 164; sexuality and theology 49
anxiety, of the real 3, 20, 67
aphanisis (fading or disappearing) 16, 112,
114
apocatastasis (restoration of all things)
152
Apollon, Willy 15
apophaticism 39, 41, 46–47, 55, 64, 69,
108, 115, 118, 129–130
apotheosis, as/or equal to God 98
Aquinas, Thomas 51n3, 61, 64, 69
Aristotle 60, 67, 144
Arius/Arians 143
ascesis (self–discipline) 7, 128, 144, 158,
164
asceticism: self–denial, essence of 49–50,
129, 141, 146, 156–157
Athanasius of Alexandria 148
atheism 58–59, 62, 109
atheist 59, 109, 153
atonement: penal substitution 39; Ransom
theory 39–40; substitutionary 126;
see also Penal Substitution theory
Aulen, Gustov 39

Behr, John 45
Bergeron, Danielle 30, 96
Boer, Roland 91–92, 93
Borromean knot 18–19, 20, 34n11, 82n11,
154
Breck, John 92
Buddhism, Zen Buddhism 4, 11, 109, 156

Canton, Lucie 29, 57
castration: anxiety 79, 95; of desire 74,
128; of the father 58, 97, 135; of Life
101; of the mother 25, 31; of object 97;
phallic 96, 145; symbolic 18, **25**, 26, 75,
96, **97**, **99**, **100**, **101**, 122, 128; threat/
complex 95–96
Cazacu, Petru 63, 164
Chaudhari, Pia Sophia 5, 63
Christ (Jesus): Church, and the 121; deity
of 51nn1–2, 56–57, 113, 118, 127–128,
132; disciples of 130, 143, 148; divinity
(nature) of 148–149; as first true human
43, 113; High Priest 113, 157; Incarnation,
revealed through 44–45, 57, 108, 110–111,
113; love of 50; person of 38, 40, 44,
148–150; pursuit of 46; sacrifices of 40,
42, 45, 142; salvation, through death of
43–44, 157; suffering of 39
Chrysostomos, Archbishop of Etna 81n1
Church, the: *asceticism* (selfless love)
49–50, 129, 141, 146, 156–157;
Bride of Christ, as the 101, 121, 131;
economy 125; *jouissance,* feminine
124–125; origin, as singular body 28;
primal father 122–123, 126–127, 135;
sexuality, belief system regarding 48–49
clinician 7, 33n3
condemnation 39, 50, 110

Constantinople 38, 133
consubstantial interiority (personal essence) 50
Copjec, Joan 81n9
Council of Chalcedon 148–149, 159n1
Council of Ephesus 148
creation: Divine, and the 40, 42–44, 48; fall of humanity, and the 6, 40, 42, 75–76, 91, 93–94, 99, 101; image of God/man 42, 58, 72, 112; narratives 5–6, 49, 92–93
Crockett, Clayton 62, 65–66
Cyril of Alexandria 148–149

das Ding. beyond of the signified, not this 27–28, 64, 66; good, essence of 113, 142–143; nothing of God 65, 67, 105, 112, 158; *see also* Thing, the
Davis, Creston 4, 60–62, 65
Davydov, Oleg 51n4
death: of ego/self 127, 157; of God 55, 57, 59, 64, 109, 112; spiritual, separation from God 42, 100
death drive 11, 15, 23, 24–25, 69, 117, 146, 157
deferred action 13
deification: thru marriage 127–128; union with God 43–44, 72–73, 94–95, 135
Deification of Man, The 159
De Kesel, Marc 28, 146
DeLay, Tad 5, 62, 64, 66–68, 82n14, 109–110
demand 22–23, 25, 51, 99
désir (desire) 21–22
desire: object, cause of 15, 17–18, 22–23, 30, 46, 138; unconscious 21, 114, 155
dialogue: Anglophonic, language barrier 11–12; Jungian 54, 138n11; psychoanalytical/religious context 6–7, 39, 47, 61, 68; Trinitarian 99, 131, 149; Winnicottian 5, 54, 159n3
Discourse to Catholics 10, 55
Dor, Joel 33n3
drive: duality of 23; psychological function of 22–23; repressed 28; sexual 25, 49, 155; *triebziel* (aim of) 24
Dunlap, Aron 5, 54, 62, 75

Eastern Orthodox Theology: Christ, as second Adam 45, 142; creation, from nothing 47–48; death, as divine compassion 42–43; foundational values 61–62, 156; Genesis narratives,

perspectives of 92–93, 94, 97, 130, 133, 148; God, essence/energy of 6, 40, 44–45, 47, 131, 133, 148–149; humanity, as center of creation 40–42; morality, concepts of 141, 145, 164; mysticism, tradition of 38–39, 45; sexual practices, traditional 48–50
École Freudienne de Paris (EFP) 10
Ecumenical Councils 112, 148, 159n2
ego: fate of 155–156; *infans* stage 14–15; Mirror Stage 12, 14, 19, 79–80, 153; narcissism and 153; the self 148, 153–154; *sinthome,* drive of the 154; *unary trace,* as non ego 154, 156, 158; *unlust* 158
Encore (Seminar XX) 54, 56, 59–60, 106, 108
eros: life/sexual drive 23, 118; true, as ecstasy 50, 73, 129
essence/energies distinction: communion with God 44, 57, 64, 75, 108; creation, regarding 47; of the unconscious (thing) 6
ethics: of psychoanalysis 66, 119
Ethics of Psychoanalysis, The 54, 56, 59, 108
eudaemonia 48, 60
Evans, Dylan 22, 34n13

fantasy 61
fasts/fasting 125, 128, 137n5
father: imaginary, influence/interpretation of 67, 95–96, 98, 100, 123 (*see also* Oedipus complex); law of the 20, 30; real 18, 26, 58, 96–98, 100; symbolic 18
feminine: position, within the church 101, 121–122, 125, 146; sexuality 81n2; subject, symbolic 101, 122, 123
filioque 133–135, 159n2
Fink, Bruce 11, 19, 26, 29, 31–32
First Council of Nicaea 148
Florovsky, Georges 163
Four Fundamental Concepts of Psychoanalysis, The 56
Freud, Sigmund 9, 13

Gallagher, Cormac 34n12
Garden of Eden: forbidden fruit 91
Genesis: 2–3 79; 2:16–17 94; 3:16–19 102, 104; creation, story of 5–6, 49, 93; creation and fall, interpretations of narratives 6, 49, 76, 79, 97
God: appearances of (incarnation) 44–45, 57, 97, 108, 110–111, 141, 156;

168 Index

communion with 44, 47, 64, 72, 150; death of (Lacan) 55, 57, 59, 64, 109, 112; energies of 47, 105, 115–116, 142; essence of 47, 95, 98, 101, 150–151; the Father 57, 76, 109, 111; humanity and 39–40, 42–43, 92, 94–95; imaginary 62, 64, 96–97, 100, **101**, 156; love of 150, 153, 157, 160n6; mercy of 101, 152; presence/absence of 66, 71–72, 99, 112–113, 118, 125, 156, 158; as uncreated light 44, 130–131

God is Unconscious: Psychoanalysis and Theology 62, 66

Grabar, Oleg 119n3

Grigg, Russell 33n9

guilt/guilty 42, 44, 77, 126

Gut (the Good) 28, 142–143

Harlow, Harry F 34n12

heaven and hell, as experiences not places 152–153

hell, nature of 40, 151, 157

henosis 135, 157

hesychasm, practice of 44

Hierotheos, Metropolitan of Nafpaktos 81n1

Holy of Holies 112–113

Holy Spirit 112–113, 131, 133–135, 159n2

Hopko, Thomas: priesthood, sexual differences and 130–131, 134; priesthood, woman and the 132–133

humanity: communion with God 44, 47, 50, 150; creation of 40–41, 75; death, fear of 42, 91; fall of 6, 94; fate of 39, 45, 153; judgement of 42, 45, 146, 152

hypostasis: being, as state of 71, 115; biological 150–151, 156; human 115–116, 136, 141, 150

hysteric 29, 32, 104

imaginary 154; father 8, 25, 30, 58, 95–98, 100, 123, 154; mother 31; object 9, 63, 95; passion 74; phallus 17–18, 26, 65, 97–98, 101, 123–124, 128, 136; schemes 28, 112; symbolism of 18, 23

immortality 41, 43, 99–101, 105n4

immortal life 24, 99, 102, 156

incest, as taboo 18, 20–21, 23, 30, 67, 98

instinct: biological need, direct object 22–24; life, immortal 31, 102

Instinkt see instinct

International Psychoanalytic Association (IPA) 10, 32n2

Interpretation of Dreams, The 58

Interstices of the Sublime: Theology and Psychoanalytic Theory 62

Irenaeus of Lyons 41–42

John of Damascus (Damascene) 110

Jouissance: enjoyment, over the top 21, 75, 128, 157; as forbidden 28; marital 121, 127–128, 135; of mother 30–31; original 64; of Other 59–60, 108, 124–126, 129–130, 141–143, 146, 159; phallic 21, 124, 128–129, 142–143; in theosis (transformation) 69–70

Kalinich, Lila J 6, 68n71, 83n21, 127, 158

Kalomiros, Alexandre 151–152, 157, 160n6

Kierkegaard, Søren 62–64

Knight, Christopher C. 51n4

knowledge: of good and evil 41, 76, 79, 94, 98–99, 103, 142, 145; natural development of 7, 45, 47, 55

Lacan, Jacques: atheist, lifelong 11, 59, 153; early life 10; God, reflections of 56–58; mysticism/sexuality, thoughts on 59–60, 105, 125; *oeuvre* 11, 22, 29, 54; pleasure principle 21, 28, 60, 69, 108, 117, 127, 142–144; silence of 165n1

Lacan, Marc–Francois 10

Lacan and Religion 62

Lacan and Theological Discourse 60

Lacanian analysis: and Christianity 4–5; Genesis narrative, interpretations 76–77, 91, 94, 97; primal repression 14, 16, 26, 28, 31, 114; religion, thoughts on 4, 10, 54–55, 71; the self, conception of 12–14, 19, 25, 146, 155, 157–158; unconscious, structure of 14, 16, 26

Lacanian literature 21, 61, 76, 82n17

Lacanian psychoanalysis: Christian theology, perspective on 4–6, 39, 54, 60, 62; concepts of 4, 9, 12, 21–22, 31; Orthodox theology, perspective on 68–69, 71, 81, 93, 105, 163–164; the Other, role of 75; sexuation, sexual position 121, 135, 137

Lacan Today: Psychoanalysis, Science, and Religion 62

lamella: object, absence of 24–25, 29, 99

language: *vel*, as a forced choice 16, 29–30, 71, 74

Law, the: domination of 17–18, 20; function of 122, 125; *jouissance* and 57, 124, 130, 143; transcendence of 128, 144–145
Leader, Darian 33n3
Leupin, Alexandre 34n11, 34n13, 62, 82n18
libido: as desire 71; as impulse, need 49; myth of 24; as pure life 102; without ego 153
linguistic: theory, Saussurean 26
Lossky, Vladimir: on apophaticism 45–46, 108; on creation 93; on the essence of God 109, 133; on the fall/death 91, 102; on personal relationship with God 41–42, 44; on sexuality 49–50
love: agape 72; demand for 22, 25, 99; of God 48, 63, 153, 157; human 49, 128
Lust–Ich, pleasure–ego 158
Lustprinzip (pleasure principle) 28, 59, 63
Luther, Martin 61, 83n22

Mantzarides, Georgio (Mantzaridis) 42, 51, 72, 159
masculinity: phallic function, relation to 122–123; priesthood and 136; symbolic 77, 135
Maximus the Confessor 73
metaphor 27, 66, 121
metonymy 27, 74
Meyendorff, John 40, 151
modalism 105n1, 149
monarchia (of the Father) 131, 134–135, 159n2
Moncayo, Raul 4, 11, 122–124, 135, 153–154, 156, 158
Moses and Monotheism 56–57, 112
Mt Athos 44

Name-of-the-Father: foreclosure, as being over 30–31; *le Nom-du-Pere* 18; *Non-du-Père* (Name-of-the-Father) 64, 77; signifier of Law 18, 79, 94; as symbolic 20, 29, 77, 154
narcissism: ideal ego and 154; primary, or pre–subjective 153; secondary 154, 156; tertiary 153, 154, 156
National Association of Evangelicals (NAE) 51n2
need: as necessity 9, 22, 46; physiological 14, 22–23
Nestorius 148
neurosis: hysterical 31–32; neurotic structure 29, 31, 96; obsessional 31, 63

neurotic 29, 31, 96
Nicene–Constantinople Creed (Nicene Creed) 133, 159n2
Nietzsche, Friedrich 10, 46
Nobus, Dany 83n20, 137n3

objet a 15, 33n6; desire, lost cause of 15, 18, 22, 31–32; in narcissism 154; pleasure, pursuit of 102, 135–136
obsessive 29, 32, 96, 104, 124, 145
Oedipus complex: ego ideal, ego as object 18, 136; ideal ego, assumption of 14–15; imaginary father 18, 25, 58, 95–96; interpretation, as dreams 17, 77; lack within 25–26; mother, object of desire 17–18; mother, symbolic 25, **25**, **97**, 99; privation (lack in the real) 18, 25–26, 58, 97
On the Absence and Unknowability of God 64, 160n5
orders: the Imaginary, The Real, the Symbolic (*see* registers)
Origen Adamantius (of Alexandria) 48, 73, 152
original sin 42, 77
Other, the: desire, object–cause 23, 25, 32; *jouissance* 59–60, 129–130, 141, 143, 159; lack in 17–18, 59, 63, 124, 128–129, 135–136, 143, 145

Palamas, Gregory 44, 72, 152, 165
paradisiacal nostalgia 49–50
par excellence: Law 20; religion 5
Parker, Kim Ian: Genesis narrative, postmodern 79–80, 91; narrative of the fall 97–98, 103
paternal function 17, 29, 97, 101, 124, 126, 135
Paul of Tarsus 11, 21, 57, 112, 113, 121, 128
Penal Substitution theory 39–40, 51n2, 126–127
persona 149
personhood, true/authentic 47, 72, 150, 156, 163
perverse 30, 31, 124, 145; desire, acting on 28, 58; structure of 29–31
Peter the Apostle 43
phallic: function 21, 60, 121–123, 126–128, 135; *jouissance* 21, 124, 128–129, 142–143
phallus: imaginary 17–18, **25**, 26, 65, 97–98, 123–124, 128, 135–136; mother's

18, 31; real, penile organ 17, 79, 104, 135; substitute 104; symbolic 18, 25, 78, 100–101, 104, 124, 135–136, 145
philosophy: *eudaemonia* of 48; theology and 18, 108–109, 148
Piskorowski, Anna 76–77, 79, 83n30, 97
points de capiton (anchoring points) 29–30
Porphyrios the Lapsokalyvite 165
postmodern: biblical studies 79; psychoanalysis 63
Pound, Marcus: Eucharist, as analytic intervention 65; liturgy, is psychoanalysis 62–63; symbolism of God 64, 67
presence/absence: of God 71–72, 100, 128–129, 158, 164; of the mother/Other 15–16, 99
privation: of immortality 100; symbolic phallus, of 101
prosopon: as deceptive, impersonal 149, 151
psychoanalysis: symptomatology 3, 30, 32; theology and 5–6, 65
psychology: analytical 5; ego psychology 19, 91
psychotic/psychosis 29–31, 71, 96, 98, 116, 124

Quinn, Malcom 83n20

Rashkow, Ilona 4, 76–77, 81
real, the 3, 5–7, 17, 21, 55, 59, 62, 64, 66, 101, 110, 144, 156
Reformation 38–39, 64
registers: analogy, three ring knot 18–19, 25, 74, 97, 111; Imaginary 11, 19–23, 30, 55, 59, 61–62, 96, 98–99, 154; Real 3–5, 11, 17, 20, 66–67; Symbolic 19–20, 135, 154
Reich, Wilhelm 83n24
repression: as defense mechanism 31; primal 14, 16, 26, 28, 31, 114; secondary 78, 110
Roman Catholic Church 3, 38, 55
Romanides, John S. 41, 47–48, 51n4, 60, 97, 151
Roudinesco, Elizabeth 32n1, 165n1

Sabellian/Sabellianism 81n7, 149
Sade, Marquis de 58, 117, 145
Sadist 145
Safouan, Moustafa 20, 26
salvation: atonement and 39–40; gift of 137n5
Satan 40

Satisfaction theory 39–40
Saussure, Ferdinand de 26
Schneider, Christoph 6, 68–75
Scholasticism, Middle Age theology 38–39
science 4, 28, 117–118, 145, 163–164
self: assertion 69, 127; concealment or oblivion 111–115; determination 51, 157; discipline 128; emptying (*kenosis*) 50, 69–70, 127, 157–158; offering 94, 141; sufficient/sufficiency 72–73, 98–100, 103–104; transcendence 72, 141, 143, 146
selfless 48, 50
separation: alienation and 17, 29, 31, 74; of the child 18, 77–78, 96; from God 42, 49, 69, 94, 100–102, 118, 153; identification and 20
serpent 41, 77, 96, 98–100
sex: drive 22, 155; marital 48, 128
sexual: differentiation (of Adam and Eve) 78–80, 103; love 49; orgasm 70, 158; release 13
sexuality 6; human 23, 25, 39, 48–50, 102–103; residue, of absence of God 118
sexuation: feminine 123–124; masculine 6, 121–123, 126
Sheridan, Alan 76, 79
signifier: binary 29, 131; master signifier 26, 29, 123; as thoughts 26–27
Silouan the Athonite 152–153
sinthome, beyond the ego 154
Skomra, Andrew 60
Société Francaise de Psychanalyse (SFP) 10
Société Parisienne de Psychanalyse (SPP) 10, 32n2
Sola Scriptura 143
Soler, Colette 32
Son, the: became man 44, 111, 134, 149
Sophrony (Sakharov) 152–153
Southern Baptist Convention 51n2
Spero, Moshe Halevi 4, 71, 76, 77–80, 97
Strachey, James 21–22
St Vladamir's Theological Seminary 70, 130
subject, the: appearance of 115; masculine/feminine position 121–122; psyche, structure of 9, 104, 119, 125; signifier of 16–17, 26–27, 108, 114
sublimation: forms of 28; inhibiting satisfaction 23, 28, 55; occurrence of 58, 112
Supreme Being 48, 60
symbolic: castration 18, **25**, 96–97, **97**, **99**–101, 122, 128; father 20, 30–31, 67, 96, 154; God 64, **100**, **101**; imaginary, of

the 51n5, 61, 82n11; mother 25, **25**, **97**, 99; order 20, 57, 61; reality, fabric of 19–20
symbolization 15–16, 66, 77–78
Symeon the Fool for Christ 143–145
symptomology 3, 30, 32

theologian: Orthodox 4, 5, 45, 71; Western 48, 112, 151
theology: Eastern Orthodox 6, 9, 39, 75, 97; mysticism within 39, 45–46, 54–55, 59–60, 105, 135; secular 4–5, 59–60, 62, 96, 118; traditional 5, 61
Theology, Psychoanalysis, and Trauma 62
Theology After Lacan: Passion for the Real 60
Theophilus of Antioch 41, 43
theosis: divine nature, partakers of 43; eternal survival, salvation 150–151, 159; grace, through God 44, 72; union, of godly energy 94, 127
Thermos, Vasileios 5, 63, 159n3
Thing, the: as absence/emptiness 55, 57–58, 108–109, 117–118, 143, 146; emptiness of the real 58, 108; as forbidden good 28, 75, 155–156; as God/not God 65–66, 67, 82n15; sublimation and 129, 144–145, 158
Totem and Taboo 20, 56–57, 92
Triebe (trieb) 22–23, 31
Triebziel 23–24
Trinity, the (Holy Trinity) 46, 133–134, 149
Triumph of Religion, The 3, 10, 55

Umbr(a), The Dark God 60
unary trace, non–self or non–ego 154, 156, 158, 160n7
unconscious: desire 21, 114, 155; functions of 14, 26; the Thing and 6
Urverdrängung: primal repression 33n7, 114

Vergote, Antoine 68–69
Verneinung (denial) 145
Verschiebung (displacement) 27, 145
Verwerfung (foreclosure) 145
Vorbewusstsein (preconscious) 27, 117
Vorstellungen (the Thing) 28, 117, 119, 127, 164; *Sache, (die Sache)* and *Wort* 27; *Sachvorstellungen* 27
Vorstellungsrepräsentanz: disavowal, of phallus 31; drive, representation of 117–118; representative of representation 27–28; signifiers, repressed 27–28, 114

Ware, Kallistos (Metropolitan) 92, 129, 152, 163
Ware, Timothy Richard 133; *see also* Ware, Kallistos (Metropolitan)
Weltanschauungen (differing concepts) 61, 163
Western Christianity: concepts, as basis for psychoanalysis 4–5; Jesus Christ, focus of 38, 51n2, 132; morality, approach to 126; salvation, theories of 39–40, 42, 56
Winnicott, Donald Woods 159n3
Wohl (well–being) 28, 142–143
Wortvorstellungen (word–presentations) 27, 117
Wunsch (wish or desire) 21, 83n21
Wyschogrod, Edith 4, 60

Yannaras, Christos: author, Orthodox 6; mysticism, stance on 9, 46, 109, 129, 138n7

Zimmermann, Robert R. 34n12
Žižek, Slavoj 4, 59
Zizioulas, John D. 134, 149–151, 155–156, 157, 159n2, 160n4

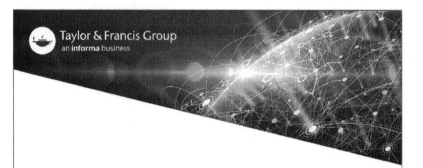

Printed in the United States
by Baker & Taylor Publisher Services